NO BULL
N~~OBLE~~ REVIEW™

REVISED SECOND EDITION

ENHANCED WORLD HISTORY

For use with the AP® World History: Modern Exam, and SAT Subject Test™

A no-nonsense approach to prepare for class and the big tests

by Jeremy Klaff & Harry Klaff

AP® and SAT Subject Tests™ are trademarks registered and owned by the College Board, which is not affiliated with, and does not endorse, this product.

About the Authors

Harry Klaff taught high school social studies in the New York City public schools system for 34 years. In 1993, he was the honored recipient of the John Bunzel Memorial Award as NYC's social studies teacher of the year. As a member of city-wide Justice Resource Center, he helped write numerous curricula in law-related education. For many years, he created the annual Model City Council project, in which students took over New York's City Hall for a day-long simulation exercise.

Jeremy Klaff has been teaching AP History classes for over a decade. His website, www.mrklaff.com has been utilized by teachers and students across the country for review materials as well as original social studies music. Jeremy has been a contributor to H2 network, and has published Document Based Questions for Binghamton University's Women's History website, womhist.binghamton.edu. He has conducted staff developments for "Entertainment in Education" at both the high school and college level.

Cover Artwork by Stephanie Strack.

Photo on pg. 15 courtesy of Steve Teran. Photo on pg. 25 courtesy of Linda Weissman. Photo on pg. 122 courtesy of Helene Begun. All other photos are of the authors.

Table of Contents

The No Bull Approach

No Bull Review…"because your review book shouldn't need a review book!"

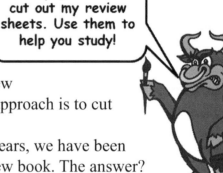

Go to page 193 and cut out my review sheets. Use them to help you study!

This book is a concise and to the point review for World History. Our goal here is to give you a great review for both in class and standardized testing. The No Bull approach is to cut through the fat and give you what you want.

We, as authors of No Bull Review, are teachers. For years, we have been speaking to students to find out what you want in a review book. The answer? No Bull. You want the facts, clear and to the point. And…you want review questions. Lots of them.

At the end of this book you will find an intense review. We advise you to know the terms and definitions on the *No Bull Review Sheet*.

The practice questions in this book are our own creation, and are based on the style of questions commonly used in the curriculum. They are questions that evaluate the important themes of World History.

We hope you enjoy the No Bull approach. Thank you, and best of luck.

– No Bull Review

Religions of the World

Religions have been around since early human existence, and through history they have affected many political, economic, and social events. Today, some of the major ancient religions are still practiced by millions of people around the globe. One cannot understand world history without being familiar with the ideas and beliefs of the major religions.

HERE IS WHAT YOU NEED TO KNOW:
Definition: Animism and Shintoism

Animism is a belief that nature's animals, rocks, weather events, and even plants contain spirits that affect the physical world. Animism was popular in ancient Africa and Asia. Similarly, in Japan, an ancient religion still practiced is *Shintoism*, which means "the way of the gods." This religion worships *kami*, which means the spirits of nature. They also practice ancestral worship.

In some places in the Western Hemisphere, Asia, and Africa, *Shamanism* was prevalent. Shamans were those with healing powers who were connected to the spiritual world.

Definition: Monotheism vs. Polytheism

Monotheism is the belief in one God. Polytheism is the belief in multiple deities (gods).

Question: What are the main things to know about Hinduism?
Answer: **RICK**

R - *Reincarnation* – This is the belief that people, or souls, are born again and again until a state of enlightenment (moksha) is achieved.

I - *India* – Typically, Hinduism's roots can be found in India near the ***Indus River Valley*** and ***Ganges River*** (explained later).

C - *Caste System* – This is a class system in India. Brahmins are the priests who make up the highest class. Then come warriors (Kshatriyas), merchants (Vaishyas), and laborers (Shudras). Untouchables are those outside of the caste who are the lowest on the social ladder. A caste can't be changed during the course of one's lifetime.

K - *Karma/Dharma* – Karma means the deeds that accumulate throughout one's life. If deeds are good, then one can rise in the caste system after reincarnation. If deeds are bad, then one's status will decrease in the next life. Dharma is a duty to honor the caste. This is done by fulfilling certain religious and societal obligations. Remember: Dharma and duty both start with a D.

Question: What other things should I know about Hinduism?
Answer:

1. Parts of the religion were brought to India by the ***Aryans***, or Indo-European people who settled in the Indus River Valley as early as c1500 BCE.

2. The sacred texts are called the Vedas. The oldest one is the Rigveda. Ancient texts were written in ***Sanskrit***.

3. Major settlements in India were along the Ganges and Yamuna rivers.

4. A long epic in Indian history is called the ***Mahabharata***. It's a poem with over 100,000 verses.

5. The ***Upanishads*** were dialogues between teachers and students. They helped explain renunciation (getting rid) of materialism (possessions) and reaching a level of perfect understanding. Like other Hindu writings, these

were written in Sanskrit.

6. The major gods to know are: Brahma the creator, Vishnu the protector, and Shiva the destroyer. During the *Bhakti Movement*, worshipers grew strong ties to deities through devotion to studying, and creative thought such as poems.

Question: What are the main things to know about Buddhism?

Answer: **BENN**

B - **B**uddha. Around 500 BCE, Siddhartha Gautama, a Hindu, was looking for ***enlightenment***. He found it during a meditation session under a tree and became "The Enlightened One."

E - **E**ightfold Path. This is the fourth of the Four Noble Truths (explained below).

N - The Four **N**oble Truths. They include:

1. That everything in life is suffering.

2. This suffering is caused by selfish desires for fleeting pleasure.

3. To end all suffering, one must stop desiring.

4. To attain enlightenment, one must follow the Eightfold Path, which is a moral staircase of proper behavior.

N - **N**irvana. If one reaches the top of the moral staircase, they are released from selfishness and darkness.

Question: What other things should I know about Buddhism?

Answer:

1. It spread from India to other parts of Asia, specifically China.

2. It has similarities with Hinduism, but Buddha did not support the caste system.

3. The Mahayana sect allows people to become Buddhas. The sect also allowed all people, not just monks, to worship. This opened up the religion to more people. In *Zen Buddhism*, all people can attain self-realization and enlightenment through meditation.

4. The Theravada sect interprets the oldest teachings of Buddha.

5. Through trade, Buddhism spread to China, Korea, Japan, and Indonesia.

6. *Buddhist monasticism* involves monks and nuns preserving Buddha's teaching while renouncing the worldly pleasures of society.

Definition: Jainism

Modern-day Jainism was reformed by Mahavira around 550BCE. The religion believes that everything has a soul and can't be harmed. This goes for all living creatures, including insects. Jainists can not harm any form of life.

Definition: Confucianism

This is a Chinese philosophy based on the writings of Confucius c500 BCE. Confucius wrote the ***Analects*** and advocated harmony, good conduct, and enlightenment. He also believed in the order of mankind. He defined the major ***Five Relationships*** as:

1. Ruler/Subject
2. Father/Son
3. Husband/Wife
4. Older Brother/Younger Brother
5. Friend/Friend

He also believed in ***filial piety***, which means a respect for one's elders, especially parents.

Definition: Daoism/Taoism

Laozi wrote the *Tao Te Ching* (*Dao De Jing*) in the sixth century BCE. He encouraged people to follow "the way." This means to accept the forces of nature, such as the balances of ***yin and yang***. These natural, yet opposite, forces complement one another. Yin is female and dark. Yang is masculine and light. The ability to live in harmony with nature is a central idea of Daoism. In studying nature, Daoists made great strides in understanding metals and medicine. See Daoist architecture on next page.

Left to right: A Daoist Temple, a Buddhist Temple, and a Confucian Temple. All three beliefs still coexist in China today.

Question: What are the Five Pillars of Islam?

Answer: **DRAFT**

D - **D**aily Prayer. One must face the holy city of Mecca and pray 5 times a day.

R - **R**amadan. This is a month where one must fast when the sun is up.

A - **A**lms. Giving charity to help the poor.

F - **F**aith in one God, Allah.

T - **T**ravel to the holy city of Mecca, Saudi Arabia. This pilgrimage is called the hajj. At some point in a Muslim's life, a trip to Mecca is necessary.

Question: What else should I know about Islam?

Answer: Remember, Islam is the religion. Those who partake in the religion are called Muslims. More specifically, Islam means to submit to the will of Allah. Muslim means one who has submitted.

1. *Muhammad* is the major historical figure to know regarding Islam. According to the religion, the angel *Gabriel* spoke to Muhammad on behalf of Allah. Muhammad then preached his monotheistic beliefs in Mecca. In 622 CE, Muhammad went on a 200 mile journey to Yathrib (later called Medina) in which he gained many followers. This is called the Hijra (Hegira).

2. The sacred text of Islam is the *Qur'an* (Koran).

3. *Sharia* is the religious law that governs the actions of a Muslim's life.

4. Muslim Empires spread Islam throughout the Middle East, western Asia, and southern Europe. *Dar al-Islam* refers to regions where Islamic rule is strong around the world.

5. *Sufism* is Islamic mysticism where intense faith and study brings people closer to God.

Question: What should I know about Judaism?

Answer:

1. Judaism is monotheistic, as Jews believe in one God.

2. The Torah is the sacred text. In the Torah, it is explained that Moses was handed the *Ten Commandments* from God. These contain the ten most important Jewish laws such as observing the Sabbath, and honoring one's parents. The Ten Commandments also outlawed adultery and murder.

3. The Kingdom of Israel was established c1000 BCE, and Jerusalem was its capital.

7

Strong kings were David and Solomon. Solomon's Temple was destroyed by the Babylonians.

4. Jews were removed from the Roman Empire c135 CE. They then scattered throughout the world. This was known as the *Diaspora*.

Question: What should I know about Christianity?

Answer:

1. Born between 6 to 4 BCE, Jesus Christ preached that people should love themselves, their neighbors, God, and even their enemies.

2. According to written accounts, or gospels, after the death (crucifixion) of Jesus, his body disappeared from his tomb and then reappeared to his followers. Many of the holy sites of Christianity are in Jerusalem in modern-day Israel. Jerusalem also has holy significance for Judaism and Islam.

3. The New Testament of the Bible was written by the disciples of Jesus known as *apostles*.

4. The head of the Roman Catholic Church is the *Pope*.

5. Christians were persecuted for hundreds of years in the Roman Empire. However, the Roman Emperor Constantine had visions of a Christian cross in the heavens. He put crosses on his soldiers' shields and won a battle. Persecution of Christians thus ended in 313 CE.

6. After the Fall of Rome, Christianity spread throughout Europe. In the much later Age of Imperialism, the religion gained strength in Asia and Africa. Note: people who spread religion are known as *missionaries*. Splits in Christianity (Eastern Orthodox and Protestantism) will be addressed later.

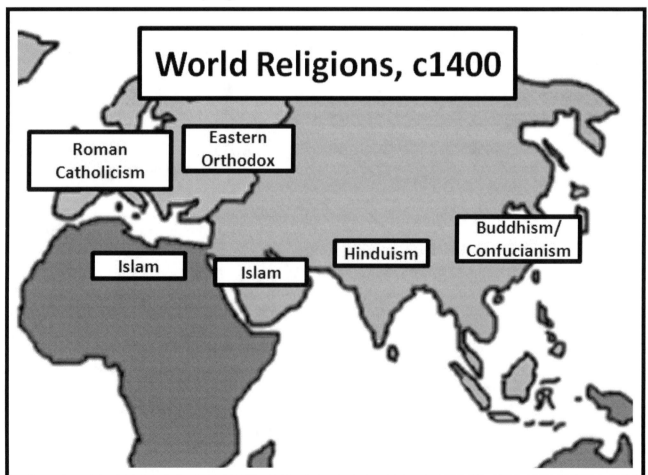

Review Questions for the AP World History: Modern Exam

Percentage of Religions Worldwide

China: Buddhist 18.2%, Christian 5.1%, Muslim 1.8%, folk religion 21.9%, Hindu < 0.1%, Jewish < 0.1%, other 0.7% (includes Daoist (Taoist)), unaffiliated 52.2% (2010 est.)

India: Hindu 79.8%, Muslim 14.2%, Christian 2.3%, Sikh 1.7%, other and unspecified 2% (2011 est.)

Ireland: Roman Catholic 84.7%, Church of Ireland 2.7%, other Christian 2.7%, Muslim 1.1%, other 1.7%, unspecified 1.5%, none 5.7% (2011 est.)

Jordan: Muslim 97.2% (official; predominantly Sunni), Christian 2.2% (majority Greek Orthodox, but some Greek and Roman Catholics, Syrian Orthodox, Coptic Orthodox, Armenian Orthodox, and Protestant denominations), Buddhist 0.4%, Hindu 0.1%, Jewish <0.1, folk religionist <0.1, unaffiliated <0.1, other <0.1 (2010 est.)

Japan: Shintoism 79.2%, Buddhism 66.8%, Christianity 1.5%, other 7.1%
note: total adherents exceeds 100% because many people practice both Shintoism and Buddhism (2012 est.)

Colombia: Catholic 79%, Protestant 14% (includes Pentecostal 6%, mainline Protestant 2%, other 6%), other 2%, unspecified 5% (2014 est.)

World: Christian 31.4%, Muslim 23.2%, Hindu 15%, Buddhist 7.1%, Folk Religions 5.9%, Jewish 0.2%, other 0.8%, unaffiliated 16.4% (2010 est.)

— Statistics courtesy of The World Factbook, Central Intelligence Agency of the United States of America

1. Which is true based on the above statistics and chronology of religious history?
   A) Christianity has become the dominant religion of Asia
   B) Islam has been confined to the Middle East
   C) Islam has been spreading at a faster worldwide rate than Hinduism and Buddhism
   D) South America and Europe have very different religious adherence

2. Which of the following has been a continuity regarding world religion?
   A) Because of globalization, it has been difficult for countries to maintain a dominant religion
   B) Religious law has affected most governments in the Western Hemisphere
   C) Religions founded after 1500 CE have become more powerful than established ones
   D) Immigration and exchange across the globe has led to religiously diverse nations

3. Which of the following statements about world religion is accurate?
   A) Judaism has a larger worldwide percentage today than at any time in history
   B) Christianity has less participation today than in c100 CE
   C) There are nations around the globe that don't contain a specific religious majority
   D) No nations utilize religion when considering government policy

Review Questions for the SAT Subject Test

1. The pilgrimage to Mecca that all Muslims must take is called
   A) Sharia law
   B) the hajj
   C) the Qur'an
   D) Ramadan
   E) Hijra

2. Which of the following religions is most associated with worshipping spirits in nature?
   A) Animism
   B) Buddhism
   C) Hinduism
   D) Judaism
   E) Christianity

3. Which of the following explains a true relationship between karma and reincarnation?
   A) Good deeds will be rewarded in the next life with a favorable promotion in the caste system
   B) A person's good karma will decrease the amount of dharma needed to be conducted
   C) Favorable karma can change a person's caste before death
   D) Reincarnation is only rewarded to people in the highest castes
   E) A person can only affect their dharma, but not their karma

4. Jainism believes
   A) in a strict interpretation of the Analects
   B) that one should follow the Eightfold Path to nirvana
   C) religion should be spread by the sword
   D) in the absolute power of the Pope
   E) everything has a soul and cannot be harmed

5. All of the following are true of Buddhism EXCEPT:
   A) Suffering is caused by selfish desires for pleasure
   B) Enlightenment must be achieved
   C) One cannot stop desiring no matter how hard they try
   D) There are Four Noble Truths
   E) To end all suffering, one must stop desiring.

6. The Five Relationships and filial piety are most associated with
   A) Hinduism
   B) Christianity
   C) Confucianism
   D) Daoism
   E) Judaism

7. A similarity between Judaism and Christianity is that they both
   A) originated in India before coming to the Middle East
   B) renounce materialism and selfish desires
   C) enforce a strict interpretation of the New Testament
   D) maintain a belief in one God
   E) are influenced by the writing of the apostles

8. Which of the following is associated with Islam?
   A) Tao Te Ching
   B) Analects
   C) Eightfold Path
   D) Qur'an
   E) The Upanishads

9. Today in China, which of the following would be practiced by the LEAST amount of people?
   A) Confucianism
   B) Daoism
   C) Christianity
   D) Buddhism
   E) Shintoism

10. A major difference between Hinduism and Buddhism is that
   A) Hindus rely on rigid class distinctions within the caste system
   B) only Buddhists believe in reincarnation
   C) Buddhism began in Japan, whereas Hinduism began in China
   D) Hinduism is monotheistic and Buddhism is polytheistic
   E) Buddhism relies on the Vedas, while Hinduism does not

Answers and Explanations

AP World History: Modern

1. **C.** Although Islam is much younger than Christianity and Judaism, the religion is second in world percentage according to the above statistics.

2. **D.** Religion used to be confined to the areas of the world where they were established. However, as time has gone by, the globe has seen religion spread.

3. **C.** There are several nations around the world which don't have a distinct religious majority.

SAT Subject Test

1. **B.** The hajj is a pilgrimage to the holy city of Mecca in Saudi Arabia. Performing the hajj is one of the Five Pillars of Islam every Muslim must honor.

2. **A.** Animism is a belief in honoring spirits and nature. Japanese Shintoism has similar beliefs in *kami*, or the spirits of nature.

3. **A.** If one has good karma, they will be rewarded with a higher status in the next life. Karma, reincarnation, and the caste system are all interrelated.

4. **E.** Jainists believe that every living creature, even insects, has a soul and cannot be harmed.

5. **C.** Buddha's teachings show that if one controls the source of their desires, they can reach a state of nirvana where no suffering occurs. This can only be done through years of discipline and introspective understanding.

6. **C.** The Five Relationships and filial piety (respect for elders) came from Confucius. The major themes of Confucian teachings can be found in the Analects.

7. **D.** Judaism and Christianity are both monotheistic religions. This means they believe in one God. Both religions have roots in the Middle East near the Holy City of Jerusalem.

8. **D.** The Qur'an (Koran) is the holy scripture of Islam.

9. **E.** Though there are Shintos in China, the other three beliefs are practiced to a greater extent. Shintoism is mostly associated with Japan.

10. **A.** Hinduism involves the caste system. Buddha disagreed with the caste system and did not incorporate it into his teachings.

Early Civilizations, Mesopotamia, and Egypt

The earliest civilizations began to develop after c10000 BCE. As humans learned to domesticate animals and harvest crops, they were able to enjoy new settled lifestyles. Major civilizations developed near sources of water such as rivers. From the *cradle of civilization* of Mesopotamia, advanced systems of writing, trade, law, and religious practice began to emerge. In nearby Egypt, incredible architecture was constructed with similar advancements in writing and worship. Eventually new civilizations, looking to amass great Empires throughout the region, waged war.

HERE IS WHAT YOU NEED TO KNOW:
• EARLY CIVILIZATIONS
Question: What do I need to know about the history at the beginning of my textbook?

Answer:

1. In 1978 an archaeologist and anthropologist named Mary Leakey found the oldest known prehistoric footprints in Tanzania, Africa. This was a hominid, or human-like creature that could walk upright. Leakey was able to examine early society by excavating artifacts, thus making her an *archaeologist*. She was also an *anthropologist* who studied culture and how people lived.

2. Early people were *nomadic*, meaning they consisted of wandering tribes. Specifically in the Middle East the term *Bedouin* is used to describe nomadic people in desert terrain.

3. Many people were *hunters and gatherers*. Men typically hunted while women gathered berries, roots, and other plants.

4. *Slash-and-burn farming* meant that people cleared land for farms by burning trees. The ashes were then used as fertilizer. These same people *domesticated* many animals, or learned to train them into creatures that could help with the farming process. Such techniques would be a part of the Neolithic Revolution (explained next). *Pastoralism* emerged, as nomads herded domesticated animals to find pasture. They utilized livestock for food, clothing, transportation, shelter, and labor.

Definition: Neolithic Revolution

By 10000 BCE, early humans learned that seeds could germinate into crops. The Neolithic Revolution involved just that, and the results were greater harvests, permanent settlements, and a decrease in nomadic lifestyle. Many were *subsistence farmers* who grew just enough to feed their families. Early societies had a *traditional economy* where agricultural goods and simple products were bartered (or traded) by families.

Thus, in the Neolithic Revolution, the hunting and gathering seen during the Paleolithic Era gave way to the taming of animals and harvesting of crops. People could now stay in one place. This led to the rise of *civilizations*. Civilizations can be classified as a settled population with a government, local economy, and cultural and scientific advancements. Even great megaliths (large-stoned structures and monuments), such as Stonehenge in England, spread across the globe.

• MESOPOTAMIA
Definition: Fertile Crescent of Mesopotamia

Mesopotamia, *the cradle of civilization*, was situated between the Tigris and Euphrates Rivers in modern-day Iraq, or the ancient Near East. *People settled near rivers for farming, water, and trade*. By 2000 BCE there was a thriving culture there, as complex ancient cities developed in Sumer, Canaan (Israel, or Palestine), and Babylon. Because of its shape and abundance of farmable soil, the area was nick-named the "Fertile Crescent" by historians. New technology emerged to help with harvests, as pottery was utilized for transporting items, and plows with wheels could be pulled by animals.

Definition: Cultural Diffusion

Probably the most important term of global studies, this means the exchange of ideas between cultures. This happened in Mesopotamia, and everywhere else in the world. Religion, technology, ideas, literature, government…you name it, it's been exchanged. You can find a list of major examples of cultural diffusion in the *No Bull Review Sheet*.

Question: What were the strongest civilizations in Mesopotamia?

Answer:

1. Sumer - Sumer was settled as early as 3500 BCE. People began to use bronze (combining copper and tin) rather than stone for their weapons. This complex knowledge of metals helped usher in the Bronze Age. In addition, the Sumerians had an elaborate system of writing called *cuneiform*, which was recorded on clay tablets. Cuneiform recounts the world's oldest legal code (c2100 BCE), the Code of Ur-Nammu.

Within Sumer was the city of Ur. They had pyramids called *ziggurats* which were used for religious worship.

2. Babylon - The Babylonians had a king named *Hammurabi* who enforced a code of law. Around 1750 BCE, *Hammurabi's Code* applied to everyone. However, sometimes it did so unfairly. The poor were treated harsher, and women had a lower status than men. Famously his code had laws that proclaimed justice to be "an eye for an eye."

3. Canaan (Israel or Palestine) - Under Kings Saul, David, and Solomon, the Hebrews established a strong Empire. Around 950 BCE,

King Solomon's great Temple was home to the Ark of the Covenant which contained the Ten Commandments. The Kingdom was over-run by the Assyrian Empire, and eventually taken over by the Babylonian King *Nebuchadnezzar II*. The Temple was destroyed, and Nebuchadnezzar II put the Jews into captivity c600 BCE.

4. Assyrians - This was a military Empire known for burning cities and slaughtering people. By 700 BCE, they had defeated nearly all of the Empires in Mesopotamia.

Question: What other Empires in the area should I know?

Answer:

1. Persians – Several Persian empires emerged near modern-day Iran. In 550 BCE, *Cyrus* became King and established the Achaemenid Empire. Cyrus was tolerant of Jews, and allowed them to resettle in Jerusalem. Under *King Darius* the Empire spread further into western Asia, towards India. One of the achievements of the Persians was the Great Royal Road which stretched over 1,500 miles and enhanced communication throughout the empire. In the time of Darius, many palaces (with ornate columns), wall carvings, great halls, and complexes were found in the capital city of Persepolis. Later in the region, the Parthians (247 BCE-224 CE), and the Sasanians (224-651) took over. Both emulated Persian strengths including military dominance, government administration, and a system of taxation. They were the last to govern the area before the spread of Islam.

2. Hittites, c1400 BCE – These were Indo-European settlers in Anatolia (Asia Minor/Turkey). Their use of iron weapons and swift-moving chariots helped them expand their Empire.

3. Phoenicians, c1500-c300 BCE – They were maritime explorers who settled many cities around the Mediterranean Sea. Phoenicians

Today, the most recognizable remains of Egyptian civilization are the pyramids and the Sphinx

are important to know because the Latin alphabet derived from them. Their writing system spread to cultures of the Mediterranean Sea, such as Greece.

Definition: Zoroastrianism

One of the oldest religions dating back thousands of years, Zoroastrianism is still followed today by a small number of participants.

It is based on the teachings of Zoroaster, a prophet in Persia. The religion teaches that the forces of good and evil battle for control of the soul. It is up to a person to fend off the urges of evil. After death, one's deeds are judged. Actions on Earth determine if one is permitted to have a blissful afterlife.

• EGYPT

Question: What is the importance of the Nile River?

Answer: The Nile is the longest river in the world (though some consider the Amazon in South America to be longer). Every year the Nile floods and leaves behind fertile soil. This natural event led to the rise of civilization in the *Nile Delta*. ***Irrigation***, or the transportation and application of water to places far from the source, was accomplished to bring water away

15

from the Nile. As in Mesopotamia, people in Egypt settled by the Nile for agriculture, water, and trade.

Definition: Lower and Upper Egypt

Lower Egypt means the area that was in northern Egypt, closer to modern-day Cairo and the Mediterranean Sea. Upper Egypt was further south and closer to the city of Thebes. Around 3000 BCE, King Menes unified the crowns of each of these two kingdoms. This was the first of 31 Egyptian dynasties (chain of family-rule).

Definition: Pharaoh/Theocracy

Egyptian kings were known as pharaohs. The Egyptians saw the pharaohs as god-kings who looked over the people and determined policy based on religion. This idea is called a *theocracy*.

Because the pharaoh had religious significance, their burials were of utmost importance. Egyptians used the process of *mummification* to dry out the body, and preserve it for eternity. Pharaoh tombs were buried all over Egypt. Notably, *pyramids* were built to house some of the mummies. The most famous pyramids are the three massive ones that dot the Giza Plateau outside of Cairo.

Definition: Hieroglyphics/Papyrus

Egyptians made use of a writing system known as hieroglyphics. They used pictures and symbols to create a written record. The hieroglyphics were preserved on stone and parchment made from the *papyrus* plant.

One of the most famous historical records is the Egyptian Book of the Dead. The book details the judgment of the deceased and their hopeful journey to the afterlife. In the quest, the deceased person meets Osiris, a central figure of Egyptian religion. Another major Egyptian deity to know is Ra, the sun god.

Question: What Egyptian Kingdoms should I know?

Answer: The 31 Egyptian dynasties are divided into several kingdoms. Though it is not imperative to know all of them, here are a few of the kingdoms from c2600 BCE-c1000 BCE. Subsequent kingdoms existed until the fourth century BCE.

The Old Kingdom was strong, but diminished in power. After a weak First Intermediate Kingdom, pharaohs grew stronger in the Middle Kingdom. Invaders known as the Hyksos took over Egypt during the Second Intermediate Kingdom. The Hyksos achieved military dominance through the use of horse-drawn chariots, and composite bows (often made from wood and animal parts such as horn). Egyptians regained power in the New Kingdom, c1550-1070 BCE.

Definition: Hatshepsut

Hatshepsut was one of the ancient world's few female leaders. During the New Kingdom, she was a strong leader. Egypt thrived with an expansion of trade during her reign c1460 BCE.

Definition: Kush and Aksum

The Kushites lived south of Upper Egypt in a place called Nubia. Nubia gained power through trade and established an Empire. Under a king named Piankhi, the Kush took control of Egypt and established a dynasty c750 BCE.

Aksum was south of the Kush Empire. Through trade with the Roman Empire and cultures further east, Aksum grew strong and extended through Eastern Africa (centered in modern-day Ethiopia) and into the Arabian Peninsula. They conquered Kush c350 CE. Aksum was weakened after Muslim invaders entered the area c700 CE. Furthermore, Islam would soon establish itself further north in Egypt.

**Review Questions for the SAT Subject Test
(NOTE: This time period is not tested on in
AP World History: Modern)**

1. Early human inhabitants before the Neolithic Revolution tended to
A) live in nuclear families on the outskirts of cities
B) congregate in urban areas
C) live a nomadic lifestyle as they searched for agricultural opportunities
D) settle closest to the equatorial regions of the continents
E) develop complex legal codes

2. What type of work is typically done by an archaeologist?
A) Studying local economies
B) Analyzing artifacts
C) Constructing maps
D) Surveying land
E) Classifying ideology

3. The Neolithic Revolution helped to do all of the following EXCEPT:
A) Create permanent settlements
B) Lead to the earliest civilizations
C) Yield more food for farmers to harvest
D) Increase the demand for Bedouin gatherers in the desert
E) Domesticate animals on a regular basis

4. The Fertile Crescent of Mesopotamia is associated with which river?
A) Ganges
B) Huang He
C) Yangtze
D) Tigris
E) Indus

5. Which of the following best exemplifies cultural diffusion?
A) Mesopotamia's soil was fertile enough to grow crops
B) Cuneiform writing techniques improved
C) Nebuchadnezzar II destroyed Solomon's Temple
D) King Hammurabi established a code of law
E) The Phoenician alphabet was utilized by the Greeks

6. Which of the following was true of Hammurabi's Code?
A) It was borrowed from the Assyrians
B) Punishments for the rich and poor were different
C) Women's rights were enforced
D) It protected natural rights by limiting the King's power
E) It was utilized in Jerusalem for centuries

7. Hieroglyphics of the Egyptians was a writing system which could be compared to cuneiform first developed by the
A) Israelites
B) Babylonians
C) Assyrians
D) Sumerians
E) Hittites

8. Which of the following was true of the Nile in ancient Egypt?

A) People only lived directly on the banks of the Nile

B) Pyramids had to built far away from the Nile because of underground flooding

C) People did not settle in the Nile Delta out of a fear of floods

D) The Nile could only be used for transportation because it is composed of salt-water

E) Water was transferred distances away from the Nile

9. The Egyptian pharaoh ruled in a theocracy. This meant they

A) used military force to gain resources from the Middle East

B) were elected by the people after the death of the previous ruler

C) administered religious law as god-kings

D) allowed the people to have a say in political affairs, but not economic ones

E) had limited power in times of war

10. Which of the following was true of the rule of Hatshepsut in the New Kingdom of Egypt?

A) Her reign was a failure as it led to the invasion of the Kushites

B) She was successful, as Egypt thrived through extensive trade networks

C) Her rule was the final dynasty of the New Kingdom

D) Egyptians did not tolerate female rule, and she was overthrown

E) She helped bring peace between Aksum and Kush

Answers and Explanations

SAT Subject Test

1. **C.** Many early human inhabitants were hunters and gatherers who lived a nomadic lifestyle. They generally moved around in search of food sources.

2. **B**. Archaeologists search and gather artifacts left behind by cultures. Anthropologists are those who study artifacts, and analyze cultures and living conditions.

3. **D**. Many Bedouins, or Middle Eastern nomads, could settle permanently because the Neolithic Revolution led to advances in agriculture. It's important to note that small desert populations of Bedouins still exist today.

4. **D**. The two rivers in Mesopotamia's Fertile Crescent are the Tigris and Euphrates. Mesopotamia is in modern-day Iraq.

5. **E.** The Greek alphabet has similarities to the earlier one used by the Phoenicians. Both alphabets have inspired languages of Western Civilization.

6. **B**. Hammurabi's Code punished the poor harsher than the wealthy.

7. **D**. The Sumerians used clay tablets to record the writing system of cuneiform.

8. **E**. Irrigation networks existed which brought water far away from its source.

9. **C**. The Egyptians believed the pharoahs were god-kings who looked over the people and determined policy based on religion. This idea is called a theocracy.

10. **B**. One of the rare female leaders in ancient times, Hatshepsut had a successful and powerful reign.

Asian and Middle Eastern Cultures

East of Egypt, empires began to grow all over Asia and the Middle East. In China, a series of dynasties pushed for technological advancements and cultural achievements. In the Indus River Valley, new Indian empires created magnificent architecture still marveled at today. Similar advances were true of Muslim empires who increased learning through math and science. As empires spread throughout the world, so too did the religion of the conquering powers. Interaction between many cultures took place on trade networks, such as the Silk Roads.

HERE IS WHAT YOU NEED TO KNOW:
• CHINA
Question: Geographically, what rivers of China should I know?

Answer: Much of early Chinese civilization was between the *Yangtze* River in the South, and *Huang He* (Yellow) River in the North. Because it regularly flooded and destroyed crops and houses, the Huang He became known as the "River of Sorrows." A large ancient construction project was China's *Grand Canal*. Whereas many rivers went east-west, this man-made structure linked north and south for communication and transport. Similar to what was seen in Mesopotamia, people settled near rivers for farming, water, and trade.

Question: What early dynasties should I know about in China?

Answer: A *dynasty* is a chain of family rule. This tends to be *autocratic*, or where total power is centered within the ruler. You should know:

1. Shang Dynasty – c1600-1050 BCE – They mostly lived in the forest, and used local wood for construction. They created wall-like structures for protection, and prayed through oracle bones. These were usually ox bones or tortoise shells which were used to communicate with the gods.

2. Zhou Dynasty – c1100-221 BCE – They made great strides in bronze-making (and later iron), silk, and script (writing). They operated under feudalism. Explained in depth during the Middle Ages chapter, this was a system where land was exchanged for military service so *lords* could maintain their property.

The later years of the empire are known as the "warring states period," as different factions struggled for power. However, the strength of the Qin Dynasty brought stability to the area in 221 BCE.

Definition: Mandate of Heaven and The Dynastic Cycle

A *Mandate of Heaven* meant that a ruler was approved by the gods to lead. Because of this, any new leader had to proclaim that they had the Mandate of Heaven. The cycle of where an old leader would lose power, and a new one would rise was called the *Dynastic Cycle*.

In the Dynastic Cycle: A strong dynasty came to power → They declined because of corruption and inner-deterioration → Natural disasters and famine complicated matters and sparked revolts →This led to a dynasty's loss of the Mandate of Heaven →Then an overthrow of the dynasty → Finally, a new dynasty received the Mandate of Heaven and brought peace. Then, the cycle repeated itself.

Definition: Qin Dynasty and Shi Huangdi (Qin Shi Huang)

Shi Huangdi (Qin Shi Huang) called himself the first Emperor of the Qin Dynasty. He dou-

The Great Wall of China was constructed to keep out foreign invaders from the north

bled the size of China by conquering land. Although much of the Great Wall of China would be built later, an early expansion of the wall was created during his reign. Peasants were forced to construct the wall *to keep out invaders from the north*. Shortly after Huangdi's death in 210 BCE, the Empire declined. Huangdi was buried in a mausoleum in the ancient capital of Xi'an, and was surrounded by an immense army of terracotta (clay) soldiers.

The Qin helped implement *Legalism*. Legalism was a belief in a strong government that kept order. It meant that the Emperor should punish those who did not carry out their civil duties. Unlike Confucianism or Daoism, Legalism meant that people had to be disciplined by the government rather than by themselves.

Definition: Han Empire

After the fall of the State of Qin, the Han Dynasty took over China for four centuries. Because the Han lost power for a short amount of time, their reign is divided into the Former/

The terracotta soldiers of Shi Huangdi (Qin Shi Huang)

Western Han (202 BCE-9 CE), and the Later/Eastern Han (25-220 CE). *Liu Bang* founded this dynasty. Both the Former and Later Han Dynasties were weakened by economic imbalances between rich and poor, weak and unstable leadership, and peasant dissatisfaction.

Question: How did the Han Dynasty control such a large area?

Answer: The Han had a centralized government where many officials controlled the legal policies. Under Emperor Wudi, this evolved into a *bureaucracy*. This means a complex network of government jobs that control a territory. To get a job in the bureaucracy, one had to pass a *civil service exam* based on Confucian teachings. Militarily, Wudi took the fight into the frontier as he helped to push back nomadic invaders from Central Asia called the Xiongnu.

Question: What were the contributions of the Han Dynasty?

Answer: The reign of the Han was known as a "*golden age*" because of its great contributions. Some of their advances were in:

1. Government – An effective centralized government with civil service jobs.

2. The invention of paper made from trees. This helped spread learning throughout the region. The Han made great strides in math, botany, acupuncture, and astronomy.

3. Farming Equipment – Creation of the wheelbarrow, iron tools, and drainage systems.

Question: What were the innovations of the Tang and the Song?

Answer: After the Sui Dynasty (581-618) constructed the Grand Canal, it was utilized by the Tang who reached it from their walled capital of Chang'an (now Xi'an) which was to the west. Founded by Emperor Tang Taizong, the Tang ruled from 618-907 CE. They took over lands in China, and under Empress Wu Zhao (Wu Zetian), parts of modern-day Korea c700. Zhao was the only female emperor in China's history.

Shortly after the Tang, the Song ruled from 960-1279 CE. It is important to know the contributions of these two dynasties. Their inventions included:

1. Gunpowder – Used at first for fireworks, this was later implemented in weaponry by the Song.

2. Porcelain – Ceramics were made out of heated clay, hence the term, "china."

3. Movable Type – The Tang made block printing, which was a way to copy images. The Song later came out with movable type, where a document's letters and words could be changed at will.

4. Both dynasties used paper money, and the Song's government issued it extensively.

Question: What was the social order of China?

Answer: Beneath the Emperor, there was an upper-class known as the *gentry*. They typically were the educated ones working the government jobs. Next was a middle class of merchants. Finally, the largest group was the peasants. These people typically farmed and worked for the landowning gentry.

As for women, they were viewed as subservient to men. *Foot binding* was commonplace in China. This was when a young girl would have each foot's toes tied to the bottom of the foot. Eventually the foot would break, causing the young woman to shuffle. This was a symbol of male dominance.

Question: What were the later Chinese Dynasties?

Answer:

1. Ming Dynasty – 1368-1644 – Much of the Great Wall was built by them, as was the Forbidden City, which is a Ming palace/city that still stands in Beijing. You need to know about *Zheng He*. He was an admiral who c1400 traveled the Eastern World on seven voyages with fleets of ships much larger than those later used by Europeans. He displayed Ming power by giving gifts, while taking in tribute by those who wished to trade with China. Tribute in-

volved the sending of diplomats with gifts in exchange for benefits such as trading rights or treaties. This tribute system legitimized the superiority of the Chinese.

The Ming Dynasty utilized the civil service system which stressed Confucian morals. People were influenced by a revival known as Neo-Confucianism, which emphasized honor, order in the family, education, and serving society. This philosophy would influence other places such as Japan and Korea who combined local cultures with those abroad.

2. Qing Dynasty – This would be the last dynasty of China. The Manchus were people from the north in Manchuria who invaded. When they conquered, they took on the name Qing. They wanted to keep China self-sufficient and leave it isolated from European influence. They didn't want Chinese people to marry Manchus or even learn their language. However, they respected Confucian ideas in government and culture. They ruled from 1644-1911.

• OTHER EAST ASIA EMPIRES
Question: What is important to know about the Mongol Empire?

Answer:

1. The Mongols were nomadic people who lived on the Steppe (grasslands) of Eastern Europe and Asia.

2. These nomads united under the rule of ***Genghis Khan*** c1200 CE. The Mongols were ruthless conquerors who utilized the horse in battle.

3. Khan conquered much of Eastern Europe and Asia, amassing an Empire greater than that of the ancient Romans. Notably, they conquered Russia and China. The Empire even extended into parts of the Middle East.

4. After Khan's death, the Empire was divided into territories known as Khanates. The Khanate of the Golden Horde contained Russia, effectively isolating it from Western Europe. In China, they established the Yuan Dynasty. The four Khanates were ruled by one of Khan's descendants and a series of administrators.

5. Kublai Khan conquered China by 1279, but failed to take over the island of Japan in the late thirteenth century. The Mongols never conquered Japan because upon their invasion, a massive storm known as a *kamikaze* destroyed their fleet of ships.

For about 100 years, there was a Mongol Peace (Pax Mongolica) that ended c1350. Much trade and cultural interaction took place during this stable time. The Empire weakened a century after Kublai's death, as famine, rebellion, overexpansion, lack of unified culture, and weak leadership broke up much of the Mongol landholdings.

6. The Mongols had strong connections with other cultures because of an extensive network of roads and trading routes that extended from India to the Middle East. European traveler Marco Polo visited China c1275. He returned to Italy with reports about Chinese life, communication networks, and the impressive Mongol palaces.

Questions: What do I need to know about early Japan?

Answer: Japan controls a chain of islands known as an *archipelago*. Island geography allowed Japan to isolate itself from the rest of the world for much of its history. Although this isolation protected them from Mongol conquest, it also kept them in a backwards, feudal lifestyle into the nineteenth century.

1. As explained in the religion chapter, the ancient religion was ***Shintoism***, which meant "the way of the gods." The religion worshiped ancestors and nature.

2. Much cultural diffusion took place between China, Japan, and Korea. Japanese culture thrived during the Heian Period from 794-

1185. Many artistic and literary achievements accompanied this time period.

3. Japan operated on *feudalism* (explained more in depth in the Middle Ages chapter). Similar to the practice in the Middle Ages where knights gave military service in exchange for land, Japanese *samurai warriors* adhered to the *bushido code*, or "the way of the warrior." Samurais were ready to die if that meant honoring the gods and their obligations. Lords known as *daimyo* provided security. The daimyo lived in castle towns, which were fortified areas where administrative decisions could be made.

4. Shogun – Similar to what took place in China, family rule existed in Japan. In 1192, Emperor Minamoto took on the title of Shogun, or dictator.

5. The Tokugawa Shogunate, founded by Tokugawa Ieyasu, united feudal Japan under military rule c1600. The capital was moved to Edo (later called Tokyo). The Shogunate controlled the daimyo by making them reside in the new capital every other year. Although they welcomed trade at first, extensive conversions of the Japanese people to Christianity led to rebellion. By 1640, Japan closed its doors to European influence. The isolation would last until the middle of the nineteenth century.

6. In terms of culture, you need to know that *haikus* were three lined poems about nature that traditionally had a 5-7-5 syllable scheme. *Kabuki theater* was a dramatic presentation that featured dance, fancy costumes, and men taking on the roles of women.

Definition: Khmer Empire and Koryo Dynasty

The Khmer Empire dominated Southeast Asia c1200 in what is present-day Cambodia. The capital of the Empire was Angkor. There, an impressive temple complex was constructed called *Angkor Wat*. It was first dedicated to the Hindu god Vishnu, and later became a Buddhist structure. The Khmer Empire established sea-trade with China and India.

In Korea, the Koryo Dynasty ruled from 918-1392. Like the Han, they had a bureaucratic government with civil service tests. The Koryo Dynasty declined after Mongol invasions in the thirteenth century.

• **INDIA**
Question: What geographic features of India are most important to know?

Note: Information on the caste system and Hinduism can be found in the religion chapter.

Answer: The *Himalaya Mountains* divide northeast India from China. You should also know:

1. Civilization in India developed in the western Indus River Valley near the *Indus River*, and to the east along the *Ganges River*.

2. India's climate is affected by great seasonal winds called *monsoons*. These impressive storms provide the rain necessary for agriculture.

3. Most of the Indian subcontinent is made up of a dry region called the Deccan Plateau.

Remember: **I DIG**...**I**ndia = **D**eccan, **I**ndus, **G**anges

Angkor Wat in Cambodia

Definition: Harappa and Mohenjo-daro

Around 2500 BCE, there were two cities called *Harappa* and *Mohenjo-daro* in the Indus River Valley. They had a complex city layout, complete with a network of roads and advanced plumbing. By 1700 BCE, nomadic people called *Aryans* took over the area and introduced aspects of Hinduism that would spread throughout the region.

Definition: Mauryan Empire and Gupta Empire

Around 300 BCE, the Mauryan Empire was founded by Chandragupta. He gathered an enormous army, fought back Greek advances, and united northern India. Once established, Chandragupta utilized a bureaucratic form of government which relied on many local officials ruling over four provinces. The Empire peaked and expanded under the reign of his grandson, *Ashoka (Asoka)*. Ashoka favored Buddhism, but was tolerant of all religions. The Mauryan capital was Pataliputra. Mostly made of wood, it had an impressive palace, thriving markets, and contained columned architecture reflectant of Hellenistic and Persian culture. Persian architecture would continue to inspire architecture (such as the Taj Mahal) in India during the Muslim rule of the Mughals.

For 500 years after Ashoka's death there was a power-struggle. The Guptas then took over in 320 CE. They made advances in astronomy and utilized the concept of zero in mathematics. Think of them as the "G000ptas." The Empire expanded westward and created trade networks within the Mediterranean. The Guptas gradually weakened, became fragmented, and were severely damaged by constant pressure from nomads in Central Asia known as the White Huns.

Definition: Mughal Empire

Led by Muslim rulers, the Mughals were a more recent Indian Empire that established itself from 1526-1707 (and weakened thereafter). Before they gained strength, much of the region was controlled by Turkish leadership. They established the Delhi Sultanate and ruled over the Hindu people. A different empire with a strong army was the *Vijayanagara Empire* (1336-1614) which established a Hindu stronghold on the southern Deccan Plateau. However, a leader from the north, Babur, mobilized an army which would help start the Mughal Empire which eventually spread throughout India. Other Mughal leaders to know include:

1. *Akbar the Great* – A strong military leader, he conquered territory on both coasts of the subcontinent of India. Akbar was known for preaching *religious tolerance*. He allowed people from different religions to hold office in the Mughal bureaucracy. Though Muslim, he gave freedoms to many Hindus, and appointed some from a warrior caste called

The Taj Mahal at Agra, India

Rajputs to lead the military. Akbar married a Rajput princess thus encouraging intermarriage. In addition, he oversaw a fair taxation policy which taxed poorer peasants at fair rates. The Mughals traded with their neighbors, but also with Europeans.

India's textiles became quite popular in Europe, and were often exchanged for gold and silver. During Akbar's reign c1600, there were also contributions in literature and education. After Akbar's time, the Mughals targeted the Sikhs (who are spiritual, nonviolent, monotheistic, and support equality) in the region as religious and political dissidents.

2. Shah Jahan – He sponsored fantastic architecture like the *Taj Mahal*, which was constructed to honor his late wife Mumtaz Mahal. Jahan's mother, Nur Jahan, exerted great power over India as wife to Jahangir. She often influenced legislation through appointed family members.

3. Aurangzeb - He was an unpopular leader who taxed the people greatly. Hindu warriors known as the Marathas broke away from the empire and founded their own state under his rule.

After overexpansion, the Mughal Empire declined when Europeans began to trade in the area. Soon after, England turned India into the "jewel in its crown" (discussed later). As British influence continued, an old system of tax collection from landholding nobles, or *zamindars*, continued. The zamindars would collect on behalf of the state.

Neighboring Sri Lanka would also be affected, as the British quickly put an end to over 2300 years of Sinhala dynasty rule off the southeast coast of India.

• **MIDDLE EASTERN EMPIRES**
Note: A Review of Islam can be found in the religion chapter.

Definition: Caliph

A *caliph* was a religious leader who was also the head of the government. Starting in 632, Abu-Bakr, Umar, and Uthman all became the caliphs who succeeded Muhammad. They were able to take over the Arabian Peninsula in the Middle East. As they expanded their power, they spread Islam.

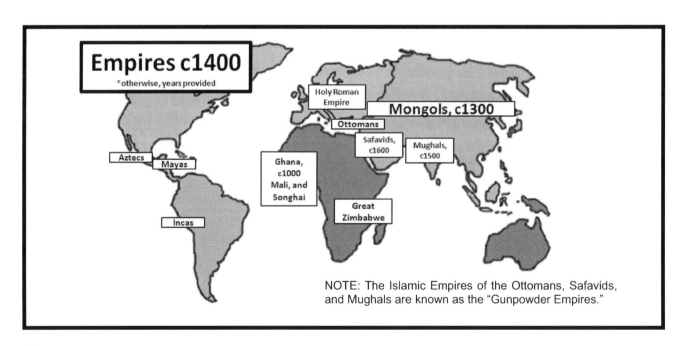

NOTE: The Islamic Empires of the Ottomans, Safavids, and Mughals are known as the "Gunpowder Empires."

The Blue Mosque in Istanbul, Turkey. Domes on mosques show similarities to Roman architecture.

Question: What early Islamic Empires should I know about?

Answer:

1. Umayyad Caliphate – 661-750 – They further spread Islam to the east and west. Although most Muslims accepted Umayyad rule, some did not. The Shi'as believed that the caliph should be a relative of Muhammad. The Sunnis disagreed and accepted rulers who led in the example of Muhammad. Still today, these two groups experience violent conflict.

2. Abbasid Caliphate – 750-1258 – They settled in modern-day Baghdad, Iraq and created a wealthy Empire with a bureaucracy to govern.

Question: Where else did Islam spread before 1500?

Answer: Through trade, cultural diffusion, and conquest, Islam spread through the Middle East, into Eastern and Northern (called Maghreb) Africa, and as far as Spain, where the Muslim state of *al-Andalus* was established. The Almoravids, Almohads, and other Islamic *Moorish* Empires had a stronghold in Spain from 711 until 1492, In Mali, Africa, a king named Mansa Musa spread Islam throughout his Empire c1300 (explained later).

By the twentieth century, Islam saw great gains in Southeast Asia, notably in Indonesia.

Question: What were the contributions of the early Muslim world?

Answer:

In the Middle Ages (during much of Abbasid rule), there was a Golden Age of Islamic thought. The *House of Wisdom* in Baghdad was devoted to learning and advanced thought. Advances of this time included:

1. Mathematics – Al-Khwarizmi had a new idea in math called al-jabr. This is modern-day algebra.

2. Astronomy – Muslims monitored the stars and planets to make calendars and maps. Nasir

al-Din al-Tusi was a scholar, mathematician, and astronomer of this period.

3. Calligraphy – This was a style of fancy Arabic (Middle Eastern) handwriting. Words were often used to make pictures. Like the Chinese, the Abbasids were skilled in making paper.

4. Architecture – Large and ornate *mosques* were constructed as a place for Islamic worship. Architecture used in Eastern Europe, such as domes and arches, were borrowed for these mosques. Hence, cultural diffusion from the Greco-Roman world was prevalent. Ornate *mosaics* (art formed from small pieces of stone or glass) were commonly found in mosques.

5. Philosophy – The writings of Averroës blended religion and the philosophy of Aristotle.

6. Medicine - Al Razi was a great physician who used observation and experimentation as he studied medicine. He wrote *Treatise on the Smallpox and Measles.*

Question: What should I know about the Ottoman Empire c1300-1920?

Answer: The Empire was named for Osman I. At its peak, the Ottoman Empire dominated Anatolia, the Balkans, and Northern Africa. Its capital was in Istanbul, previously Constantinople (in modern-day Turkey).

Their strategic location between Europe and Asia led to commercial benefits, as they had a strong trade presence in the Mediterranean and Black Seas, as well as the Persian Gulf of the Middle East. Much revenue was raised through taxes both on trade and within the Empire. Europeans looked for new trade routes to avoid clashes with the powerful Ottoman Empire.

As with earlier Islamic empires, religion spread with expansion. *Ghazis* were warriors seen as necessary for such diffusion of religion. The Ottoman Empire's military strength became dependent on gunpowder for muskets and artillery (cannons). They utilized a system called *devshirme*, whereby boys were taken from Christian families of the conquered. They would be converted, and turned into soldiers. Ottoman elite soldiers were called *janissaries*.

Rulers of the Ottoman Empire were called **sultans**, and rule was based on family lineage. The Ottomans relied on a complex bureaucracy where policy would trickle down from the top to local governments. You need to know **Suleiman the Magnificent**, or Suleiman I. His reign was the true peak of the Empire. By 1530, Suleiman had pushed as far west as Central Europe. **He gave religious freedom to Jews and Christians.** He also devised a law code for political, social, and economic matters. The code coexisted with Sharia (Islamic) law.

As will be shown, the Ottoman Empire would weaken by the middle of the nineteenth century due to many factors including nationalism from the diverse populations within. At that time, a westernizing policy called the *Tanzimat reforms* looked to move towards secular studies in schools, a legal system that did not discriminate based on religion, and westernization in government. The reforms also altered taxation. Before the changes, *iltizām* existed, which was a tax farming system where wealthy elites would collect taxes on behalf of the state and keep some revenue for themselves. The Tanzimat reforms divided both religious and secular (not stressing religious law) leaders.

Definition: Safavid Empire

From 1501-1722, they were the Shi'a Muslims (unlike their Ottoman rivals who were Sunni) who conquered Persia (Iran). Their peak occurred under Shah Abbas. Because it was situated in the Middle East, there was great trade with Europe and the Ottoman Empire. After Abbas died, the Empire weakened militarily, economically, and was susceptible to corruption. Despite surviving a series of seventeenth century battles along the Safavid-Mughal border (modern-day Afghanistan), the Safavid Empire eventually dissolved in the eighteenth century and fell to Afghan invaders.

Definition: Silk Roads and Indian Ocean Trade

The Silk Roads were trade routes c130BC to 1453 that went from China, through India, and into the Middle East and Rome. Spices (used for seasoning and preserving food), exotic animals, metal goods, gold, silk, and many other products made their way from the Eastern World into the West. Because of the popular and valuable silks that came out of China, the path of trade was called the Silk Roads. This network is a great example of cultural diffusion.

China did much trading in the Indian Ocean, as did India, Eastern Africa, Indonesia, and eventually European powers. Gold, silk, porcelain, iron, agricultural items such as cotton, and much more, made its way from continent to continent. Not only did tangible goods pass hands on trade routes, but religion did as well. Islam and Christianity would make its way across Asia for centuries. From c1000-c1500, a true complex interregional exchange emerged in the Indian Ocean.

The *Srivijaya Empire* in modern-day Java, Indonesia was one such empire in the Indian Ocean that was strong c1200. Its geographical ties to India and China enhanced trade while making it a Buddhist stronghold in the region. A later strong empire in the area was the *Sultanate of Malacca* (c1400-1511) which grew strong from trade due to its natural harbors and location in the Indian Ocean. They gave tribute and gained trade from the Ming Dynasty. In addition, after a Malaccan leader converted to Islam, this further brought trade from places such as Gujarat in western India.

Review Questions for the AP World History: Modern Exam

Use the following map for Questions 1-3.

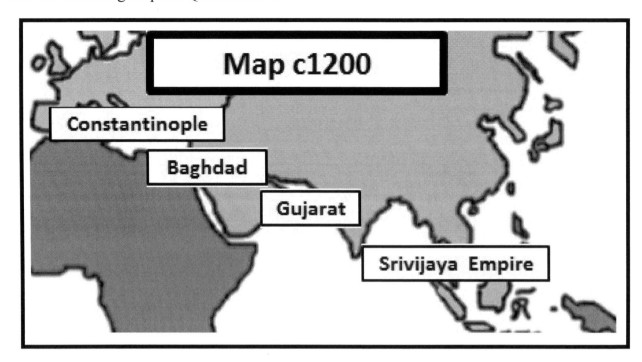

1. Which of the following was true of the above map?
   A) The spread of Christianity halted east of Baghdad
   B) Both land and sea routes linked Europe to Asia
   C) Extension of tribute to Zheng He reached the Byzantine Empire
   D) The proximity of land-based empires led to the inevitable fall of Muslim empires

2. Which of the following would not be exchanged across the cities above?
   A) Exotic animals
   B) Metal
   C) Spices
   D) Maize

3. Which of the following time periods helped foster the greater exchange of goods?
   A) Pax Mongolica
   B) Edo Period
   C) Heian Period
   D) Reign of Aurangzeb

Review Questions for the SAT Subject Test

1. Two important rivers of ancient China were the Huang He and the
   A) Ganges
   B) Tigris
   C) Indus
   D) Yangtze
   E) Brahmaputra

2. All of the following were components of the Dynastic Cycle EXCEPT:
   A) Natural disasters devastating the people
   B) The rise of a new dynasty
   C) Decrease in religious adherence
   D) Revolts of the people
   E) A time of peace or conflict

3. The above structure was built to
   A) keep out invaders from the north
   B) prevent people from escaping the country
   C) imprison those who did not pay taxes
   D) act as a dam to control flooding rivers during monsoon season
   E) act as a trading post on the Silk Roads

4. The Han Dynasty c100 BCE, and the Koryo-Dynasty c1300 CE, both governed their Empires through
   A) edicts from one dictator
   B) a network of officers based on family relationship
   C) representative democracy
   D) direct democracy of the local peasants and farmers
   E) a government bureaucracy based on civil service exams

5. Which was invented by the Tang and Song Dynasties?
   A) Wheelbarrow
   B) Iron tools
   C) Slash-and-burn farming
   D) Drainage systems
   E) Movable type

6. Women in ancient China were
   A) often foot bound and kept subservient
   B) allowed to be part of the lawmaking gentry
   C) an important component of the Dynastic Cycle
   D) given the Mandate of Heaven more often than men
   E) forced into military service after marriage

7. Which of the following was true of the voyages of Zheng He?
   A) He opened up China to Western trade from England and Spain
   B) His fleet of boats reached North America
   C) His ships were larger and predated European exploration by a century
   D) He discovered the fastest route possible to the West Indies
   E) He refused to take tribute from leaders

8. The Mongol Empire never permanently took over parts of modern-day
    A) China
    B) Japan
    C) Russia
    D) Middle East
    E) Korea

9. In the Umayyad Caliphate, Shi'a and Sunni Muslims conflicted most over the
    A) interpretation of the Qur'an
    B) length of the holy month of Ramadan
    C) relationship of the caliph to Muhammad
    D) architecture styles used for mosques
    E) role of women in society

10. Both Ottoman ruler Suleiman and Akbar the Great of the Mughal Dynasty
    A) expelled Catholics from Asia Minor
    B) converted to Buddhism
    C) favored the spread of Hinduism throughout Asia and Asia Minor
    D) permitted certain religious freedoms
    E) controlled land in the Balkans

Answers and Explanations

AP World History: Modern

1. **B.** The Silk Roads and the Indian Ocean proved to be locations of great exchange at this time.

2. **D**. Maize was a plant from the New World. Native American culture was isolated from the Silk Roads.

3. **A**. It was in the interest of the Mongols to support a mostly peaceful transition of goods across the Silk Roads.

SAT Subject Test

1. **D**. Today, the Yangtze River is still a major fishing and transportation hub in China.

2. **C**. The Dynastic Cycle was used to explain the transfer of power throughout hundreds of years of Chinese dynasties. Once an Emperor had the Mandate of Heaven, they ruled until their power naturally declined.

3. **A**. The Great Wall was constructed in stages over more than a thousand years. Shi Huangdi was an Emperor who expanded the wall's early construction. It was built to keep out invaders from the north. Over China's history, invasions continued to occur despite the wall.

4. **E**. A bureaucracy is a complex network of specialized government jobs. The Han Dynasty used civil service tests to determine who would work such jobs. A similar bureaucratic testing system (civil service exams) is used today in the United States.

5. **E**. The Tang provided block print, which would print images. The Song went one step further and invented movable type, which allowed a printer to change letters, or different parts of the image.

6. **A**. Women were kept inferior to men in ancient China. It wouldn't be until the twentieth century, mainly during communist rule, that women would see political gains in China.

7. **C**. Zheng He's fleet of ships c1400 was greater than those used in European exploration missions during the fifteenth and sixteenth centuries. He traveled great distances to places such as the Persian Gulf, Africa, and modern-day Indonesia.

8. **B**. Japan's island geography made it difficult for the Mongols to conquer. A terrible storm wiped out Mongol ships when they attempted to invade.

9. **C**. The dispute was over the relationship of the caliph (religious leader) to Muhammad. Today, these two sects still experience conflict in the Middle East.

10. **D**. Suleiman gave freedoms to non-Muslims within the Ottoman Empire. The same can be said of Akbar the Great of the Mughal Empire.

Greece and Rome

The greatest influence on today's Western Culture of North America and Europe comes from ancient Greece and Rome. Many Western ideas such as government, architecture, literature, math, science, and philosophy, had their roots in Greece. The Romans adopted many of these ideas and spread them throughout their Empire. After Rome fell, the culture was brought East by the Byzantine Empire. Many of the achievements and ideas of the Greco-Roman world have influenced the last two thousand years of global history.

HERE IS WHAT YOU NEED TO KNOW:
• GREECE
Question: How did Greece's geography affect its development?

Answer: Early Greek culture emerged c1600 BCE near Mycenae. These people were the Mycenaeans.

Mainland Greece is:

1. Mountainous, which made it difficult to link ancient city-states. This led to isolation.

2. Surrounded by water on three sides, which made the peninsula perfect for sea-travel and trade. The Greeks also controlled nearby islands.

Definition: Polis

A polis is a Greek city-state. Major business and government proceedings were conducted atop a hill called an *acropolis*. A polis could function as a:

1. Monarchy – Ruled by a king.

2. Aristocracy – Ruled by wealthy nobles.

3. Oligarchy – Ruled by a powerful and wealthy elite.

Definition: Homer, c750 BCE

Homer wrote epic poems such as the *Iliad* and the *Odyssey*. The *Iliad* was set during the Trojan War between Troy (in Anatolia, or Turkey) and Greek city-states. This is the story where the Greeks hid inside a wooden horse to sneak into Troy. The *Odyssey* portrays the aftermath of the Fall of Troy.

Question: What was the difference between Athens and Sparta?

Answer:

Sparta was a strict military society. From a young age, boys were trained and drilled for military service. It was also an oligarchy, which meant it was ruled by a select few citizens, including two kings who controlled the army. *Athens*, whose leader was Pericles c450 BCE, supported a ***direct democracy***. This meant that many of the local male citizens could govern over the affairs of the polis. Women and slaves had no political power. Education, more than military training, was favored in Athens.

Both Athens and Sparta teamed up to defeat invaders in the Persian Wars from 490-479 BCE. The victory helped Athens usher in a new golden age of culture in the fifth century BCE.

Definition: Peloponnesian War

In 431 BCE, Sparta declared war on the Athenians. Because of Sparta's military advantage, Athens surrendered in 404 BCE. The war devastated the Athenian government and led many to question the efficiency of democracy.

Question: What were some of the cultural accomplishments of the Greeks?

Answer:

1. Classical Art and Architecture – As seen in the Athenian *Parthenon*, symmetry and columns were major components. The famous types of columns to know are Doric

The Parthenon's symmetry and use of columns makes it an excellent example of classical architecture. Note that restoration of this great piece of history is an ongoing project.

(representing strength), Ionic (wisdom), and Corinthian (beauty). Like architecture, Greek sculpture was also symmetrical. It often portrayed cultural events, war scenes, and the human body.

2. Drama – Theatrical performances of both comedies and tragedies were popular.

3. Literature – Besides Homer's poems, writers to know are Sophocles (*Oedipus the King* and *Antigone*), Aeschylus (*The Oresteia*), and Euripides (*Medea*).

4. Philosophy after the Peloponnesian War – A new era of thinking began (explained next).

5. Math – Pythagoras had a famous theorem regarding the triangle, Euclid's *Elements* laid the foundation for geometry, and Archimedes used the measurement of π (pi).

6. Science – Aristarchus studied astronomy and the movement of the planets and sun. Hippocrates made great strides in medicine.

7. Olympics – These games that were once held to honor the god Zeus are still held today for international athletic competition.

Question: Who were the "Big Three" philosophers of Ancient Greece?

Answer: **SPA**

1. **S**ocrates (469-399 BCE) – He believed in questioning the world around him. Socrates stated that "***the unexamined life is not worth living.***" The government found him guilty of corrupting the youth of Athens. He was sentenced to death.

2. **P**lato (427-347 BCE) – A student of Socrates, he constructed much of his writings as dialogues between more than one person. He wrote ***The Republic***, where he outlined an efficient government controlled by the most intelligent leaders, or philosopher-kings.

3. **A**ristotle (384-322 BCE) – A student of Plato, he used logic to test sciences such as biology, psychology, and metaphysics. Alexander the Great was one of his students.

Another important philosophy of the Greek

and Roman world was *Stoicism*, which encouraged people to embrace natural law and virtue, while controlling human desires for power, pleasure, and material gain.

Definition: Hellenistic Age

North of Greece is Macedonia. There in 359 BCE, Philip II became king. By the time of his assassination in 336 BCE, Macedonia controlled or occupied much of the Greek peninsula. Philip's son, Alexander, declared himself the new king. Alexander the Great, as he would later become known, defeated King Darius III of Persia. After that victory, he marched into Egypt, and spread as far east as India.

After his conquests, a blending of Greek, Persian, Egyptian, and Indian cultures took place. This cultural diffusion was known as *Hellenistic culture*, and the exchanging of ideas occurred in architecture, religion, art, and literature. Much of this exchange took place in the Egyptian city of Alexandria which was a center for Mediterranean exchange.

• ROME
Definition: Etruscans

The Etruscans (768 BCE-264 BCE) controlled much of northern and western Italy, and influenced Roman religious rituals, art, architecture (arches), use of iron, and even their system of writing. The Roman alphabet was influenced by the Etruscans, who had been influenced earlier by the Greeks.

Question: How did Rome's early republic function?

Answer: A republic is a type of government where the citizens vote for others to represent them. In later centuries, different styles of the Roman Republic would be adopted all over the world. The Roman Republic was comprised of:

1. *Patricians* – The *aristocracy*, or rich property owners who had the most power.

2. *Plebeians* – Commoners such as merchants and farmers. They were not allowed to hold high office. Eventually, in the Roman Senate, they became elected officials called *tribunes*.

3. Senate – Controlled by the aristocracy, this strong legislative group served for life. As mentioned above, plebeians eventually received a voice here.

4. Dictators – The Roman Republic was allowed to appoint a dictator, or absolute ruler, to govern in times of war or conflict.

5. *Twelve Tables of Law*, c450 BCE – These were written laws that expressed individual rights within the Republic. They were displayed at the Roman Forum (meeting center) for all to see.

Question: What was the extent of the Roman Empire before the rise of Julius Caesar?

Answer: Land-owning citizens had to perform mandatory military service in the Roman Legion.

1. The Legions conquered what is now modern-day Italy.

2. Competing for trade in the Mediterranean, Rome fought the *Punic Wars* with Carthage in northern Africa. There were three wars fought between 264-146 BCE.

3. The Second Punic War saw Carthaginian leader *Hannibal* take his troops, horses, and elephants through the French Alps and attack Rome from the north. He never captured the city, and a Roman general named Scipio defeated him near Carthage.

4. In the third war, Senator Cato's belief that, "Carthage must be destroyed" became a reality when in 146 BCE, it was set on fire. Rome's victory in battle gave them control of the Medi-

terranean Sea. Less than 100 years later, their Empire expanded from Western Europe to Anatolia (Turkey).

Question: What should I know about Julius Caesar?

Answer:

1. He was elected to the high office of consul in 59 BCE, and along with two others, comprised a *triumvirate* of rulers. After civil war plagued Rome, Julius Caesar emerged to secure power.

2. Caesar became a dictator, or absolute ruler, and conquered land in Greece, Western Europe, Egypt, and Asia Minor. For centuries, the Roman Empire would control trade in the Mediterranean Sea. Through land and sea travel they would take in textiles, animals, food such as fruit and grain, oil, and raw materials/metals. Slaves were also traded.

3. He gave citizenship to some in the conquered territories, and preached land reform to aid the poor.

4. He became dictator for life in 44 BCE, but was assassinated shortly thereafter on March 15, 44 BCE...the Ides of March.

Question: What happened after Caesar's assassination?

Answer: Caesar's relative Octavian, along with General Mark Antony, banded together to rule Rome. After the two experienced conflict, Octavian emerged as the true leader of Rome and took on the title of *Augustus*.

Definition: Pax Romana

Pax Romana was a time of about 200 years of peace from 27 BCE to 180 CE. It coincided with the rise of Augustus. This tranquil period led to greater expansion of the Roman Empire, vast trade, and cultural advances.

The arches of the Roman Colosseum

Question: What cultural advancements of Rome should I know?

Answer:

1. The great architectural project of the Roman Colosseum provided a meeting center for entertainment. Gladiators were known to fight to the death in this arena. On smaller structures, domes were used by the Romans to create vaulted ceilings.

2. As stated earlier, you need to know about the Twelve Tables of Law.

3. *Aqueducts* were stone and concrete structures, typically on arches, that distributed water to the population. In addition, an impressive network of roads linked the Empire.

4. Virgil's *Aeneid* was modeled after the epics of the Greeks. Such cultural diffusion of the Greeks was common in Rome. Roman literature, art, and architecture all showed Greek influence. This combination of Greco-Roman culture laid the foundation for *Western Civilization*, or *Western Culture* in Europe.

5. As stated in the religion chapter, Christianity spread through the Roman Empire. In

313 CE, persecution of Christians ended after Emperor Constantine won a battle which he attributed to Christianity. The Edict of Milan promoted religious tolerance.

Question: What led to the Fall of Rome?

Answer: Rome fell in 476 CE. It collapsed because of economic issues such as inflation and failing agriculture, and political factors such as overexpansion.

A century earlier, Emperor Constantine moved the capital of the Empire eastward from Rome to Byzantium (Constantinople). This also hastened the decline of Rome. After invasions from tribes such as the Huns (first led by Attila), Rome weakened from famine and political unrest. In the end, the depleted Empire fell quietly.

Question: What should I know about the Byzantine Empire?

Answer: The Eastern Roman Empire survived as the Byzantine Empire. You need to know about Emperor Justinian. Under his leadership c560, the Byzantines controlled most of the Mediterranean Sea, including northern Africa, southern Spain, modern-day Italy, the Balkans, and Asia Minor. He ruled alongside his powerful wife Theodora. She was consulted on laws, supported women's rights, and became the most powerful woman in the Empire. Justinian:

1. Established a code of Roman law c530 CE. Justinian's Code contained social laws expanding the rights of women (marriage rights) and slaves. It also provided laws against *heresy* (clashing with the established religion).

2. He supported a unification of church and state. His most ornate church was called the Hagia Sophia and was a center for Byzantine Christianity.

3. After Justinian, the Empire gradually lost power over several centuries, as invaders from various locales took over territory.

When the great capital of Constantinople (now called Istanbul) was overrun by the Ottomans in 1453, the Hagia Sophia was converted into a mosque. Most of all, you need to know that the Byzantine Empire preserved the learning established by Greece and Rome. This includes advancements in literature, philosophy, and architecture.

Question: What happened to Christianity in the Byzantine Empire in 1054?

Answer: There was a *schism*, or split. This East-West schism occurred partly because there was a controversy over the use of *icons*, or images used in prayer, in the Eastern parts of the Byzantine Empire. In 730, Emperor Leo III declared icons to be synonymous with idol worship. Other issues continued to separate religious leaders by 1054.

Thus, the religious practices of Eastern and Western Europe drifted apart, and there was an eventual split where the Eastern faction became *Eastern Orthodox*, while the Western one continued to practice *Roman Catholicism*.

Question: How did Byzantine culture affect Russia?

1. Vladimir the Great and Yaroslav the Wise supported adopting Byzantine Christianity in Kiev c1000 CE. Kiev was a center of trade for Russians, Vikings, and northern Slavic people. The Vikings, used *longships* to control the Baltic Sea, and Eastern European rivers and ports. They took settlement in Russian trading centers such as Kiev and Novgorod.

2. The Mongol Empire controlled the Russian people for about 250 years.

3. When Russia became independent from Mongol rule in 1480, influences of Byzantine culture were still present. One example is the *Cyrillic alphabet*, which has connections to Slavic people who traded in Constantinople. Many Russians had a Slavic heritage.

Review Questions for the SAT Subject Test (NOTE: This time period is not tested on in AP World History: Modern)

1. How did geography influence the development of the Greek polis before 500 BCE?
    A) Flatlands led to immense cultural diffusion throughout the peninsula
    B) Proximity to the Nile River created opportunity for trade with Africa
    C) The Romans were able to conquer Greece in 400 BC because of its position on the Aegean Sea
    D) Greece's open terrain made it an easy target for Persian conquest
    E) Mountains isolated individual city-states

2. The Golden Age of Athens came after which conflict?
    A) First Punic War
    B) Persian Wars
    C) Peloponnesian War
    D) Trojan War
    E) Second Punic War

3. Which of the following best describes Spartan society?
    A) Immense concentration on art and architecture
    B) Development of a disciplined military-state
    C) Presence of an absolute monarchy
    D) Promotion of a direct democracy
    E) Concentration on Socratic philosophy

4. The philosophy of Socrates can best be described as
    A) a belief in a republic controlled by a philosopher king
    B) great research in biology and metaphysics
    C) asking questions to discover the truth
    D) arguments for rigid class structure
    E) a strong belief in filial piety

5. Which of the following best classifies Pax Romana?
    A) A time when the Twelve Tables of Law established women's rights
    B) Pericles' creation of a direct democracy
    C) Julius Caesar's extension of the Roman Empire into India
    D) A period of war with Carthage
    E) A lasting peace that helped develop culture

6. Aqueducts were important to the Roman Empire because they
    A) improved the architecture of Catholic churches
    B) helped to distribute water to the Empire
    C) provided a defense from invading tribes from the north
    D) became a means for trading on the Silk Roads
    E) linked the Roman Empire with India

7. The end of religious persecutions against Christians within the Roman Empire coincided with
   A) the early years of Pax Romana
   B) Octavian's rise to power
   C) the fall of the Roman Empire
   D) a military victory by Emperor Constantine
   E) the fall of the Byzantine Empire

8. All of the following were causes for the Fall of Rome in 476 CE EXCEPT:
   A) Overexpansion of the Empire
   B) Corruption of public officials
   C) An increase in taxes
   D) Decay of the infrastructure of Roman roads
   E) pressure from foreign lands

9. Which of the following was true of Justinian's Code?
   A) It increased rights among women
   B) New prayer rituals were instituted for Muslims
   C) Christian prayer was made illegal inside the Hagia Sophia
   D) It was the first code of law ever created by an Empire
   E) It encouraged heresy

10. The Byzantine Empire was different from Rome in all of the following ways EXCEPT:
    A) Language
    B) Geography
    C) Religious practice
    D) Trade partners
    E) Greek heritage

Answers and Explanations

SAT Subject Test

1. **E**. Greece is a mountainous peninsula. Mountains made it difficult for the Greeks to unite, and led to the creation of independent city-states. An ancient Greek city-state is referred to as a polis.

2. **B**. Greek victory in the Persian Wars (490-479 BCE) ushered in a Golden Age of cultural achievement.

3. **B**. Whereas Athens concentrated more on cultural achievement, the Spartans were a disciplined military state.

4. **C**. Socrates believed that "the unexamined life is not worth living." He questioned as a way to create dialogue and analysis. This *Socratic Method* is still used today.

5. **E**. Pax Romana was the Roman peace. It strengthened the Empire and led to cultural advancements within Rome.

6. **B**. Aqueducts were stone structures built on arches that helped distribute water to areas within, and outside of, Rome.

7. **D**. Once before a battle, Emperor Constantine had visions of crosses in the sky. After the subsequent military victory, he ended the persecution of Christians with the Edict of Milan.

8. **D**. There were many causes for the Fall of Rome. However, some Roman roads are still present today in Italy and elsewhere. A great number of them were still intact by 476 CE.

9. **A**. Justinian's Code, though not the first code in the history of the world, gave more rights to women within the Byzantine Empire.

10. **E**. Although the Byzantine Empire was considerably east of Rome, they still maintained a Greek heritage similar to the Romans.

Middle Ages, Renaissance, and the Protestant Reformation

After the Fall of Rome, Western Europe went into intellectual decline. The Middle Ages, or Medieval Period, saw a fragmented Europe that mostly operated under a system of feudalism. Complicating matters were the harsh realities of war and disease. However, these Dark Ages gave way to the Renaissance where Europe experienced a rebirth and flowering of culture. This rebirth was also accompanied by controversy. When Martin Luther hammered the 95 Theses to the Church at Wittenberg, a shockwave was sent throughout the religious establishment of Europe. The Protestant Reformation would lead to new religious sects by the seventeenth century.

HERE IS WHAT YOU NEED TO KNOW:
• THE MIDDLE AGES
Definition: Middle Ages

"The Middle Ages" are what historians call the time period in Europe between roughly 500-1500. This was an era when Europe slowly evolved after the Fall of Rome. Because of a slow growth in intellectual thought, parts of this time are referred to as the Dark Ages. A synonym for Middle Ages is ***Medieval***.

Definition: Carolingian Dynasty/Charlemagne

The Franks were Germanic people from Gaul (France). Their first Christian king was Clovis. When he died, Charles "The Hammer" Martel took over and gained territory. He prevented Islam from spreading to the region in the 732 Battle of Tours. Later, his son, Pepin the Short, was given the title of "King by the Grace of God." This began the Carolingian Dynasty.

Pepin's son was ***Charlemagne***. Under his reign from 768-814, his Carolingian Empire controlled more land than the Byzantines. Charlemagne's Frankish Kingdom conquered or controlled areas in Central, Eastern, and Western Europe. Charlemagne was crowned Holy Roman Emperor in 800. Charlemagne's title inspired the Holy Roman Empire, which dominated Central Europe for centuries beginning c1000.

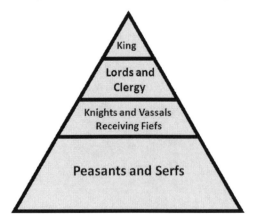

Definition: Feudalism

The Middle Ages were a harsh time where invaders (Vikings, Magyars, and Muslims) looked to plunder European lands.

Feudalism was a political and economic system that involved land ownership and military service. Feudalism was strong in most of Europe until about 1500. It was still prominent in Japan into the nineteenth century.

The general pyramid of feudalism involved a king on top, followed by nobles known as lords. Beneath were ***knights*** who protected the lord's ***manor***, or estate. Some knights received a fief (piece of land) for their service and were known as vassals. At the bottom were tax-paying peasants, and serfs. ***Serfs*** were bound to the land and could not freely travel. There was also often an unpaid ***corvée*** labor system whereby serfs and free peasants could be assembled by landlords for short-term projects

King

Lords and Clergy

Knights and Vassals Receiving Fiefs

Peasants and Serfs

such as building roads or improving the natural landscape. Serfdom existed in Russia until the nineteenth century, when Czar Alexander II emancipated (freed) them.

Definition: Chivalry

Chivalry was a code of conduct where a knight fought honorably for the lord and his lady. This was similar to the Japanese *bushido code* of the *samurai warrior*.

Chivalry affected the way knights treated women. Though not equals, women were seen in a pure and virtuous light. *Troubadours*, or musicians in castles, sang about the themes of love and honor. Women who were nobles could inherit land in many places. Such women were also more likely to receive an education. As for peasant women, they were usually confined to homes tending to children, and working agriculture.

Question: What should I know about the Middle Age economy?

Answer:

1. It was mostly agricultural, with a *Three-Field System* whereby land would be farmed in sections. One of those sections would be left unfarmed so the soil could rejuvenate.

2. Many worked in business and were artisans. The merchant class was known as *burghers*. *Guilds*, similar to today's unions, protected the working rights of artisans of a similar craft. The guild members were *masters* of their trade. Before becoming a master, one had to be an *apprentice* for another master, and then a wage-earning *journeyman*.

3. In Northern Europe near the Baltic Sea, there was a commercial organization known as the *Hanseatic League*. States in modern-day Germany, Sweden, Poland, Latvia, Estonia, and others, formed this organization to protect trading rights such as freedom of the seas, and fair weights and measures. The League was strong from the thirteenth through fifteenth centuries.

Question: What should I know about the Roman Catholic Church of the Middle Ages?

Answer: Because the Church was incredibly important and powerful, the Middle Ages was also known as the *Age of Faith*. You should know:

1. The Church was in charge of giving out *sacraments* (sacred rites) which were necessary for *salvation*, or being delivered from sin to ultimately go to Heaven. The Church's clergy was comprised of first the Pope, then archbishops and bishops, and finally local priests. The law of the church was called canon law.

2. *Lay investiture* - This was when kings and rich nobles appointed religious officials. This would give them an unfair influence over the Church. Though the Church was powerful, activities such as lay investiture were viewed by many as corrupt.

3. *Excommunication* - This meant to kick one out of the Church.

4. The Church struggled for power with the Holy Roman Emperors. At the Concordat of Worms in 1122, the Pope and Emperor compromised their issues.

5. Still, corruption continued. *Simony* occurred when Church positions were sold.

6. Churches were in Romanesque and *Gothic* architecture styles. Romanesque churches were symmetrical with rounded arches and towers. Gothic churches were ornate with pointed arches, stained-glass windows, and *flying buttresses* that linked walls. (See photo of St. Vitus Cathedral in Prague on next page.)

7. Some attacked the church, such as John Wycliffe and Jan Hus. Around 1380, Wycliffe said that Jesus Christ was the true head of the Church, not the Pope. Around 1400, Hus preached that the Bible was of a higher author-

St. Vitus Cathedral in Prague is a gothic church with pointed arches, flying buttresses, and stained-glass windows

ity than the Pope. Hus was excommunicated and burned at the stake.

Definition: The Crusades, 1095-1291

These were religious wars fought between European Christians and Muslims from Africa and Asia Minor (Anatolia/Turkey). Both were fighting to secure the Holy Land of Jerusalem. In total, there were nine Crusades. You don't need to know all of them, but you should know:

1. The First Crusade was called for by Pope Urban II in 1095. The Crusaders were mainly Roman Catholic armored knights with crosses on their shields. They briefly captured land near Jerusalem, but could not hold onto it. Turks from the former *Seljuk Empire of Anatolia* prevented a Crusader victory.

2. In the Second Crusade, Jerusalem was taken by the Muslim commander *Saladin*. In the Third Crusade, Crusader and English King *Richard the Lionheart* reached an agreement that allowed Christians to enter the Holy Land as visitors in 1192.

3. Though violent and creating much religious strife, the Crusades created new trade networks between Europe, Asia, and Northern Africa. Not only were goods and innovations exchanged, but scientific and mathematical thought as well.

4. The Crusades further weakened the system of feudalism, as money became more valuable and cities began to rise.

Definition: Spanish Inquisition

This was a movement in Spain that looked to maintain the orthodoxy of the country through forced conversions and deportation. A tribunal interrogated those seen as heretics (people with beliefs that clashed with the Catholic Church). Typically the oppressed were Jews, Muslims, or recent converts to Christianity. Confessions were often forced through torture. Remnants of the inquisition existed into the nineteenth century.

The Inquisition came amidst the *Reconquista*, which was a plan to remove Muslims from Spain. Christians kicked out the remaining Muslim kingdoms in 1492. For almost 800 years before that, the Moors (Muslim invaders from northern Africa) had conquered much of the Iberian Peninsula (Spain and Portugal).

Definition: Thomas Aquinas, Dante Alighieri, Margery Kempe

Aquinas was a religious scholar who wrote the *Summa Theologica* c1274. His work is a combination of Christian theology (study of religious faith) and Greek philosophical thought, specifically from Aristotle. Aquinas' followers were called *scholastics*.

Dante Alighieri's *Divine Comedy* is an epic poem from c1321 that portrays a soul's journey. The book travels through Hell, Purgatory, and Heaven. In the book, Dante incorporates some of the same religious philosophy used by Aquinas.

Margery Kempe was a traveling mystic who wrote an early autobiography about her religious experiences and pilgrimages in the Medieval world c1400. Her work is considered by many to be the first autobiography ever written in English, as she recorded both the power of her devotion and the power of the Church at the time.

Definition: Great Schism, 1378-1417

Unlike the schism of 1054 that divided religion between Eastern Orthodox and Roman Catholicism, this schism was *within* the Catholic Church. Two people declared themselves Pope; Pope Urban VI in Rome, and Clement VII in Avignon, France. Eventually, a different Pope was elected.

Definition: Bubonic Plague/Black Death

Approximately one-third of Europe's population died of this dreaded disease. The plague was believed to be brought to Italy from Asia in 1348. It then spread to the entire continent. The Black Death ultimately hurt the prestige of the Church as prayers went unanswered. The plague further weakened the stability of the feudal system.

Definition: Hundred Years' War, 1337-1453

England and France had a history of conflict. In 1066, **William the Conqueror** from Northern France (Normandy) took the English throne. His descendants continued to rule England. That included King Henry II, who married Eleanor of Aquitaine. She had been a wife to both an English and a French king.

This war wasn't really 100 years. But from 1337-1453 England and France were engaged in battle. In the war, a French girl named ***Joan of Arc*** saw visions from God and felt compelled to save France. Although Joan led the army to victory, she was later captured and accused of heresy and witchcraft. She was burned at the stake in 1431.

The Hundred Years' War was mostly a standoff, as England won very little territory by war's end.

• THE RENAISSANCE
Definition: Renaissance

This was a time period from about 1350-1550 that saw a "rebirth" of learning and culture. There was also a push for individualism, as unlike those born into wealth, a new merchant and artistic class believed that one should be judged by achievements. The movement affected art, literature, political thought, and science.

Question: Where did the Renaissance begin?

Answer: Italy. Italy borders the Mediterranean Sea, and is a perfect port for economic commerce and trade. In addition, Italy's social roots were based on the classical traditions of Greco-Roman culture. The Italian Renaissance was centered in Florence where the influential Medici family ruled the city by 1434.

Definition: Humanism

Humanism was a cultural and philosophical movement that celebrated a person's achievements. Whereas the Middle Ages stressed studying Christianity, humanism looked to investigate the classical teachings of ancient Greece and Rome. Humanists expanded education in subjects called humanities (social studies, literature, philosophy, languages). They wanted to ***secularize*** society, or make it worldly instead of religious.

A replica of Michelangelo's David *stands in Florence for all to see*

Question: What should I know about Renaissance Art?

Answer: Whereas Medieval art was concerned with religious themes that were often out of proportion, many of the Renaissance paintings were secular and done in *realism*. This meant breathtaking detailed images proportional to the human body. Renaissance art was colorful and done in perspective, or three dimensions. Some artists to know are:

1. Michelangelo – His statue of the *David* was completed in 1504 and today can be found in Florence. The statue is both a symbol of strength and a celebration of the human body. Michelangelo also painted the ceiling of the Sistine Chapel in Rome (Vatican City). He sculpted the *Pietà* which portrays the Virgin Mary holding her son Jesus after the crucifixion. The statue is currently at St. Peter's Basilica in Vatican City.

2. Raphael – He painted *Madonna and Child*. He also painted the *School of Athens*, which is a c1510 masterpiece where Plato walks with Aristotle. It is a *fresco*, which is a work of art painted on damp plaster, typically on walls.

3. Leonardo da Vinci – c1500, he was truly a "Renaissance Man," as his talents went beyond art. Among other things he was an inventor, scientist, sculptor, and writer. His best known paintings were the *Mona Lisa* and *The Last Supper*. In both, one can sense the emotions of the subjects.

4. Donatello – He was a sculptor who also was able to convey emotions into stone.

5. Outside of Italy, Flemish painter Jan van Eyck was successful using oil paints. In Germany, Albrecht Dürer and Hans Holbein were famous for their paintings of realism that brought people to life.

Definition: Gutenberg's Printing Press, c1440

Literature became more widely available because of *Johann Gutenberg's* invention of the printing press. The *Gutenberg Bible* was one of the earliest works printed in Europe. Because of this new use of movable type, learning spread throughout Europe at a much faster pace. Further increasing education, many writers abandoned Latin and wrote books in *vernaculars*, or local/native tongues.

Question: What should I know about Renaissance literature?

Answer:

1. Niccolò Machiavelli wrote *The Prince* in 1513. In this work he explained that a strong leader must rule harshly to keep order. Otherwise, people would walk all over that leader. Therefore, a ruthless personality is needed to not only secure power, but hold onto it.

2. The *Elizabethan Age* refers to the reign of Queen Elizabeth where great literature was being produced in England (explained next).

3. England's Thomas More wrote *Utopia* which is a commentary about a fictitious, perfect, and peaceful place.

4. Erasmus was a humanist who wrote *The Praise of Folly*. He supported Biblical study and condemned corruption of the Church.

Definition: Elizabethan Age

This refers to the Renaissance period in England that coincided with the reign of Queen Elizabeth I from 1558-1603. Elizabeth Tudor was a patron of the arts who sponsored artistic endeavors. During this time, William Shakespeare of England wrote and produced comedies such as *The Merchant of Venice*, and tragedies like *Hamlet* and *Macbeth*.

Note: The Renaissance experienced in England, France, and Germany is known as the ***Northern Renaissance***.

• PROTESTANT REFORMATION

Question: What was the Protestant Reformation?

Answer: This was a movement by people who ***protest***ed, and wanted to reform (change for the better) the Roman Catholic Church. From 1517 through the next century, new sects of Christianity were formed.

Question: What were the causes of the Reformation?

Answer: For centuries there had been critics of the Roman Catholic Church, such as John Wycliffe and Jan Hus during the Middle Ages. By 1500, the causes for discontent were:

1. Selling of ***indulgences***. An indulgence reduced or removed punishments to those who sinned. Dominican priest Johann Tetzel sold indulgences to raise money to renovate St. Peter's Cathedral in Rome. Many objected to the selling of such "pardons."

2. Resentment to the power of the Pope and clergy.

3. A belief that the Bible was far more important than the power of church officials.

Definition: Martin Luther/95 Theses

On October 31, 1517, a religious monk named Martin Luther hammered a list of grievances to a church in Wittenberg, Germany. These were the *95 Theses*. They were quickly copied and distributed throughout Germany and Western Europe. The main ideas of Luther included:

1. The Bible was the authority of Christianity, not the clergy.

2. Only God could give salvation to heaven.

3. To achieve salvation, one must exercise faith in God's forgiveness.

4. Church practices created during the Middle Ages were not binding.

Luther also attacked the selling of indulgences. These ideas helped start the Protestant Reformation.

Question: What was the Church's reaction to Luther's ideas?

Answer: Pope Leo X excommunicated Luther (kicked him out of the Church) when he refused to take back his words.

In 1521, Luther stood trial in front of the Diet (assembly) of Worms at Worms, Germany. Again, he wouldn't retract his statements. Holy Roman Emperor Charles V issued the Edict of Worms, which labeled Luther a heretic. It also banned his writings and ideas. Still, ***Lutherans*** followed his teachings.

Question: What was the immediate impact of the Reformation in Germany?

Answer: As people began to preach Luther's teachings, violence ensued as peasants revolted in Germany looking for more political rights. In addition, German princes were divided as to which religion to support. Eventually, Holy

Roman Emperor Charles V was able to bring peace between the Catholic and Protestant princes. In the 1555 *Peace of Augsburg*, the princes agreed to allow the ruler of each German state to determine if it would be Catholic or Protestant.

Question: Why did Henry VIII of England abandon the Roman Catholic Church?

Answer: The Church would not allow Henry to annul, or declare his marriage invalid. He decided to break away from the Church, and in 1534, Parliament (the legislature of England) passed the *Act of Supremacy*. This made Henry the head of the Church of England. Because he was now independent of Rome, Henry could divorce his wife, Catherine.

Henry married six women in total. His second wife, Anne Boleyn, was accused of adultery and executed. Earlier, she gave birth to a daughter…who later became Queen Elizabeth I. For generations, England had religious conflicts between Protestants and Catholics.

Question: What should I know about the family tree of Henry VIII?

Answer: Henry had a son who ruled for six years. His first daughter, Mary, favored Catholicism during her reign and put to death many Protestants (hence her nickname, Bloody Mary). After Mary, Elizabeth I took the throne and brought England back to Protestantism. She became the head of the *Anglican* Church of England.

Definition: Calvinism and Predestination

Many different sects of Protestantism evolved. It is important to know about Calvinism.

Influenced by the teachings of John Calvin, Calvinists preach *predestination*, or the concept that God has planned the fate of all people. This means that only certain souls can find salvation. Calvinist principles spread to France, Netherlands, and Switzerland. It was also adopted by Presbyterians in Scotland.

Question: I'm confused – on a map, who is what religion?

Answer: Protestants lived in every country in Europe. However, you should know these generalizations c1600:

Protestant – Strong in England, Germany, and Scandinavia (Norway and Sweden)

Roman Catholicism – Strong in Spain, France, Italy, and Ireland. (Austria and Hungary were mixed between Protestant and Roman Catholic.)

Eastern Orthodox – Greece and Russia

Definition: Counter-Reformation/Catholic Reformation

This was an attempt by the Catholic Church to reform itself and keep church members from leaving. Beginning in 1545 at the *Council of Trent*, Catholics condemned the unwarranted selling of indulgences, and reaffirmed the importance of the Bible. They also stated that good works, as well as faith, were necessary for salvation.

One of the most influential reformers was Ignatius of Loyola. His followers became the Society of Jesus, or *Jesuits*. Their goal was to spread the teachings of Jesus and convert people to Catholicism. To a degree, they were successful in slowing the spread of Protestantism.

Question: What were the results of the Protestant Reformation?

Answer: The major outcome was division between religious sects. Furthermore, the Roman Catholic Church, which had been so powerful during the Middle Ages/Age of Faith, was negatively impacted. The recent invention of the printing press helped spread the ideas of new beliefs.

Review Questions for the AP World History: Modern Exam

"Upon this a question arises: whether it be better to be loved than feared or feared than loved? It may be answered that one should wish to be both, but, because it is difficult to unite them in one person, it is much safer to be feared than loved, when, of the two, either must be dispensed with. Because this is to be asserted in general of men, that they are ungrateful, fickle, false, cowardly, covetous, and as long as you succeed they are yours entirely; they will offer you their blood, property, life, and children, as is said above, when the need is far distant; but when it approaches they turn against you. And that prince who, relying entirely on their promises, has neglected other precautions, is ruined; because friendships that are obtained by payments, and not by greatness or nobility of mind, may indeed be earned, but they are not secured, and in time of need cannot be relied upon; and men have less scruple in offending one who is beloved than one who is feared, for love is preserved by the link of obligation which, owing to the baseness of men, is broken at every opportunity for their advantage; but fear preserves you by a dread of punishment which never fails."

— Niccolò Machiavelli, *The Prince*

1. Which of the following statements is most consistent with Machiavelli's point of view regarding the governed?
  A) Democracy benefits both the leader and the citizens
  B) A representative democracy is the best form of government
  C) Citizens would take advantage of weak leadership
  D) It is more important to love a leader than to fear one

2. Which of the following reflects the historical time period which influenced Machiavelli's writing?
  A) Early Middle Ages feudal period
  B) Before the second Crusade
  C) Reign of Charlemagne
  D) During the Renaissance

3. Which action taken reflects the sentiments of the above writing?
  A) Queen Elizabeth's defeat of the Spanish Armada
  B) Henry VIII's imprisonment of rebels against his religious doctrine
  C) Pope Urban's call for the Crusades
  D) William the Conqueror's invasion

Review Questions for the SAT Subject Test

1. Which Carolingian in 800 was the first to be crowned Holy Roman Emperor?
  A) Henry VIII
  B) Richard I
  C) Charlemagne
  D) Alexander the Great
  E) Richard III

2. The Medieval practice of lay investiture within the Catholic Church involved
  A) kings and nobles appointing religious officials
  B) selling sacraments which would lead to salvation
  C) forcefully removing a member from the Church
  D) enforcing strict interpretation of the Bible
  E) charitable donations to the poor

3. A result of the Crusades was
  A) peace in the Middle East for centuries
  B) an increase in cultural diffusion
  C) European control of Jerusalem
  D) revolutions in France
  E) the beginning of the Middle Ages

4. The Reconquista was a movement to
  A) expel Jews from the Roman Empire and distribute them across Europe
  B) recapture the Holy Land in and around Jerusalem
  C) convert those seen as heretics to Protestantism
  D) reclaim Spain from centuries of Muslim influence
  E) spread Islam throughout Western Europe

5. Unlike the schism of 1054, the Great Schism that began in 1378
  A) created the new religion of Eastern Orthodox
  B) united the Church of both the East and the West
  C) brought Roman Catholicism to Greece
  D) divided power between the Holy Roman Emperor and the Church
  E) involved a dispute as to who was the true Pope

6. Renaissance art and literature
  A) moved away from Greco-Roman traditions and styles
  B) originated in England, then moved through Central Europe
  C) lacked emotion and realism
  D) celebrated humanism, and individual achievement
  E) was confined to only Italy

7. Johann Gutenberg's influence on the Renaissance included the
  A) creation of fresco paintings
  B) spreading of the written word throughout Europe
  C) introduction of Flemish painting styles
  D) questioning of the importance of religion
  E) analysis of how a prince should rule

8. The selling of indulgences c1500 was unpopular to many because it meant
   A) one could sin, yet avoid punishment
   B) church officials would be appointed based upon wealth
   C) nobles, who were outside of the Church, could gain clergy offices
   D) the Holy Roman Emperor would control the Church instead of the Pope
   E) the Holy Land could not be reclaimed

9. Martin Luther's 95 Theses were written
   A) in response to the declining faith of Catholics
   B) to promote religion after its decline during the years of the Black Plague
   C) in protest to practices he found corrupt within the Catholic Church
   D) on behalf of Calvinists looking to break away from the Church
   E) as a plea to Crusaders in the Holy Land

10. Henry VIII became the head of the Church of England c1534 because he
   A) hoped to secure land in Italy which was controlled by the Church
   B) wanted a solution for the Great Schism
   C) was denied sacraments needed for salvation
   D) had a deeply religious adherence to Lutheranism
   E) wanted to end his marriage and the pope would not allow it

Answers and Explanations

AP World History: Modern Exam
1. **C**. Machiavelli asserts that if a leader permits too much in the way of leniency and freedom, the citizens would take advantage.

2. **D**. Nation-states gained strength during the Renaissance. This historical context is important in understanding Machiavelli's writing.

3. **B**. Censoring and imprisoning those who criticized him, Henry VIII instilled fear into his dissenters.

SAT Subject Test
1. **C**. Charlemagne, King of the Franks, was crowned as the first Holy Roman Emperor in 800.

2. **A**. Lay investiture meant giving kings and nobles the power to appoint church officials. This was one of several Church practices seen as corrupt.

3. **B**. Odd that war would lead to trade. But that was the case for the Crusades. This is an important fact to know.

4. **D**. Muslims had a strong presence in Spain for centuries. The Reconquista looked to drive them out, and reclaim the country for Roman Catholicism. The last Muslims left in 1492.

5. **E**. During the Great Schism there were two men who claimed to be Pope. One was in Rome, and one was in Avignon, France.

6. **D**. Humanism was a big component of Renaissance culture. It celebrated human achievement and stressed Greco-Roman culture.

7. **B**. Gutenberg's printing press spread the written word throughout Europe.

8. **A**. Indulgences reduced or removed punishments from those who sinned. Their sale was heavily criticized by those who wanted to reform the Catholic Church.

9. **C**. In 1517, Martin Luther hammered the 95 Theses to a church in Wittenberg, Germany. He was protesting what he believed to be corruption within the Church.

10. **E**. Under Church law, Henry VIII could not annul his marriage. To get around this, he became the head of the Church of England and granted himself the divorce.

Africa, Native America, and the Age of Exploration

African and Native American Empires thrived for centuries. Kingdoms in Western Africa depended on a valuable gold-salt trade. Culturally diverse because of its challenging geography, Africans had contact with different cultures from Europe, to the Middle East, to Asia. Unlike Africans, Native Americans were isolated from the rest of the globe living in what would become known as the New World. Much of their history and culture is still a mystery to the Western World. However, their impressive architectural creations and cultural symbols still impress historians and tourists alike.

The Age of Exploration brought Europeans to the New World, and within decades, the Empires of Native America were destroyed. Europeans extracted great wealth from these new lands. Explorers would capitalize on Africa as well, especially in the coming centuries.

HERE IS WHAT YOU NEED TO KNOW:
• AFRICA

Question: How diverse is Africa's climate?

Answer: Very. The various climate zones include:

1. Desert – The Sahara is the largest hot desert in the world. It experiences hot temperatures and dry soil. Traders, such as the Berbers of North Africa, would utilize the camel for tough treks across the desert. The desert has been expanding southward to a region called the *Sahel*. When grassy regions dry up, it's called *desertification*.

2. Savanna – Wet and dry seasons combine to create tall grassy plains that support agriculture. About one-half of Africa is Savanna.

3. Rain Forest – The middle of the continent has a wet climate with an abundance of trees. People do not typically populate the jungles near the Equator.

4. Steppe – Extreme temperatures and little rainfall.

5. Mediterranean – High temperatures with wet winters and autumns.

Question: What was early African society like?

Answer:

1. Nomadic people formed clans, or small groups. Rather than living in nuclear families (with just parents and children), people typically resided with extended families (grandparents, aunts, uncles, etc).

2. Most were *hunters and gatherers*, as often men hunted and women gathered vegetation. Cultivation was dependent on geography, as bananas and root-based crops were harvested in forests, while a grain called millet could be taken from the savanna grasslands.

3. An early religion was *animism*, which believed in the spirits that existed in nature (see religion chapter).

4. Some families were patrilineal, meaning they traced ancestry through the father. The opposite would be matrilineal, as some societies traced it through the mother.

Definition: Bantu-Speaking People

Because of the diversified geography, many different cultures emerged south of the Sahara Desert. However, tribal languages had similarities because they derived from the migrations of the *Bantu* people as early as 2000 BCE. Many of today's African languages date back to these ancient travelers.

Question: What African Empires should I know c800-1500?

Answer: The most important early trade network in Africa was the *gold-salt* exchange. Western Africa had abundant gold, but a lack of salt. Salt from the north towards the Sahara was available for trade. You should know the following Kingdoms of Africa's West Coast:

1. Ghana – During their Golden Age, c800-1050, they grew rich from their trade of gold. There was much cultural diffusion with the Muslim world.

2. Mali, c1200-c1450 – **Mansa Musa** was a powerful King. He performed the hajj, **and brought Islam into the Empire**.

3. Songhai, c1375-1591 - Controlling the trading city of Timbuktu, Songhai was the largest Empire in Western Africa. Like Mali, Songhai was influenced by Muslim leaders. The Songhai Empire dissolved after losing the Battle of Tondibi to neighboring Morocco in 1591.

4. Hausa – They built city-states c1000 in modern-day Nigeria. They traded with Africa and Europe…as did the Benin culture.

5. You should also know Axum and Kush, as explained in the second chapter. They were trading centers near Egypt that linked Africa and the Mediterranean.

6. In Eastern Africa, because of contact with Middle Eastern countries, a new language called **Swahili** emerged. This is a combination of African Bantu and Arabic. Contact was strong between Arabia and Eastern African Empires along the Swahili Coast in places such as Zimbabwe (c1300) and the Mutapa (c1500). (See *Empires c1400* map on pg. 26.) Zimbabwe had impressive stone wall enclosures that were used for defense. They utilized copper and bronze metals, and had long-distance trading networks where items were exchanged such as gold. Muslims in the region, some of whom established communities, also traded for slaves in Eastern Africa. The city-state of Kilwa had Muslim leaders. Kilwa grew rich c1300 due to locally mined gold and its proximity to Asian markets along the Indian Ocean.

Definition: Ibn Battuta

He was a North African traveler who ventured throughout the African and Muslim world for 29 years between 1325-1354. He also went as far as Asia, and Eastern and Western Europe. His observations are of interest to those comparing the strengths of World Empires, and cultural diversity in the mid-fourteenth century.

• NATIVE AMERICA

Question: Who were the first Native American people?

Answer: During the Ice Age, people traveled over a land bridge known as Beringia that connected Asia to North America (Alaska). These migrants settled and populated what would become known as the *New World*. They lived as hunters and gatherers, and were especially good farmers. They grew **maize** (corn) in particular.

Question: What were the early Native American Empires?

Answer:

1. Olmec – c1200-c400 BCE – Earliest civilization in Mesoamerica (Mexico). Many historians believe they were the first society in North America to have a writing system. They most likely worshipped jaguars. They produced enormous stone-carved heads which are still visible today.

2. Zapotec – c1000 BCE – Western Mesoamerican culture that had some vast building structures such as pyramids and religious centers.

3. Chavín – c900-c200 BCE – Populating the Andes Mountains in South America, they had advanced canals and drainage systems.

4. Nazca – c200 BCE-c500 CE – Living in the dry lands of Peru, they created elaborate irrigation systems. Mysterious lines detailing insects and animals still highlight the area.

5. Moche – c100-c800 CE – They used riv-

ers for irrigation and established a strong agricultural society.

6. Anasazi – c200-c1300 CE – They lived in the modern-day American Southwest. They constructed *pueblos*, or cities made from adobe architecture (clay-bricked). One enormous pueblo community was at Chaco. Pottery, jewelry, and irrigation networks have been excavated there.

7. Northwestern Native Americans used totems, or totem poles, to represent a family or group in the community.

8. Mississippian – Within the Mississippi River Valley, a complex society emerged c700-c1450. Today, the Cahokia Mounds of Illinois contain many religious and archaeological remains of this society.

Question: What should I know about the Mayan Empire?

Answer: The Mayans lived in Mesoamerica, peaking from about 250-900 CE. Some of their cities were Tikal in Guatemala, and Chichen Itza in the Yucatán Peninsula of Mexico.

1. They built elaborate cities. In Chichen Itza, there were pyramids, a ball court, and an observatory.

2. They had a great understanding of math and astronomy.

3. They had a written language composed of glyphs, or symbols. The books were called codices (or codex for singular).

4. Their most celebrated work was the Popol Vuh, which is their story of creation.

5. Once a great civilization, they mysteriously began to shrink in numbers. Some historians think there was war. Others believe there was a plague or famine.

Question: What should I know about the Aztec Empire?

Answer: The Aztecs lived in Mexico, near modern-day Mexico City. An early city was Teotihuacan. The Aztecs took it over after the fall of the Toltecs.

1. Teotihuacan established trade networks. One item traded was a razor-sharp rock known as obsidian. Obsidian was used to cut out the hearts of sacrifices to the sun god Huitzilopochtli.

2. Another major deity to know in Mesoamerica was Quetzalcoatl, the Feathered Serpent.

3. Tenochtitlan, near Lake Texcoco, was a major Aztec city with palaces and pyramids.

4. The Aztec Empire expanded by 1400 but then weakened under Montezuma II in the sixteenth century.

5. Montezuma and the Aztecs fell to the Spanish (explained later). Many Aztecs believed that the Spanish were Quetzalcoatl.

6. The Aztecs utilized *chinampas*, which were "floating gardens" of agriculture in freshwater swampy areas. Large crop-yields could be accumulated from these creative man-made structures.

Question: What should I know about the Inca Empire?

Answer:

1. The Incas had a vast empire in western South America along the *Andes Mountains*.

Incas built impressive structures with stones that often fit together like puzzle pieces. No mortar was used.

55

Terraces were used for agriculture in the Andes

They were strong in Peru. Mountain ranges like the Andes are visible on *physical maps*, which color and depict the Earth's land features.

2. There was great observance to the sun god, Inti.

3. Immense stone structures displayed advanced architectural skills. Notably, the impressive city of Machu Picchu is today a tourist attraction in Peru. The city of Cuzco was a cultural center. Many of the structures in the city were draped with gold. Some Incan structures were constructed from large stones that did not use mortar to fasten them. They instead fit together like puzzle pieces.

4. The Incas had an organized government and a strong network of roads. There was a labor system called Mita. This meant public service, or citizens aiding in construction.

5. Because it was in the mountains, there was a need for *terrace farming* (explained next). For irrigation, the Incas used the *waru waru* technique, whereby soil would be raised so rain-water could collect and be stored during periods of drought. The process also helped to control erosion.

6. Like the other Native American Empires, the Incas were conquered by the Europeans.

7. The Inca used *quipu* to record information on stringed knots.

Definition: Terrace Farming

Farming done in the mountains meant that crops had to be harvested in a certain manner. Terraces were like steps that went up a mountain. This allowed farming to be done on the slopes of the Andes. In addition, when it rained, water and nutrients would be washed down the steps, as opposed to running off. Terrace farming was used all over the world where sloped terrain was present.

• THE AGE OF EXPLORATION

Question: Why did Europeans want to explore the New World?

Answer: **GGG** (see below). The Age of Exploration was from roughly 1492-1700. New technologies in shipbuilding emerged. The Portuguese built **caravels**, which were small fast-moving boats with large *lateen* sails that could gather wind for speed from either side. Large cargo ships called carracks could make long voyages. An **astrolabe** (or mariner's astrolabe) was used to locate stars, the moon, and planets to aid in navigation at sea.

G - Gold - A promise of wealth. Specifically, explorers such as Christopher Columbus were looking for a quicker route to Asian trade markets. Such a route would prevent traveling through the Muslim controlled lands of the Middle East.

G - God - The Europeans wanted to spread Christianity.

G - Glory - Explorers wanted their own personal fame and fortune, as did the countries that sponsored the voyages.

During the Age of Exploration, European countries traveled and conquered the Empires of the New World (Native America). *The Encounter* of cultures across Hemispheres inspired more exploration and had major social, political, and economic effects on Africa, Native America, Europe, and eventually Asia.

Definition: Line of Demarcation /Treaty of Tordesillas

Spain and Portugal were the two early powers of exploration, and they fought over land in the New World. In 1493, Pope Alexander VI attempted to bring peace. He drew a *line of demarcation* on a map and said that Spain would get everything west of it, and Portugal would get the land to the east. In 1494, the Treaty of Tordesillas moved the line a bit to the west to give Portugal more territory in modern-day Brazil. Today, this is why most people in South America speak Spanish, yet Brazil to the east speaks Portuguese.

Question: What explorers should I know about c1500?

Answer:

1. Christopher Columbus – Italian, but exploring for Spain. He was sent by King Ferdinand and Queen Isabella in 1492 to find a quicker western route to India. Instead, he found the New World. Spain hoped to stay economically ahead of its rivals, especially Portugal.

2. Vasco da Gama – Portuguese. He found a direct sea route to India for spices and other trade. He reached the trading post of Calicut, which would be utilized by other European nations shortly after.

3. British and Dutch East India Companies - England and the Netherlands set up powerful trading companies in India (explained later). By the middle of the seventeenth century, the Dutch had the largest fleet of ships, and extended their trade to the Indian Ocean. They utilized ships called fluyts to carry cargo.

4. Ferdinand Magellan – Portuguese. He was the first to circumnavigate (completely sail around) the Earth.

Definition: Conquistadors

These were Spanish explorers who looked to *conquer* and liquidate the resources of Native America, such as gold. Two of them to know:

1. Hernán Cortés – After defeating Montezuma II, the Aztec capital fell in 1521. Though outnumbered, *use of advanced weapons and gunpowder*, as well as the recruitment of the Aztec's enemies, led the Spanish to victory.

2. Francisco Pizarro – With the use of advanced weapons, he conquered the Incan Empire and their capital of Cuzco, c1533.

Definition: *Encomienda* System

Victories for the Spanish in the New World led to a massive collection of gold and other riches. The Spanish forced Native Americans to help remove such resources in a labor system called **encomienda**. Though it was supposed to be fair, *encomienda* resembled slavery, as rights were denied to the natives. Reformer **Bartolomé de las Casas** believed this system was immoral and brutally cruel to the natives. By 1550, Spain reformed the system.

Haciendas, or self-sufficient plots of land which sold crops for profit, were utilized by the aristocracy in the colonial period (and beyond) with the help of labor (often exploited or indebted) which lived on the land.

Definition: Columbian Exchange

One of the greatest examples of cultural diffusion, the Columbian Exchange was the trading of all plants, animals, resources, and diseases between the Americas and the rest of the world. Did you know that in 1491 there were no pumpkins in Europe?

To Europe and the Eastern Hemisphere came peanuts, avocados, turkey, pumpkins, corn, and potatoes.

To the New World came horses, wheat, cows, olives, and diseases such as smallpox and influenza. Food such as rice and okra were brought from Africa as the slave trade occurred (see next).

The transfer of diseases ultimately depleted Native American populations. African slave-labor became more prevalent in the Americas, as after centuries of European contact, Africans acquired better immunity to such diseases.

Definition: Middle Passage

The Middle Passage was the **Triangular Trade's** central journey which brought slaves from Africa to the Caribbean. As for the Triangular Trade, molasses from the Caribbean was brought to New England, distilled into rum, and then traded to African kings for the slaves. Kingdoms in Africa also continued to trade captive slaves for military equipment, textiles, money, and luxury items. The slave trade was prevalent on the west coast in places such as the Kingdoms of Ashanti, Benin, and Dahomey (see map on pg. 67).

By the eighteenth century, many slaves worked on plantations where they would farm

Mestizos adopted Christianity. Above is a painting of The Last Supper *by Marcos Zapata from Peru. The main course has become guinea pig, a local delicacy.*

cash crops (agricultural goods to be harvested for great profits) such as tobacco near Virginia and sugar in the West Indies. Slaves were controlled by their masters as private property, or *chattel*. The human rights violation of slavery existed for centuries in the New World.

Definition: Mercantilism and Commercial Revolution

Mercantilism is an economic system where the European Mother Country (whether it be Spain, France, Netherlands, or England) extracted raw materials, such as gold or tobacco, from their colonies. They sold finished goods to the colonies as well. The sole purpose of the colonies was to make the Mother Country rich and self-sufficient. Silver from the Spanish colonies made it as far as Asia in a network of trade.

The expansion of international trade and colonization led to new business ventures and joint-stock companies (see pg. 91). This time of opportunity was called the *Commercial Revolution* and lasted from the late fifteenth century until the seventeenth century. Individuals looked to profit as well, as private boat owners (privateers) were sponsored by nations to use their naval might. In the Caribbean some with boats became pirates who attacked merchant ships.

Question: What was the Spanish social hierarchy of the New World?

Answer: From most powerful to least, you should know:

Peninsulares – People who were born in Spain and could hold the highest offices in the New World.

Creoles – Spanish people who were born in the New World. Along with the Peninsulares, they controlled most of the wealth.

Mestizos – People of European and Native American ancestry.

Mulattos – People of African and European ancestry.

Native Americans – Most numerous, but had the fewest rights.

Question: What important conflicts should I know concerning Native Americans in North America?

Answer: In 1680, the Pueblo Indians revolted against Spanish rule and the spread of Christianity in modern-day New Mexico, causing many Spaniards to resettle in modern-day Texas. From 1675-1676, English colonists fought and ultimately defeated Metacom (King Philip), despite the destruction of colonial settlements in Massachusetts. When the United States received independence from Great Britain, policies continued to be hostile towards American Indians. In the winter of 1837-38, the Cherokee Nation suffered the Trail of Tears as thousands died after being forced to move from the east coast to west of the Mississippi River. Another clash took place in 1890 as the US Cavalry opened fire, killing over 150 protesting Sioux at Wounded Knee, South Dakota.

Question: How were Australia and New Zealand affected by exploration?

Answer: Oceania, or the area in the Pacific which includes Australia, New Zealand, and other island nations, was not as quickly affected by exploration and imperialism. The Maoris of New Zealand, and semi-nomadic Aborigines of Australia, populated the area. Europeans arrived in the seventeenth century, and slowly began to colonize. Captain James Cook of Britain came to the area in 1769.

In 1788 Britain established Australia as a penal colony, or a place for criminal prisoners. Many free settlers, Christian missionaries, and those looking to profit from the wool trade soon came over. By 1838, Britain controlled New Zealand as well. From 1845-1872 the Maoris were defeated in a series of wars.

Review Questions for the AP World History: Modern Exam

"There are all kinds of green vegetables, especially onions, leeks, garlic, watercresses, nasturtium, borage, sorrel, artichokes, and golden thistle; fruits also of numerous descriptions, amongst which are cherries and plums, similar to those in Spain; honey and wax from bees, and from the stalks of maize, which are as sweet as the sugar-cane…

"Every kind of merchandise is sold in a particular street or quarter assigned to it exclusively, and thus the best order is preserved. They sell everything by number or measure; at least so far we have not observed them to sell anything by weight. There is a building in the great square that is used as an audience house, where ten or twelve persons, who are magistrates, sit and decide all controversies that arise in the market, and order delinquents to be punished…

"This great city contains a large number of temples, or houses, for their idols, very handsome edifices, which are situated in the different districts and the suburbs; in the principal ones religious persons of each particular sect are constantly residing, for whose use, besides the houses containing the idols, there are other convenient habitations..."

— Hernán Cortés in a Second Letter to Emperor Charles V, 1520

1. Which society is being described by Cortés in the letter?
  A) Mayan
  B) Incan
  C) Aztec
  D) Olmec

2. Which of the following was a short-term effect of the observations in the first paragraph?
  A) Columbian Exchange
  B) *Encomienda* System
  C) Middle Passage
  D) Treaty of Tordesillas

3. What long-term effect would result from the Encounter observed above?
  A) An alliance made by Portugal and the Incas
  B) Spanish missionaries spreading Christianity
  C) A banning of intermarriage between the Spanish and Native Americans
  D) Increased isolation of Mesoamerican societies

Review Questions for the SAT Subject Test

1. Desertification has been most concerning in Africa's
   A) Sahel
   B) Savanna
   C) Rain Forest
   D) Steppe
   E) Mediterranean zones

2. The Bantu were most associated with
   A) the Trans-Atlantic Slave Trade
   B) expanding Islam throughout Africa
   C) establishing a gold-salt trade in the east
   D) creating great walled structures
   E) spreading language through migration

3. Mansa Musa of Mali was instrumental in
   A) spreading Islam throughout his Empire
   B) establishing trade in Eastern Africa
   C) defeating the Mutapa Empire
   D) selling slaves to Europeans as part of the Triangular Trade
   E) controlling trade on the Silk Roads

4. African Kingdoms of Western Africa c1000 found their greatest profits in the trading of
   A) slaves
   B) gold and salt
   C) pottery
   D) spices
   E) porcelain

5. Pueblos in the southwest of the modern-day United States were constructed by which culture?
   A) Olmec
   B) Chavin
   C) Zapotec
   D) Nazca
   E) Anasazi

6. The Aztec and Inca were similar in their
   A) worship of a sun deity
   B) settlements construction in the Andes
   C) ability to defeat European invaders
   D) use of Cuzco as a trading center
   E) translation of scriptures into English

7. Terrace farming was a productive method of agricultural harvest. It was achieved by
   A) leveling land on mountains
   B) burning forests and using ashes for fertilizer
   C) rotating crops across three fields
   D) leaving land unfarmed for one year
   E) creating tunnels through mountains

8. *Encomienda* was
   A) an exchange of goods
   B) a technique for sailing a great distance
   C) the middle passage of the Triangular Trade
   D) a system of forced labor
   E) a political club in Spain

9. Conquistadors were those Spaniards who
   A) brought European crops and goods to the New World
   B) used their technologically advanced weapons to take over New World Empires
   C) refused to use caravel ships for exploration
   D) mined gold in Asia
   E) sought to take wealth from Philip II

10. Which of the following was true of the Columbian Exchange?
   A) The Pope ended all exchanges of plants and animals after the Treaty of Tordesillas
   B) The turkey was brought from Europe to the New World
   C) Horses were introduced to Europe
   D) Diseases were brought from Europe
   E) Maize found its way to the Americas

Answers and Explanations

AP World History: Modern

1. **C**. Cortés conquered the Aztecs. The Aztecs had impressive cities, such as Tenochtitlan.

2. **A**. The Columbian Exchange led to the transfer of plants, animals, and diseases across hemispheres.

3. **B**. Christianity would eventually become the dominant religion in both North and South America.

SAT Subject Test

1. **A**. The Sahel borders the Sahara Desert. As desertification takes place, it grows larger in size.

2. **E**. Bantu migrations brought the roots of many languages that are still spoken today south of the Sahara Desert.

3. **A**. Mansa Musa incorporated Islam into his Empire. He personally went on the hajj.

4. **B**. The gold-salt exchange was a valuable trading system that benefited Western Africa.

5. **E**. The Anasazi were known for constructing adobe (clay-bricked) structures known as pueblos.

6. **A**. Worshipping the sun god was an important aspect of both Incan and Aztec culture.

7. **A**. In order to plant crops in the mountainous regions of the Andes, the Inca needed to level off the land in a process known as terrace farming. Terrace farming was used all over the world, notably in Southeast Asia.

8. **D**. *Encomienda* was a system of forced labor used in Native America by the Spanish Conquistadors.

9. **B**. Although Native American Empires were advanced, militarily they were no match for the weapons of the Conquistadors.

10. **D**. The most catastrophic result of the Columbian Exchange was the transfer of European diseases. Because Native Americans were not immune to diseases such as influenza and smallpox, millions died after contact.

The Age of Absolutism and the Enlightenment

For centuries, absolute monarchs ruled Europe. In most cases, individual rights were limited and kings grew stronger. Because the monarch claimed to be a representative of God, few questioned the extent of their power. However, in the seventeenth century a movement in philosophy known as the Enlightenment began. Popular philosophical thought led to a demand for natural rights and liberty. Some monarchs extended rights to their people. Others did not. By the middle of the eighteenth century, demands for freedom grew louder and more violent.

HERE IS WHAT YOU NEED TO KNOW:
• THE AGE OF ABSOLUTISM
Definition: Absolutism

Monarchs (kings and queens) ruled with complete power from c1500-c1740. Similar to ancient China (Mandate of Heaven) and Egypt (theocracy), religion impacted rule. In Europe, *divine right* reflected the belief that the monarch was a representative of God.

Definition: Louis (Bourbon) XIV - France

Before Louis took the throne, Cardinal Richelieu governed. A cardinal is a Catholic clergy title. Because Louis XIII was a weak king, Richelieu became his powerful official. Richelieu favored Catholicism in France, and legislated against French Protestants called *Huguenots*. Huguenots had been given freedoms previously with the 1598 Edict of Nantes.

Louis (Bourbon) XIV was the prototypical absolute ruler c1700. Nicknamed "The Sun King," Louis said *"I am the state."* He expanded the *Palace of Versailles* into one of the most elaborate compounds in the world. Complete with thousands of rooms, ornate statues, and extensive gardens, this symbol of France was built at the expense of the suffering and starving peasants.

Louis XIV fought many wars during his 72 year reign. Although France became a strong force, weaker countries teamed up against them to keep French territorial gains minimal. During his rule, the debt of the country increased because of his lavish spending. Louis took power away from the nobles, as government officials called *intendants* had great influence over state affairs.

The famous Hall of Mirrors at Versailles. Endless chandeliers and mirrors were constructed while many in France were starving.

Definition: Philip II of Spain

Gaining much power from the riches of the New World, Philip's Spain was the wealthiest nation in Europe c1580. Philip defended Catholicism as Protestantism spread throughout Western Europe. Spain ultimately squandered its fortune and went into economic decline. In 1588, Philip's *Spanish Armada* was defeated by England. In time, the British became the supreme naval force in the world.

Question: What wars plagued Europe from 1618-1763?

Answer: Wars took place on the continent during this time period. Here are three:

1. Thirty Years' War – 1618-1648 – This war began with the **Defenestration of Prague** when Protestants threw three Catholics out of a window (they survived). Thus, the war was caused by religion. However, it evolved into a larger conflict over French and Hapsburg (explained next) dominance on the continent. In the **Peace of Westphalia** that ended the conflict, the Hapsburgs lost power in the region and France gained some land.

2. War of Spanish Succession – 1701-1714 – This was a battle to see if a French Bourbon (Louis XIV's grandson) could take the Spanish throne and unite the Kingdoms. It was agreed that a Bourbon could take the throne, but Spain and France would have to remain separate entities.

3. Seven Years' War – 1756-1763 – Known as the French and Indian War in North America (which began in 1754), this world war saw Britain defeat France to maintain their colonial Empire in the New World and India. Thus began the coexistence of English and French-speaking residents in Canada. A movement known as the *Quebecois separatist movement* gained strength over the years, as those identifying as French looked to protect their interests as Canada strengthened under the British flag.

Definition: Hapsburgs

The Hapsburgs were an Empire in Central Europe, notably Austria and Hungary. After the Thirty Years' War their Empire expanded, as they conquered lands once controlled by the Ottoman Empire in the Balkans of Eastern Europe. *Maria Theresa* is the most relevant name

to know. A devout Catholic, she was not tolerant of other religions.

The thorn in Maria's side was **Frederick the Great** of **Prussia** (in modern-day Germany). When Maria took the throne, Frederick looked to gain land from her in the **War of the Austrian Succession**. Frederick eventually secured the territory of Silesia in 1748.

Definition: Ivan the Terrible

Ivan IV was a *czar* (Russian king) who restricted the powers of Russian nobles called **boyars**. After his first wife died in 1560, Ivan went on a killing spree, executing thousands of boyars. He then took their land. Ivan also killed his son in a fit of rage. Because his other son was unfit to rule, Russia went through a few decades of czar uncertainty. Eventually it was the **Romanov** family that came to power. The House of Romanov would rule from 1613-1917.

Definition: Peter the Great

Peter Romanov was a czar who wanted to imitate Western Europe, or **westernize** c1680. This meant to modernize Russia militarily, culturally, economically, and technologically. Peter traveled to the west with his army. Examples of westernization were: increasing the size of the army, expanding education, and removing Mongol influence from society in the way people dressed and presented themselves. Because all great nations of the West had impressive capitals, the new city of **St. Petersburg** was constructed in Russia. It was built with serf labor.

Peter the Great also raised the status of women. In addition to easing restrictions on dress, he allowed women to mingle with men at social gatherings. Furthermore, he encouraged greater educational opportunities for women.

Definition: Stuarts of England

After Elizabeth Tudor (Elizabeth I) died with

no heir in 1603, the Stuart family ruled England. You need to know:

1. James I – A cousin of Elizabeth, he assumed the throne. During his reign came a new interpretation of the Bible (King James Bible).

2. Charles I – He did not consult Parliament in governing affairs, and ruled absolutely. Charles and his supporters, known as Cavaliers, were defeated by *General Oliver Cromwell* in the *Puritan Revolution/English Civil War*. Charles was brought to trial by the Puritan victors, and was executed for treason in 1649. Cromwell ruled as a military dictator until 1658.

3. Charles II – With the people longing for a return of the monarchy, Charles II resumed Stuart rule in 1660. This was called the *Restoration*. During his reign, the *Habeas Corpus Act* was passed by Parliament. It guaranteed the accused a right to go before a judge. One could not just be thrown into prison.

4. James II – He took power in 1685 and favored Catholicism. This upset English Protestants, including his daughter Mary.

5. William and Mary – Aided by her husband, a Dutch prince, Mary overthrew James in the bloodless *Glorious Revolution* of 1688.

Definition: Constitutional/Limited Monarchy

Under the rule of William and Mary, the absolute monarchy ceased to exist. Instead, a new *limited,* or *constitutional, monarchy* prevailed with Parliament having immense strength in the creation of laws. Parliament drafted the Bill of Rights in 1689 to ensure freedom of speech, fair taxation, and other personal liberties. To recap, the three documents that limited the monarchy over the years were:

1. Magna Carta – 1215 – The Great Charter was forced upon King John to sign. This document limited the king's power and gave rights to the people.

2. Habeas Corpus Act – 1679 – Guaranteed the accused the right to go before a judge.

3. Bill of Rights - 1689

• THE ENLIGHTENMENT
Definition: Scientific Revolution c1550-1700

The Enlightenment was mostly a political and philosophical movement, but it coincided with new discoveries in science. Philosophers such as Francis Bacon and René Descartes attacked the scientific conclusions made by Aristotle. Descartes relied on math and reason to prove his theories. This use of observation developed into the *Scientific Method*. The Scientific Method was a new sequence of investigation that was used to test a hypothesis through experimentation. After logical steps were taken, a conclusion could be derived.

What you should also know about the Scientific Revolution:

1. *Heliocentric model*, 1543 – This was Nicolaus Copernicus' belief that the planets revolved around the sun. This idea contrasted with the geocentric model that declared the Earth as the center of the universe.

2. *Galileo Galilei* – He was a scientist who discovered that objects of different weights fall at the same speed (this went against Aristotle's theory). He also observed the moons of Jupiter and confirmed Copernicus' theories. His findings upset the Church, and at trial in 1633 he was forced to retract his observations. Despite his retraction, Galileo spent his remaining days under house arrest.

3. Andreas Vesalius – Gave new ideas on anatomy and how to perform surgery.

4. Isaac Newton – Researched universal gravitation and created three laws of motion.

Definition: Enlightenment/Age of Reason
Coinciding with the Scientific Revolution was the Enlightenment. This Age of Reason was a

movement from the mid-seventeenth century through the eighteenth century. It looked to reform (progressively change) society through knowledge and reason. A goal of most Enlightenment thinkers was to protect natural rights. Regarding faith, many during this time supported *Deism* believing that God created the world, and then allowed natural law take over.

Question: Which Enlightenment writers should I know?

Answer: Enlightenment philosophers used reason to define the liberties they thought people should have in nature. You should know:

1. Thomas Hobbes (English) – *Leviathan*, 1651 – He believed that people created government, calling this notion a "social contract." A Leviathan is a monster, and a metaphor for government. Like Machiavelli before him, Hobbes believed that people are greedy and need to be kept in check by a strong and absolute ruler. Despite his support for a strong monarchy, Hobbes is included in the Enlightenment. Generally, the following three philosophers are more relevant to know.

2. John Locke (English) – *Two Treatises of Government*, 1690 - He believed that people were born free with natural rights such as life, liberty, and property. His ideas were adopted by Thomas Jefferson in the American Declaration of Independence. That document used the term "consent of the governed" referring to Locke's belief that legitimate governments, while respecting basic rights and liberties, gain permission from their citizens to exert power.

3. Jean-Jacques Rousseau (French) – *Social Contract*, 1762 – He said that government should rule for the common good. A famous quote of his was that, "Man is born free, and everywhere he is in chains." Here, Rousseau was describing unjust laws which prevent natural rights and liberty.

4. Baron de Montesquieu (French)-- *The Spirit of the Laws*, 1748 – He illustrated the concept of *separation of powers*, where the legislative branch (makes laws), executive branch (enforces laws) and judicial branch (interprets laws) controlled the government. All three would operate under a system of *checks and balances* that would prevent one branch from getting too strong. Separation of powers was adopted by numerous nations, including the United States.

5. Voltaire (French) – In the eighteenth century he wrote hundreds of essays regarding the themes of freedom of speech, religion, and other social reforms. He was a supporter of separation of church and state.

Definition: Mary Wollstonecraft

In 1792, this British activist published *A Vindication of the Rights of Woman*. She argued that women should receive an equal education to men, and should participate in politics and the economy outside of the home. Still, it would be decades before women received equality in Europe.

Definition: *Encyclopédie*

c1760, Denis Diderot was an editor for this publication in France that printed many essays. The essays supported Enlightenment ideas and looked to change the way people viewed government.

Question: How did the Enlightenment impact the arts in Europe?

Answer:

1. Classical music began to thrive in Central Europe c1780 under the likes of Wolfgang Amadeus Mozart (*The Magic Flute*), and later Ludwig van Beethoven (renowned for his symphonies).

2. In the Age of Absolutism, many castles displayed *baroque* architecture. This was a colorful and lavish style. In the late 1700s, a

Ornate baroque statue at the Palace of Versailles

music, literature, and even architecture that evolved in the late eighteenth century. It emphasized spontaneous emotions and heroism, and was a reaction to the rational balance of the Classical Period. By the nineteenth century, the harsh working conditions of the Industrial Revolution made people want stories they could relate to. This led to a rise in *realism*, or entertainment that reflected what was really going on in society.

4. In the nineteenth century, French artists such as Edouard Manet, Edgar Degas, and Claude Monet froze their impressions of a moment in time. This art movement is called *impressionism*. Some artists, such as Dutch painter Vincent van Gogh, concentrated more on emotions. These artists are known as post-impressionists.

Definition: Enlightened Despots

A despot is another term for an absolute ruler. Enlightened despots were those who supported the Age of Reason. Rulers such as Frederick the Great of Prussia and *Catherine the Great* of Russia supported modernization. They embraced the arts, education, religious toleration, and an end to certain torture punishments.

less elaborate movement called *neoclassical* emerged. This was inspired by the architecture of Western Civilization (Greece, Rome, and the Renaissance). Another movement in France, called rococo (or late baroque), was elegant, elaborate, and decorative.

3. *Romanticism* was a movement in art,

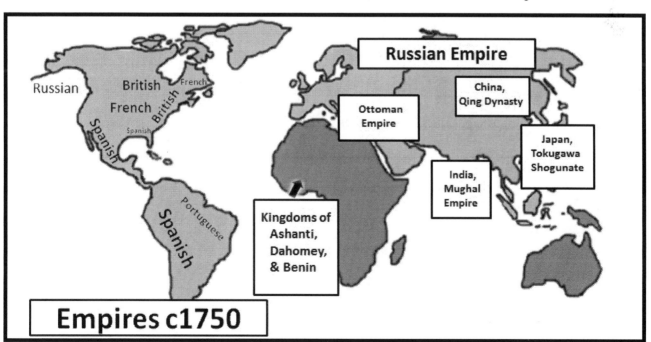

67

Review Questions for AP World History: Modern Exam

Right to Petition

That it is the Right of the Subjects to petition the King and all commitments and prosecutions for such petitioning are illegal.

Standing Army

That the raising or keeping a standing Army within the kingdom in time of peace unless it be with Consent of Parliament is against law.

Subjects' Arms

That the subjects which are Protestants may have arms for their defense suitable to their conditions and as allowed by law.

Freedom of Election

That election of members of Parliament ought to be free.

Freedom of Speech

That the freedom of speech and debates or proceedings in Parliament ought not to be impeached or questioned in any court or place out of Parliament.

Excessive Bail

That excessive bail ought not to be required nor excessive fines imposed nor cruel and unusual punishments inflicted.

— Excerpts from The English Bill of Rights, 1689

1. Which of the following was an immediate cause for the issuing of the document above?
   A) English Civil War
   B) Glorious Revolution
   C) The Restoration
   D) Defeat of the Spanish Armada

2. Which of the following can be considered a continuity of the above document?
   A) The Renaissance
   B) The Enlightenment
   C) The Protestant Reformation
   D) The Thirty Years' War

3. The immediate effect of the above document was
   A) religious freedom in Europe
   B) a questioning of scientific thought throughout the world
   C) the elimination of class titles in England
   D) a move towards a limited monarchy

Review Questions for the SAT Subject Test

1. Which was true of France's economy under Louis XIV?
   A) A new fair code of taxation was passed to aid the peasants
   B) The debt of the country greatly increased during his reign
   C) Industrialization began in the first decade of his rule
   D) There was vast economic prosperity for all classes
   E) Mercantilism had a decreased importance

2. Peter the Great wanted Russia to
   A) isolate itself from the rest of the world
   B) trade only with countries in the East
   C) imitate the nations of Western Europe
   D) abolish serfdom in the Empire
   E) decrease its naval presence in the Baltic

3. Divine right is most accurately defined as the
   A) seizing of noble lands by a king
   B) centralization of power within a two-house legislature
   C) protections given to property and free speech
   D) belief that the monarch is a representative of God
   E) westernization of the justice system

4. All of the following were influential in limiting the monarchy of England from 1215-1689 EXCEPT:
   A) Habeas Corpus Act
   B) Bill of Rights
   C) The Restoration
   D) Magna Carta
   E) Glorious Revolution

5. Religion and the Peace of Westphalia were associated with which war?
   A) Thirty Years' War
   B) War of Spanish Succession
   C) War of the Austrian Succession
   D) Seven Years' War
   E) Puritan Revolution

6. Which of the following best describes the heliocentric model?
   A) The Earth and planets revolve around the sun
   B) A body in motion stays in motion
   C) The Earth is at the center of the universe
   D) Planets and the sun all revolve around Earth
   E) The earth is the center of the galaxy

7. The laws of gravity are attributed to which scientist?
   A) Isaac Newton
   B) Andreas Vesalius
   C) Nicolaus Copernicus
   D) René Descartes
   E) Galileo Galilei

8. Belief in life, liberty, and property are most associated with the writings of
   A) Jean-Jacques Rousseau
   B) John Locke
   C) Voltaire
   D) Baron de Montesquieu
   E) Thomas Hobbes

9. In *The Spirit of the Laws*, Baron de Montesquieu advocated for

A) speech rights
B) women's rights
C) property qualifications to vote
D) freedom of religion
E) separation of powers

10. Enlightened despots were those monarchs who

A) censored all philosophers who promoted human rights
B) wanted to limit educational opportunities
C) actively experimented and took part in scientific discovery
D) looked to extend their Empires overseas
E) were open to some of the ideas brought forth by philosophers

Answers and Explanations

AP World History: Modern Exam
1. **B**. With the Glorious Revolution, William and Mary took the throne. The Bill of Rights followed shortly after.

2. **B**. The document looked to expand rights. This was the focal point of the Enlightenment which continued into the eighteenth century.

3. **D**. The monarchy continued to limit itself throughout Europe, as citizens gained legislative power in various ways.

SAT Subject Test
1. **B**. Louis spent money lavishly during his reign. Most notably, he renovated the elaborate Palace of Versailles. His spending left France in debt.

2. **C**. Peter wanted to imitate Western Europe and modernize Russia.

3. **D**. Similar to a theocracy in Egypt, or Chinese Mandate of Heaven, divine right meant that the absolute monarch of Europe was a representative of God.

4. **C**. The Restoration of 1660 meant a return to monarchy in England. Charles II did not rule as absolutely as his father Charles I. Parliament passed the Habeas Corpus Act during his reign, which extended rights to the accused.

5. **A**. Although the Thirty Years' War escalated into a larger conflict, it began as a religious war.

6. **A**. Nicolaus Copernicus' model stated that the Earth and the other planets revolve around the sun.

7. **A**. Isaac Newton was best known for his laws of motion and universal gravitation.

8. **B**. These were John Locke's ideas that helped inspire the American Declaration of Independence. Locke's *Two Treatises of Government* was his most famous work.

9. **E**. Montesquieu favored a government with three branches (Legislative, Executive, Judicial) where a system of checks and balances kept each branch from becoming too powerful.

10. **E**. Enlightened despots, such as Catherine the Great and Frederick the Great, were open to some of the ideas set forth by Enlightenment thinkers.

The French Revolution, Napoleon, and Latin America

Enlightenment thought was one of the major inspirations behind the bloody revolution that consumed France in the late 1700s. By 1789, France was controlled by a regime that did not fairly represent most of the population. Swiftly, the people revolted and established a Republic in France. However, what was in name a Republic was really a radical government that looked to eliminate all opposition. After a Reign of Terror bled France, Napoleon Bonaparte took over the country and ruled as a military dictator. Napoleon's thirst for an Empire eventually led to his downfall, as overexpansion and war losses led twice to his exile.

HERE IS WHAT YOU NEED TO KNOW:
Question: What were the main causes of the French Revolution?

Answer: Mnemonic Device: **MEAT**

M - **M**onarchy. The rule of King Louis XVI and Queen Marie Antoinette was inefficient and did not meet the needs of the people.

E - **E**nlightenment. Ideas of liberty and equality made citizens further resent the absolute monarchy of France.

A - **A**merican Revolution. The King and Queen spent a lot of money to help America defeat the British. All the while, people were starving in France. In addition, there was a belief that if the Americans could be successful in a revolution that brought liberty, so too could the French.

T - **T**axes/**T**hird Estate. The Third Estate made up about 98% of the people. Despite not having most of the wealth in France, they paid more than their fair share in taxes. They also had little say in government.

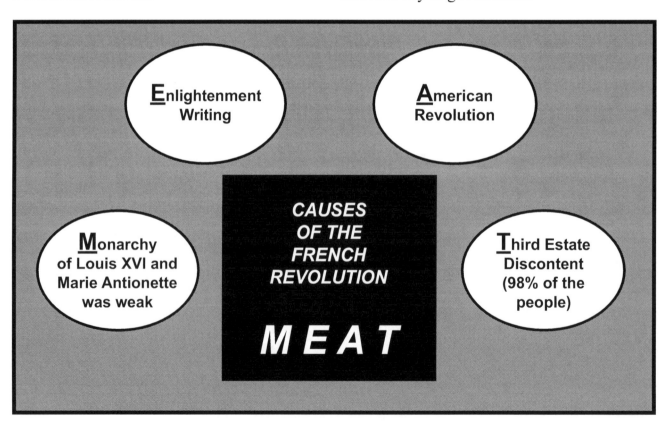

Enlightenment Writing

American Revolution

CAUSES OF THE FRENCH REVOLUTION

Monarchy of Louis XVI and Marie Antionette was weak

Third Estate Discontent (98% of the people)

MEAT

Definition: Old Regime/Three Estates

The Old Regime was the historic class and political structure of France. From most powerful to least, it included:

The First Estate – Clergy, who owned a great deal of land.

The Second Estate – Nobles, who also controlled a great amount of wealth.

The Third Estate – The Third Estate was divided into the bourgeoisie (explained below) and the peasants. Peasants made up most of this Estate.

Definition: Bourgeoisie

A branch of the Third Estate was the bourgeoisie. They were well-educated artisans and capitalists who familiarized themselves with Enlightenment thought. The bourgeoisie believed they were entitled a say in government because of their education and standing in society.

Definition: National Assembly, June 17, 1789

France was spending more money than it had. When Louis XVI asked the Estates General (representatives from the three Estates) for more tax revenue, the Third Estate became enraged for multiple reasons. Though comprised of 98% of the people, they had the same amount of representatives as the other two Estates. To make matters worse, each Estate only had one vote. This meant that the First and Second Estates could always outvote the Third Estate. Enraged by the structure, and inspired by Enlightenment ideas, the Third Estate declared itself the *National Assembly* of France that could pass laws for the people.

Definition: Tennis Court Oath, June 20, 1789

Locked out of an Estates General meeting, National Assembly (Third Estate) members broke into an indoor tennis court. There, they took an oath to make a new constitution for France.

Definition: Storming of the Bastille, July 14, 1789

A symbol of absolutism in France, the Bastille was a prison that housed political criminals. Although King Louis XVI began to listen to the demands of the people, he also called in neutral (Swiss) troops to protect France from mob rule. Nonetheless a crowd overtook the Bastille. This event triggered the first bloodshed of the Revolution, which today is celebrated in France as Bastille Day.

In the aftermath of the Bastille there were riots and mob chaos. Fueled by rumors that both the King and the first two Estates were going to imprison or kill peasants, hysteria unfolded known as the *Great Fear*. Peasants armed themselves with whatever they could and paraded through the streets. Many looted the homes of nobles.

Question: What other events from the French Revolution should I know?

Answer:

1. Women in Paris took to the streets to protest the inflation of bread prices. They broke into the Palace of Versailles (just outside of Paris), and demanded that the King and Queen rule from Paris. In 1791, the royal family attempted to escape to Austria, but was recognized near the French border and captured.

2. The National Assembly finished the constitution (as pledged on the tennis court). The lawmaking power was then given to a new *Legislative Assembly*.

3. Austria, which was loyal to Louis, demanded that he be restored to power. The Legislative Assembly declared war on Austria in 1792, and lost many early battles. Austria never did conquer Paris though, and the Legislative Assembly, and later a newly elected *National*

Convention, maintained power.

4. In 1793, a powerless Louis was put on trial and found guilty of treason. He was executed via the **guillotine** (device used to chop off heads). The Queen was executed months later.

Definition: *Declaration of the Rights of Man and of the Citizen*, **1789**

This was a document, similar to the American Declaration of Independence, that declared all men to be created equal. It promised to protect the natural rights of individuals. The words had far-reaching implications, as they would inspire revolution as far away as Latin America. In France, the demands for *liberty, equality, and fraternity* could be heard throughout the countryside.

However, women were not included. *Olympe de Gouges* spoke out for female equality. She was unsuccessful in her campaign, and was executed during the Reign of Terror (explained later).

Definition: Political Spectrum: Radicals, Moderates, and Conservatives

In the Legislative Assembly, there were:

Radicals (who sat on the left) – They represented people such as the **sans-culottes**, or those laborers and merchants who wanted to totally change the way France conducted its government.

Conservatives (who sat on the right) – They were fine with having a limited monarch. Many of them were aristocratic émigrés, or royal supporters who emigrated from France during the violence.

Moderates (who sat in the middle) – They were still undecided on the role of the monarchy in France.

Related, you should know the *political spectrum*, or the explanation of ideologies in politics. To generalize, those who favor more government reform (change) to promote individual liberties are called *liberals*. Those who favor less government reform are *conservatives*. The *moderates* can lean either way. *Revolutionaries* are radicals who want much more change than legally possible. *Reactionaries* wish to "turn back the clock" on society. In the case of the French Revolution, reactionaries would be those looking to restore the absolute monarchy.

Definition: Jacobins

The Jacobins were a revolutionary political club that wanted to eliminate all aspects of monarchy and make France a Republic. The Jacobins turned to violence to achieve their goals. Their leaders were Jean-Paul Marat, Georges Danton, and Maximilien Robespierre.

Definition: Maximilien Robespierre and the Reign of Terror

Robespierre seized power. He wanted to rid France of people who supported nobility and the monarchy. To do this, he established the **Committee of Public Safety** to sniff out enemies of the Republic. Between 1793 and 1794, thousands of so-called traitors were executed in what would be known as the **Reign of Terror**. Even Danton, a once loyal Jacobin, was executed. Marat was stabbed to death in a bathtub by a female political opponent named Charlotte Corday.

Definition: The Directory

Robespierre's killing-spree was too much to endure for the French people. Robespierre was guillotined in 1794. In the aftermath of the terror, a moderate five-member executive branch known as the **Directory** took over alongside a two-house legislature. The Directory appointed **Napoleon Bonaparte** to lead France's army.

Definition: Coup d'état, 1799

Napoleon Bonaparte's popularity as a General was growing. When the French Directory was internally falling apart, Napoleon pounced on the government. He suddenly seized power in 1799. Such a "blow of state" is called a *coup d'état*.

Question: Under Napoleon, what parts of Europe did France control?

Answer: Napoleon had a foot in just about every country in Europe. His great victory at *Austerlitz* in 1805 was enough to defeat the *Third Coalition* (European nations who banded together to fight France). The Napoleonic Wars were fought from 1803-1815. At his peak:

1. Napoleon controlled modern-day France, Belgium, Netherlands, Spain, Italy, and Poland.

2. Austria, Prussia, Denmark, and Russia were allies through treaties.

France gave up much of its New World territory, as a slave uprising by Toussaint L'Ouverture in Haiti made it difficult to control the sugar crop. A great deal of land in the New World was sold to the United States in the Louisiana Purchase of 1803.

Definition: Battle of Trafalgar, 1805

This was a naval battle that Napoleon lost to British commander Horatio Nelson off the coast of Spain. The defeat proved Britain's navy was supreme. Napoleon would never conquer the island of Britain.

Definition: Napoleonic Code

Napoleon crowned himself Emperor in 1804. He placed the crown on his own head rather than have the Pope do it for him. To legislate for the Empire, a legal code was named for him. Although the code gave equal rights to all men under the law, it limited freedom of speech. Furthermore, women's rights were decreased and male dominance was proclaimed.

Question: What were Napoleon's three mistakes?

Answer: **CPR**

1. **C** - *Continental System*. Despite conquering much of Europe, Napoleon never defeated Britain. Geographically, Britain is an island. Beginning in 1806, Napoleon hoped to blockade, or surround Britain with ships, to prevent all trade. This was a failure because Britain's navy was strong enough to resist, and other European nations did not like being told whom they could trade with. Many illegally traded with Great Britain anyway.

2. **P** - *Peninsular War*, 1808-1814. Napoleon controlled Spain, but wanted to control the entire Iberian Peninsula, including Portugal. He marched his soldiers through the peninsula and attacked. Napoleon lost much of his army in this war, and never took over Portugal. His forces had a hard time combatting *guerrilla warfare*, or unorganized ambushes led by French adversaries, including civilians.

3. **R** - *Invasion of Russia*, 1812. He invaded his former ally, Russia. When Napoleon got deep enough into the country, Czar Alexander I ordered the land to be burned (called scorched-earth policy). This destruction of agriculture left Napoleon's army to starve through the harsh Russian winter. He lost almost his entire force during the campaign.

Definition: Elba and Hundred Days

After his defeat in Russia, Napoleon was banished to the island of *Elba* near Italy. Not guarded too tightly, he escaped in 1815 and marched through France's countryside to gather supporters. He attempted to regain his Empire for about one hundred days. This attempt ended on June 18, 1815 when he lost the *Battle of Waterloo*. Napoleon was banished to the island of *Saint Helena* in the Atlantic. There, he died in 1821.

Definition: Congress of Vienna

This was a meeting in Austria from 1814-1815. Led by Austrian Prince *Klemens von Metternich*, diplomats embraced ideas such as establishing a *balance of power* in Europe and restoring the *legitimacy* of the monarchs dethroned by Napoleon.

Fearful of revolutions similar to the one seen in France, coalitions such as the *Holy Alliance* and Metternich's *Concert of Europe* were formed. It was agreed that if an uprising broke out in one country, the members of the alliances would put it down. These alliances did not prevent the wars to come in the nineteenth century.

Question: How did South American countries get their independence from European nations?

Answer: For centuries there had been resistance against Spanish rule and a demand for labor and social rights. In Peru, *Tupac Amaru II* helped lead a rebellion from 1780-1783 comprised largely of Incan descendants. Supported by mestizos and Creoles, he was ultimately captured and executed. However, anti-Spanish sentiment continued. Inspired by the French Revolution and the Enlightenment, Latin America saw revolutions c1820 led by:

1. *Simón Bolívar* – He relied mostly on volunteers as he marched through the Andes to solidify a major victory in 1819 in modern-day Colombia. Known as the *Liberator*, he helped bring self-rule to much of South America including Colombia, Bolivia, Peru, and Venezuela.

2. *José San Martin* – He fought alongside Bolívar, and helped free Chile, Peru, and Argentina.

3. *Toussaint L'Ouverture* – As mentioned above, in 1801 he led an uprising of slaves in Haiti that eventually led to its independence from France in 1804. Haiti, like Brazil, had strong *Maroon societies*, or communities of former and runaway slaves. These societies were loyal to freedom causes.

4. Mexico also declared independence in 1821. With the help of *Miguel Hidalgo* and *José Morelos*, Mexico received independence from Spain after bloody conflict. In the middle of the nineteenth century, Mexican politician *Benito Juárez* presented liberal reforms in a movement called La Reforma. He advocated for separation of church and state, and increased education for the poor. Napoleon III of France sent over an army in 1862, and fought to control Mexico. France appointed Austrian Archduke Maximilian to lead the country as emperor. Amidst immense resistance, Maximilian's government collapsed, the French pulled out, and he was executed in 1867. Juárez continued to lead the country.

5. In contrast, Brazil received its independence from Portugal in 1822 through mostly peaceful measures. However, Portugal did not recognize their independence until 1825.

Review Questions for the AP World History: Modern Exam

Article I – Men are born and remain free and equal in rights. Social distinctions can be founded only on the common good.

Article II – The goal of any political association is the conservation of the natural and imprescriptible rights of man. These rights are liberty, property, safety and resistance against oppression.

Article III – The principle of any sovereignty resides essentially in the Nation. No body, no individual can exert authority which does not emanate expressly from it.

Article IV – Liberty consists of doing anything which does not harm others: thus, the exercise of the natural rights of each man has only those borders which assure other members of the society the enjoyment of these same rights. These borders can be determined only by the law.

— Excerpts from the *Declaration of the Rights of Man and of the Citizen*, 1789

1. The above Declaration can be seen as a continuation of which event?
   A) Peninsular War
   B) Venezuelan War of Independence
   C) Continental System
   D) American Revolution

2. The major purpose of the above Declaration was to
   A) bolster the strength of the Old Regime and affirm the importance of Bourbon rule
   B) apply Enlightenment ideas to the government of France
   C) reserve trial by jury and property rights for the aristocracy
   D) pledge an oath to make a new Constitution for the French people

3. Which of the following was a long-term effect of the above?
   A) English Civil War
   B) Glorious Revolution
   C) Haitian Revolution
   D) Establishment of the Old Regime

Review Questions for the SAT Subject Test

1. All of the following were causes of the French Revolution EXCEPT:
   A) A lack of representation for the Third Estate
   B) Enlightenment philosophy
   C) The appointment of Napoleon Bonaparte to command the military
   D) Inspiration from the American Revolution
   E) An unfair system of taxation

2. The violent spark of the French Revolution began on July 14, 1789 at the
   A) Bastille
   B) signing of the Tennis Court Oath
   C) Palace of Versailles
   D) Cathedral of Notre Dame
   E) Estates General

3. The bourgeoisie was mainly represented by
   A) nobles who supported the king
   B) clergy members of the first estate
   C) educated merchants and artisans
   D) the poorest class of peasants
   E) the king and his court

4. The Jacobins and King Louis XVI both would agree with
   A) dividing all noble lands amongst the people
   B) imprisoning or executing opponents of their policies
   C) ridding the country of organized religion
   D) accepting rule through divine right
   E) eliminating autocratic rule

5. Which never became part of Napoleon's Empire?
   A) Spain
   B) Italy
   C) Netherlands
   D) Belgium
   E) Great Britain

6. Napoleon's final defeat in the Hundred Days occurred as a result of which battle?
   A) Moscow
   B) Waterloo
   C) Elba
   D) Trafalgar
   E) Austerlitz

7. Historians consider all of the following to contribute to Napoleon's downfall EXCEPT:
   A) Peninsular War
   B) Invasion of Russia
   C) Battle of Austerlitz
   D) Continental System
   E) Alliances of his enemies

8. An outcome of the Congress of Vienna was
   A) restoration of the monarchs dethroned by Napoleon
   B) the handing over of the French government to the Legislative Assembly
   C) execution of King Louis XVI
   D) the ratification of a French constitution
   E) the removal of the Jacobins from power

9. The *Declaration of the Rights of Man* inspired which of the following?
   A) Napoleon's coup d'état
   B) The Congress of Vienna
   C) Latin American independence movements
   D) The American Revolution
   E) The Russian invasion

10. Who of the following led a slave revolt against the French?
   A) José San Martin
   B) Simón Bolívar
   C) Benito Juárez
   D) Miguel Hidalgo
   E) Toussaint L'Ouverture

78

Answers and Explanations

AP World History: Modern

1. **D**. The American Revolution, with its Declaration of Independence, had similar themes of liberty. That successful revolution helped to inspire the one in France.

2. **B**. The above articles reflect Enlightenment ideas which, when applied to government, aimed to increase the rights of French citizens.

3. **C**. The American Revolution inspired the French Revolution. The French Revolution helped to inspire Latin American independence movements.

SAT Subject Test

1. **C**. Napoleon took command of the military in a coup d'état years after the Revolution began.

2. **A**. The Bastille was a prison, and a symbol of the King of France.

3. **C**. Many of the revolutionaries of France were part of the bourgeoisie of the Third Estate. They were well educated and usually accumulated some degree of wealth.

4. **B**. Although the Jacobins were against the King, they used some of the monarch's methods to intimidate opponents of the Revolution. During the Reign of Terror thousands were executed under Maximilien Robespierre.

5. **E**. Napoleon attempted to harm Britain through battle and trade embargoes. Britain never became part of Napoleon's Empire.

6. **B**. Waterloo, in Belgium, was the scene of Napoleon's final defeat. He was exiled to the island of St. Helena shortly thereafter.

7. **C**. The Battle of Austerlitz in Central Europe was one of Napoleon's greatest victories. There, he defeated a group of European nations known as the Third Coalition.

8. **A**. The Congress of Vienna "turned back the clock" on Europe, and under the leadership of Prince Klemens von Metternich, former monarchs dethroned by Napoleon were restored to power.

9. **C**. The ideas of the French Revolution spread to Latin America. Led by Simón Bolívar, and others, South American nations began to declare their independence from European powers.

10. **E**. Toussaint led a slave revolt in Haiti. By 1804, Haiti received its independence. At about the same time of the revolt, Napoleon sold the Louisiana Territory to the United States.

Nationalism, the Industrial Revolution, and Nineteenth Century Western Europe

A wave of nationalism swept over Europe in the middle of the nineteenth century, as revolution and war led to the formation of new nation-states. As this was occurring, an Industrial Revolution was taking place in Britain and spreading to the rest of the world. Goods were being produced by machines in factories. In addition, new methods of transportation led to urbanization. However not everyone was thrilled with capitalism, as socialist writers encouraged the working class to fight for more rights. Regarding rights at this time, citizens within Great Britain and its colonies received more liberties during the nineteenth century.

HERE IS WHAT YOU NEED TO KNOW:
• NATIONALISM
Definition: Nationalism

Nationalism is a belief that one's loyalty rests with the people of a nation-state because of a common culture, heritage, set of beliefs, or interest. Typically, nationalism is accompanied by strong pride for one's nation-state/country.

In the bloody year of *1848*, revolutions broke out all over Europe as nationalism and dissatisfaction with governments ran wild. France, and modern-day Germany and Italy, were greatly affected. People wanted more democracy, individual liberties, and improvements to working conditions.

In France, conflict resulted with Napoleon's nephew Louis-Napoleon winning a presidential election. He would adopt the title of Emperor Napoleon III and bring stability and modernization to France.

As nineteenth-century nationalism escalated among Greek, Armenian, and Slavic populations, the Ottoman Empire gradually weakened. The Austrian Empire was also transforming borders due to nationalism. Hungarian pride helped split the Empire into the states of Austria and Hungary. Thus, Austria-Hungary was born in 1867.

Definition: Italian Unification, 1848-1870

Giuseppe Mazzini was a revolutionary who founded Young Italy (for those under 40) in 1831 as a means of bringing attention to an independent Italian republic. Italy was not a country until *Camillo di Cavour* of Sardinia linked up with northern Italy, and *Giuseppe Garibaldi's* army of Redshirts marched through Southern Italy. They helped unify the entire boot (Italy is shaped like a boot). The Pope provided the large area containing Rome known as the *Papal States*. The Church kept a small piece of land which is called Vatican City.

Definition: German Unification, 1848-1871

As stated earlier, nationalistic revolutions tore through modern-day Germany in 1848. In 1862, Otto von Bismarck became prime minister of *Prussia*, which would evolve into Germany. Bismarck unified Germany with *"Blood and Iron,"* as through war, Prussia won land. Bismarck used the diplomacy of *realpolitik*. This meant to rule with authority for practical, realistic, and material reasons…not for idealistic or moral ones.

In a short Seven Weeks' War, Prussia took land from Austria. In the Franco-Prussian War of 1870-71, they received the territories of *Alsace and Lorraine* from France. King Wilhelm I of Prussia declared himself *kaiser*, or the first German Emperor. Thus formed the *Second Reich* (the Holy Roman Empire being the first one, and Adolf Hitler would become the Third Reich).

In the new united Germany, Bismarck supported social legislation such as healthcare, accident insurance, and old age pensions.

Definition: Crimean War, 1853-1856

The Russians also hoped to gain land, as the Ottoman Empire was falling apart by 1853. Britain and France helped push back Russian advances. Note: This was the war where British nurse Florence Nightingale became famous for her work with wounded soldiers.

The Ottoman Empire continued to lose land in the Balkans (areas near Romania, Bulgaria, and Bosnia) before World War I. The once mighty Empire would become known as the "sick man of Europe."

• THE INDUSTRIAL REVOLUTION
Definition: Industrial Revolution

During the second half of the eighteenth century, there was an enormous increase in the number of machine-made finished goods being produced in factories across England. Such ideas of industrialization spread to mainland Europe, the United States, and eventually the world. Because factories offered jobs, people migrated to cities in a process called ***urbanization***.

Urbanization was enhanced by railroads that linked rural and urban (city) areas. Steam-powered vehicles, such as Robert Fulton's steamboat, were available because of James Watt's fuel-efficient steam engine. Urbanization had its share of problems, as pollution, child labor, and unsanitary living conditions were common in cities. In the late nineteenth century, cities would improve sanitation and plumbing which helped control outbreaks of cholera. This was a reaction to the findings of researchers such as Louis Pasteur who studied germ theory and disease prevention. Also regarding health, modern vaccines against smallpox and other diseases were administered throughout the nineteenth century. However, it wouldn't be until the 1920s that antibiotics would be used to fight bacteria.

Definition: Agricultural Revolution

Farming techniques improved shortly before the Industrial Revolution. In order to have successful industrial output, an abundance of food would be needed for workers and the people of Europe. Some of the new techniques used were:

1. Crop Rotation – Similar to the Three-Field System of the Middle Ages, this technique was used by farmers to ensure good harvests. It was learned that some crops would grow better in the soil if they were planted in the same spots where specific crops bloomed the year before. Farmers had to be resilient and creative with crop methods, as for centuries a *"Little Ice Age"* had shortened growing seasons and fostered a need for more efficient methods.

2. Enclosures – After buying up smaller farms, landholders added fences to create larger farms.

3. Seed Drill – Invented by Jethro Tull, this invention planted seeds evenly in rows, instead of randomly scattering them.

4. Farmers used breeding to yield larger animals to feed the population.

Indeed, industrialization led to a high demands for raw materials, such as cotton for clothes, metals, and guano (bird/bat droppings) from Peru for fertilizer. Even palm oil (used for soap, candles, and lubricants) from the Niger Delta became a lucrative trade for Europeans in the nineteenth century. Much wealth was brought to Buenos Aires due to Argentina's valuable meat trade.

Question: Where did the Industrial Revolution begin c1750?

Answer: England. England, though an island, has abundant natural resources such as coal and hydroelectric (water) power. Resources used to produce finished goods are called *factors of production*. These factors include capital, laborers, land/natural resources, and *entrepreneurship* (explained later). In addition, because it's an island on the English Channel, there are ample harbors suitable for trade. England also has rivers for domestic travel.

Question: What were some of the early inventions of the textile industry in England?

Answer: England's textile factories dominated industry. You should know these eighteenth century inventions:

1. John Kay's *flying shuttle* doubled the speed at which yarn could be spun.

2. James Hargreaves' *spinning jenny* could spin yarn on eight spindles at a time.

3. Samuel Crompton's *spinning mule* spun with the help of hydroelectric (water) power.

Eli Whitney's invention of the cotton gin in the United States helped provide the raw material of cotton for English textile production. Whitney also invented the system of *interchangeable parts*. This meant that if a part of a firearm broke, you could just replace that part…instead of the entire weapon. When the American cotton trade was disrupted by the Civil War, Egypt and South Asia expanded a rich cotton trade.

Definition: Adam Smith and Capitalism

In 1776 Adam Smith wrote *The Wealth of Nations* where he argued that the government should take its *hands off* the economy and permit a free market. This non-interference concept is called *laissez-faire*. In the coming centuries, a *mixed economy* would become prevalent, as a combination of both private enterprise and government regulation has been seen in many countries.

In the economic system of *capitalism*, business ventures are controlled by private owners who have an incentive to gain from their investments. There is *free-enterprise*, or private ownership of businesses. One who takes the financial risk of operating a business is called an *entrepreneur*. Corporations were also formed. They could issue stock to outside investors looking to own a share of the company.

Definition: Karl Marx and Socialism

During the Industrial Revolution, people were suffering from hard work and an increasing gap between the rich and the poor. Germans Karl Marx and Friedrich Engels wrote *The Communist Manifesto* in 1848 to criticize these situations. They believed the lower class, the *proletariat*, would rise up and eliminate all distinctions of classes. Marx favored a *classless society*. In a classless society, there would be *socialism*, where the means of production can be shared by the people. This is the opposite of capitalism, which has individuals striving for the incentive of profit. In an equal socialist state, such incentive would not exist. In an economic, political, and social sense, extreme socialism would be defined by Marx as communism (explained more in depth later).

Also unhappy were the *Luddites.* Luddites were those who protested the massive changes brought forth by the Industrial Revolution. They were upset that machines were replacing skilled laborers.

Definition: Unions

As the Industrial Revolution spread, so too did unionization. Still prevalent today, unions are organizations that look to provide protection against the exploitation of the working class. They aim for higher wages and better working conditions. When demands aren't met, unions can go on *strike*, or stop working.

Unions fought for *collective bargaining,* where the union would negotiate a contract with the employer for all its workers.

In Britain during the mid-nineteenth century, there was labor reform legislation. The 1832 Sadler Report was a parliamentary investigation into harsh child labor and poor working conditions. Parliamentary action reforming child labor followed.

Definition: Jeremy Bentham/John Stuart Mill

These men believed in "the greatest happiness principle" where the government should provide the greatest good for the greatest number. This notion of the morality of actions being judged by their consequences is called *utilitarianism*. In other words, a government's actions would be deemed good if they provided for the happiness of many.

Definition: Thomas Malthus and David Ricardo

Unlike many who thought society would continue to improve, Malthus believed that increased birthrates would not keep pace with food supplies. Therefore, poverty and even starvation would be experienced by some. Ricardo agreed that there would always be a poor class. He believed that the larger the size of the working class, the smaller the wages would be. According to such an "iron law of wages," workers would make just enough to get by (subsistence wages). With such a large labor force available, employers would have no incentive to pay high wages.

• NINETEENTH CENTURY WESTERN EUROPE

Questions: Question: What were some domestic reforms under Queen Victoria? How did women's rights evolve around the world?

Answer: Queen Victoria was known for spreading democracy to the people. During her reign there was a working class *Chartist Movement* which demanded more rights, such as suffrage (voting privileges) for men. These rights coincided with a more educated population, as free schooling emerged throughout Western Europe during the second half of the nineteenth century.

Just before Victoria's reign, slavery was abolished in the British Empire through actions of abolitionists such as *William Wilberforce.* Parliament agreed to end the human rights violation of slavery in 1833. Slavery would continue in the United States until 1865.

During her reign, Parliament's House of Commons (which was elected unlike the House of Lords) gained much power. The Queen became mostly a figurehead, or ceremonial leader.

In terms of women's rights in Britain, suffrage was gradually gained, as women such as Emmeline Pankhurst of the Women's Social and Political Union (WSPU) were arrested for militant activity c1910. Full suffrage equality was achieved in 1928. In the United States, women gradually gained rights as well. At the Seneca Falls Convention of 1848, women demanded that all men and women were created equal. After helping out on the homefront during World War I, American women received the right to vote in 1920. This political achievement was coupled with social freedom, as women called *flappers* pushed the envelope in terms of dress, makeup, and social activity. Other countries followed with women's suffrage rights, such as Brazil in 1932. Voices continued to emerge, as **Lola Rodríguez de Tió** was an advocate for women's rights and the rights of her fellow citizens of Puerto Rico. Her poetry helped to inspire others around Latin America. Discrimination against women and minorities was legislated to be illegal in the United States under the Civil Rights Act of 1964.

Question: In which of its colonies did Great Britain allow self-rule?

Answer: Self-rule meant that Britain would allow certain colonies to govern themselves, despite still being controlled by the British Empire. You should know:

1. Canada became a **dominion** in 1867, meaning it could self-govern. This didn't end the *Quebecois separatist movement* (see pg. 64).

2. Australia was founded as a **penal colony** for convicted criminals. After persecuting the local Aborigines, the British settled Australia, as well as neighboring New Zealand. In the early 1900s, both became dominions like Canada. Australia adopted the White Australia Policy in 1901, which permitted only white immigrants to come to the continent. Like the Chinese Exclusion Act (1882) of the United States, this was aimed to prevent immigration and cheap labor from Asia.

3. Ireland received **home rule** much later. The **potato famine of the middle 1840s** caused a rift between Ireland and Great Britain, as the British did little to help the starving people of Ireland. An estimated one million people died during the famine. Ireland protested for home rule for decades. In 1921, Southern Ireland received it after a War for Independence. The country formally became the Republic of Ireland in 1949.

It's important to note that Northern Ireland remains part of the United Kingdom. When Ireland received home rule, the northern (and more Protestant part) was kept by the British. The area experienced much political and religious conflict in the decades following independence. Unionist Protestants wanted Northern Ireland to remain British, while Nationalist Catholics believed the area should become part of the Republic of Ireland. From 1968-1998, a time period known as "The Troubles" was marked by much violence in the area, resulting in the deaths of over 3,500 people. Until 2005, the Irish Republican Army, founded as a military organization seeking independence for Ireland, utilized violent tactics in protest of British control over Northern Ireland.

Definition: Charles Darwin's Theory of Evolution

First published in 1859, Darwin wrote **On the Origin of Species**. He preached "survival of the fittest," and that species who don't adapt, die. He stated that species evolve and adapt through a survival process called natural selection. Darwin made many of his observations at the Galapagos Islands off the west coast of South America. His theory of evolution was very controversial because it went against the creation teachings of the Bible.

Theories of Darwin were used to justify European imperialist policies of the nineteenth century (Social Darwinism explained in next chapter).

Definition: Dreyfus Affair

France operated under what was called the **Third Republic** during the late 1800s. It was an unstable representative democracy. Captain Alfred Dreyfus was a Jewish military officer who was accused of selling secrets to the Germans. He was convicted in 1894 on bad evidence and sentenced to life in prison. It was later proven that other officers set him up for conviction. Dreyfus was ultimately pardoned of the charges, and allowed to return to the military. The case was an example of *Anti-Semitism*, or prejudice against Jews.

Question: What major communications inventions occurred in the nineteenth century?

Answer:

1. Telegraph – Electrically sent messages across great distances.

2. Telephone – Alexander Graham Bell's invention brought voices together in the US and later throughout the world.

3. Radio – Guglielmo Marconi helped bring about the ability to transmit messages wirelessly.

By the end of the century, American Thomas Edison showed moving pictures on his kinetoscope. Of course, later in the twentieth century, television would become the medium for both audio and visual content.

Review Questions for the AP World History: Modern Exam

"As every individual, therefore, endeavors as much as he can both to employ his capital in the support of domestic industry and so to direct that industry that its produce may be of the greatest value; every individual necessarily labors to render the annual revenue of the society as great as he can. He generally, indeed, neither intends to promote the public interest, nor knows how much he is promoting it. By preferring the support of domestic to that of foreign industry, he intends only his own security; and by directing that industry in such a manner as its produce may be of the greatest value, he intends only his own gain, and he is in this, as in many other cases, led by an invisible hand to promote an end which was no part of his intention."

— Adam Smith, *The Wealth of Nations*, 1776

1. Which of the following is an accurate point of view of the above passage?
   A) Socialism is a superior economic system
   B) Foreign industries are more important than domestic ones
   C) The factors of production should be shared by the workers
   D) Hard work through capitalism could benefit others

2. Who of the following would disagree most vocally with the above statement?
   A) Karl Marx
   B) John Stuart Mill
   C) Eli Whitney
   D) John Kay

3. Which of the following was not relevant to the historical time period described above?
   A) Child Labor in factories
   B) Women's suffrage in England
   C) Religious conflicts in Europe
   D) Urbanization to cities

Review Questions for the SAT Subject Test

1. Nationalism is most likely to develop in regions that have
    A) isolated city-states
    B) diverse religious practices
    C) vast trade networks that accumulate wealth
    D) people who share a common culture or history
    E) a lack of raw materials and resources

2. German unification in the nineteenth century was accomplished mostly through
    A) peaceful negotiations with France and Poland
    B) treaties and land purchases through Switzerland
    C) war with neighboring countries
    D) negotiations with the Church for the Papal States
    E) international pressures for reform

3. Why did the Industrial Revolution begin in England in the eighteenth century?
    A) England's vast overseas Asian Empire gave it the raw materials necessary to industrialize
    B) The geography of England provided rich resources and water transportation needed for industrialization
    C) Napoleon's Continental System forced England to become self-sufficient
    D) Because of failed farming techniques, British people looked for other avenues to achieve economic success
    E) It was an inevitable location for the continuation of the Columbian Exchange

4. Luddites and Socialists were similar in that both
    A) believed in laissez-faire economics
    B) wanted free enterprise and entrepreneurialism
    C) resented the Industrial Revolution's impact on society
    D) supported the election of wealthy business owners to Parliament
    E) openly supported dictatorships

5. What was the greatest influence on urbanization in Britain c1800?
    A) Readily available jobs in factories
    B) Crop failures in rural areas
    C) Universal male suffrage
    D) International trading opportunities
    E) Decreased education in cities

6. Which inventor's creation led to an increase in crop harvests?
    A) Samuel Crompton
    B) James Watt
    C) John Kay
    D) Jethro Tull
    E) James Hargreaves

7. Karl Marx and Friedrich Engels would most likely support
    A) a classless society where the workers share the factors of production
    B) laissez-faire capitalism as advocated by Adam Smith
    C) survival of the fittest in business, and educational opportunities for the elite
    D) elimination of labor unions as a means to bargain wages
    E) imperialist policies in foreign countries

8. Queen Victoria's reign in Britain in the nineteenth century was known for

A) limiting suffrage rights and the number of elected officials

B) decreasing the legislating power of the House of Commons

C) restoring absolute monarchy, and decreasing the power of Parliament

D) increasing democracy, and limiting the role of the monarch

E) the beginnings of the Industrial Revolution

9. Which of the following had the greatest impact on urban health in the nineteenth century?

A) Railroad transportation of medicines

B) An increase in medical professionals

C) Universal healthcare programs

D) Widespread use of antibiotics

E) Improvements in sanitation and plumbing

10. Charles Darwin's research was controversial mostly because

A) he did not take into account issues of natural selection

B) his discoveries went against the basic teachings of the Church

C) he did not acknowledge advanced human intelligence

D) humans never lived in the Galapagos Islands

E) he openly criticized the scientific method

Answers and Explanations

AP World History: Modern

1. **D**. According to Smith, although people strive for profit, an "invisible hand" could deliver some benefits to others in the process.

2. **A**. Karl Marx would be an advocate for socialism, not capitalism.

3. **B**. Women's suffrage would be seen later, during the twentieth century.

SAT Subject Test

1. **D**. Nationalism is one of the most important terms of the course. It involves strong pride in one's nation, and develops because of a common culture, history, language, or set of beliefs.

2. **C**. Otto von Bismarck helped unify Germany through "Blood and Iron." This strategy was accompanied by war.

3. **B**. Geographically, England was the perfect spot for the Industrial Revolution because of an abundance of natural resources and water travel.

4. **C**. Not everyone was happy during the Industrial Revolution. Socialism was supported by workers looking to gain more rights. Luddites opposed the mechanization of industry because machines replaced skilled workers.

5. **A**. People moved to cities (urbanized) because jobs were readily available. Similar urbanization took place all over Europe and the United States.

6. **D**. Jethro Tull's seed drill helped plant seeds in even rows deep within the soil.

7. **A**. If all classes were eliminated, true equality would occur. In the *Communist Manifesto*, Marx and Engels advocated for a classless society.

8. **D**. Gradually over centuries, monarchs lost absolute power in Great Britain. Queen Victoria continued this trend by giving more authority to Parliament in the nineteenth century.

9. **E**. In the late nineteenth century, cities would improve sanitation and plumbing. This was a reaction to the findings of researchers such as Louis Pasteur who studied ***germ theory*** and disease prevention. ***Antibiotics***, such as penicillin, would see widespread use later c1928.

10. **B**. Darwin's theories still remain controversial among many today because his conclusions dispute the creation teachings of the Bible.

Imperialism and World War I

Nationalism helped fuel the Age of Imperialism of the nineteenth century where nations took over territories for political and economic gain. Socially, the culture of the conqueror was often enforced as well. Around the globe, Western nations competed for the raw materials and markets that weaker territories had to offer. The riches most sought after were in Africa and Asia. Imperialism was one of the causes for World War I, where fighting on the Western and Eastern fronts left millions of soldiers and civilians dead by 1918. After the war, Germany was held accountable by the Treaty of Versailles.

HERE IS WHAT YOU NEED TO KNOW:
• IMPERIALISM
Definition: Imperialism

Imperialism is when one powerful nation takes over a weaker territory and enforces their political, economic, and social ideals onto the conquered. Typically, this was rationalized through **Social Darwinism**, or a belief in "survival of the fittest." Many European nations imperialized in the middle to late nineteenth century. Britain amassed the greatest Empire. Their main focus was on Africa and Asia.

Question: Why did nations imperialize?
Answer: **MGM**

1. **M** - **M**oney – To capitalize on rich resources such as gold, jewels, and ivory.

2. **G** - **G**od – To convert to Christianity those seen as "savages." **Rudyard Kipling** wrote the poem, **The White Man's Burden** which spoke of imperialists civilizing races believed to be inferior. **Assimilation** is the process whereby the conquered adopts the imperializing nation's culture.

3. **M** - **M**arket – Heavily populated countries were ideal markets for selling finished goods. China and India were the most populous imperialistic markets.

Another G you could use is *geopolitics*. This means to take over locations around the globe for strategic purposes. Islands, for example, could be used as army bases.

Definition: Berlin Conference, 1884-85

The Conference was part of an imperialistic "Scramble for Africa." European nations assembled in Berlin, Germany to divide up the lands of Africa. Of course, no African leaders were present to object to this division. Britain and France came away with the most territory after the conference. Belgium took the Congo. In Africa, Liberia maintained independence. Ethiopia, under *Menelik II*, pushed back the Italian military to also remain independent. Resistance failed elsewhere, however. In West Africa, a Muslim leader named *Samory Touré* unsuccessfully utilized guerrilla warfare in an attempt to push out the French. After years of rebellion, the French proved to be stronger, more organized, and soon took a stronghold over the western area of the continent.

A few years before the conference, Egypt lost control of the Suez Canal to the British, and became occupied by European powers. A nationalist rebellion failed in 1882. The British also used superior weaponry to put down a jihad, or holy war, in neighboring Sudan to give them overwhelming control of northeast Africa.

Definition: Boer Wars, 1880-81, 1899-1902

South Africa was thriving under the military strength of Zulu chief **Shaka** c1800. However, years later the Boers (Dutch settlers) took over the region with the help of advanced military weaponry. When diamonds and other riches were discovered there, the British swooped in. Two wars were fought, the first from 1880-81, and the second from 1899-1902. The British used concentration camps against the Boers which upset other European nations. The British won, and the Union of South Africa remained in their hands until 1961.

Definition: British East India Company

This was a *joint-stock company* (venture where investors could buy stock in the company) that controlled much of the trade in India by the first half of the nineteenth century. As the Mughal Empire weakened, Britain continued a policy of imperialism in the subcontinent of India. Because India had a population hovering over 300 million, it was a great market for selling finished goods. Indian people were encouraged to purchase only British items. Eventually, India became known as the *"jewel in the crown,"* as its resources and market made it the most valuable of all of the British colonial treasures.

Definition: Sepoy Mutiny, 1857

In 1857, a rebellion was caused by Indian nationalism and discontent with the British Empire. A *sepoy* was an Indian soldier of Hindu or Muslim descent who was hired to fight for the British.

The spark that triggered conflict was talk of the British using grease from meat in their firearm cartridges. Since soldiers bit open these cartridges when reloading, the grease would go against the religious dietary restrictions of the sepoys. At first, protesters were thrown in jail. Later, violence ensued. The British put down the uprising by 1858, and strengthened their grip over India. Strict British rule, known as the *British Raj*, continued until 1947.

Question: What disrupted China's policy of isolation?

Answer: China attempted to prevent European control. They were self-sufficient, yet traded many goods with the West. However, things changed by 1830 because of an addiction to a narcotic called opium. Millions of Chinese people became addicted to opium supplied by the profiting British. The drug trade eventually led to war.

Definition: First Opium War, 1839-1842

Because of the drug trade mentioned above, there was extreme discontent in China. The first Opium War (there were two), saw Britain's powerful steamships and technologically advanced weapons defeat the Chinese. The war began in 1839, and the *Treaty of Nanjing* (Nanking) of 1842 gave England control of *Hong Kong*. Hong Kong would become a booming metropolis over the next century. The Chinese lost a second Opium War in 1860. In 1997, the British handed Hong Kong back to the Chinese.

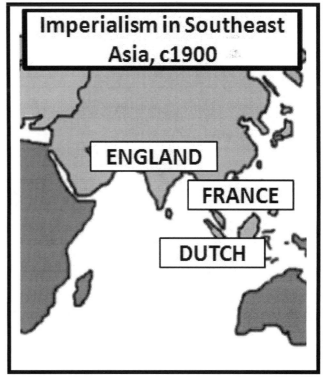

Imperialism in Southeast Asia, c1900

ENGLAND

FRANCE

DUTCH

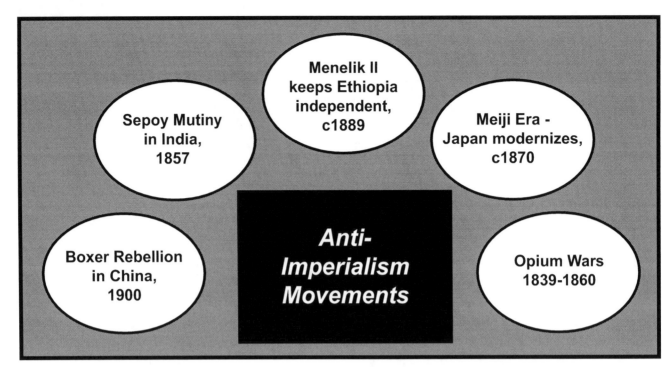

Anti-Imperialism Movements
- Menelik II keeps Ethiopia independent, c1889
- Sepoy Mutiny in India, 1857
- Meiji Era - Japan modernizes, c1870
- Boxer Rebellion in China, 1900
- Opium Wars 1839-1860

Definition: Spheres of Influence

Britain wasn't the only nation who entered China. Other European countries, Japan, and the United States were also present. Each nation carved out a "sphere of influence," meaning they each began to control the trade within a piece of territory within China.

Definition: Open Door Policy, United States Imperialism

Generally, US Secretary of State John Hay's 1899 policy was created to protect American trading interests in China. The United States did not want to lose Chinese trade to other European countries, so it declared China open to all countries who wanted to trade. Of course, China could not object. One thing that was not open for China, was immigration to the United States, as the 1882 Chinese Exclusion Act forbid immigration from China to the US due partly to fears of job competition.

Deprived of their rights from imperial Spain, the Philippines saw a time of revolution in the late nineteenth century. This partially stemmed from a *Propaganda movement* where Enlightenment thought was used to challenge Spain and gain sympathy for rights. Ultimately, the United States would gain control after defeating the Spanish in the Spanish-American War (1898). After the war, the US received Puerto Rico, Guam, and purchased the Philippines from Spain for $20 million. US rule over the Philippines was quite harsh and led to massive resentment. The military had to put down a rebellion from 1899-1902. This was the *Philippine-American War*.

Countries such as Great Britain looked to invest and lend money with interest to Latin American countries. However, the US became the police powers in the Western Hemisphere c1900. They supported the 1903 Panamanian Revolution against Colombia, who had backed out of a treaty to build a canal. Once Panama became free, a treaty granted the US the canal zone. The Panama Canal was an immense building project which linked the Atlantic to the Pacific for commerce and travel. Doctors aimed to control malaria and yellow fever (spread by mosquitoes) which killed many during the early years of its construction.

Businesses increased investment in Central and South America throughout the twentieth century, as the United Fruit Company harvested bananas, and sold them in the US and abroad.

Definition: Boxer Rebellion, 1900

Boxers were Chinese people who wanted to drive out foreign imperialist nations. In addition, they resented Chinese conversions to Christianity. In 1900, their rebellion escalated, and was supported by the conservative Dowager Empress Cixi. Imperialist nations ended the uprising rather quickly. In addition, Qing Dynasty power deteriorated and war reparations were high. China would not rid itself of all foreign interests for another fifty years.

Decades before from 1850-64, there was a religious and political civil war called the Taiping Rebellion. It was led by Chinese Christians who wanted to redistribute wealth across the country. The Qing Dynasty put down the rebellion with the help of European powers. It was at this time that the Qing began a "self-strengthening" movement where they imitated western industrial and military weaponry. However, China would not strengthen nearly as much as the Japanese in terms of westernization c1900.

Question: How did Japan's experiences with imperialism differ from those of China?

Answer: Whereas China did not adapt to westernization, Japan did. In 1853, American Commodore Matthew Perry landed in Tokyo. Japan had no choice but to open its once isolated doors to trade. However, unlike China, Japan industrialized and grew stronger. When shogun rule ended in 1867, the emperor was returned to power in the Meiji Restoration. Japa-

nese Emperor Mutsuhito looked to enlighten Japan with modernization.

In the **Meiji Era** from 1868-1912, the Japanese embraced Western technology and modernized their factories. Not everyone supported it, as thousands of disenchanted samurai warriors unsuccessfully rebelled against this new governmental structure in the 1870s.

Unlike the Chinese who were imperialized, the Japanese **became** imperialists. One can compare the expansion of Japan's Empire to that of Britain after their Industrial Revolution. However, Japan's Empire would be far less global. Because Japan did not have extensive reserves of resources, they looked elsewhere for raw materials, such as coal and iron. This quest for raw materials escalated into the twentieth century. Remember: M for Meiji. M for Modernization.

Question: Where did the Japanese imperialize?

Answer: The Japanese fought several wars. You should know:

1. Sino-Japanese War, 1894-95 – Japan swiftly defeated the Chinese and took some land.

2. Russo-Japanese War, 1904-05 – Japan's victory over the much larger Russia shocked the world. The war paved the way for Japan's eventual domination of Northern China (Manchuria) and Korea. In both places, the Japanese ruled harshly and enforced their culture upon the imperialized.

• WORLD WAR I
Question: What were the causes for The Great War (World War I)?

Answer: Mnemonic device: **MANIA**

M - **Militarism** – European nations began amassing large armies that were prepared for war.

A - **Alliances** – These militarized nations created alliances. Germany, Austria-Hungary, and Italy joined the Triple Alliance in 1882. Russia, France, and Britain entered the Triple Entente in 1907.

N - Nationalism – Different nations believed that they should dominate the European continent.

I - Imperialism – Nations wanted to gain territory and make their Empires more powerful.

A - Assassination – The spark that started the war was the assassination of ***Archduke Franz Ferdinand*** who was shot by Serbian nationalist Gavrilo Princip in Sarajevo on June 28, 1914. Serbia was one of several nations who broke free from the weakening Ottoman Empire. The Ottomans were known as the "sick man" of Europe in the "powder keg" of the Balkans.

After the assassination, Austria-Hungary declared war on Serbia, and a ***chain reaction*** of war declarations spread throughout Europe.

Question: What military events of World War I (1914-1918) are important to know?

Answer:

1. The war was fought on both the Western and Eastern Fronts. The Western Front was on the French and German border. The Eastern Front was on the German/Austro-Hungarian and Russian border.

2. The Triple Entente became known as the Allies. The Triple Alliance lost Italy, and became the Central Powers (Germany and Austria-Hungary).

3. The early German strategy was called the Schlieffen Plan. Its goal was to swiftly defeat France, and then move eastward to defeat Russia. This never happened.

4. Russia dropped out of the war because of the Russian Revolution (explained in next chapter).

5. The war moved outside of the two European fronts, as Gallipoli in modern-day Turkey (Ottoman Empire) saw fierce fighting.

6. Months after American reinforcements arrived, Kaiser Wilhelm II agreed to an ***armistice*** to end the fighting on November 11, 1918 (the eleventh hour of the eleventh day in the eleventh month).

Question: What caused the United States to enter World War I in 1917?

Answer: Before the war, the United States remained neutral. However, certain international events changed this. It's good to know... ***The Boat and The Note.***

1. The Boat – The ***Lusitania***. It was a passenger ship (with Americans on board) sailing off the coast of Ireland. It was sunk by a German submarine (U-boat) on May 7, 1915. The US warned Germany to refrain from continued submarine warfare. However, the Germans would not stop.

2. The Note – ***The Zimmermann Telegram***. In 1917, the British intercepted a telegram from Arthur Zimmermann of Germany. He was writing to Mexico seeking an alliance. The Germans proposed that, if victorious at the end of the war, land from the United States would be given to Mexico.

The Germans continued their policy of unrestricted submarine warfare. President Woodrow Wilson asked Congress to declare war in April of 1917. He was hoping to make the world "safe for democracy."

Question: What were the technological innovations of World War I?

Answer: This modern war saw:

1. Trench Warfare – Though used in earlier wars, trenches were most prevalent in World War I. Trenches involved the digging of large holes/tunnels in the ground. They were used to take cover from enemy fire. Ultimately in World War I, soldiers could not move very far in a day, as new trenches would have to

be dug. The trenches were filthy, and full of vermin and disease.

2. *U-boats* (Unterseeboots), or submarines – The Germans enhanced the invention of the submarine. They used these U-boats to sink ships and control the high seas early in the war.

3. Airplane – The Wright brothers of the United States successfully flew the first flight in 1903. A decade later, the plane was able to drop bombs, spy, fight, and transport materials.

4. Poison/Mustard Gas and Gas-Masks – A German innovation that was soon used by the Allies, chemical weapons were common in the Great War. Gas-masks were used by both sides to prevent respiratory failure.

5. Tanks – A British invention. Early tanks were not very reliable. However the Germans would improve on the technology during World War II.

6. Machine guns and flamethrowers were also used in this war.

Definition: Fourteen Points

United States President Woodrow Wilson presented his plan for peace. In a 1918 speech, Wilson addressed issues of fair trade, freedom of the seas, treatment of the imperialized, and constructing new borders. Most important was his fourteenth point, which was to create an international peace-keeping organization. This would become the *League of Nations*. Unlike today's United Nations, the League could not raise an army to enforce peace.

Definition: Treaty of Versailles, June 28, 1919

The *Big Four* who helped influence the peace treaty were Woodrow Wilson of the US, David Lloyd George of Britain, Georges Clemenceau of France, and Vittorio Orlando of Italy. The Treaty of Versailles was signed on the fifth anniversary of the Ferdinand assassination. In the treaty:

1. Germany lost Alsace-Lorraine to the French. They also surrendered other international colonies.

2. Germany had to shrink the size of its army and could not manufacture weapons. In addition, they had to stop constructing U-boats.

3. Germany was found guilty of causing the war and had to pay $33 billion in war reparations (money paid by the defeated country).

This harsh treatment of Germany in the aftermath of the war has led many historians to believe that the Treaty of Versailles was a cause for World War II.

Note: The United States never ratified the Treaty of Versailles because the US Senate feared that joining the League of Nations would encroach on their neutrality.

Question: What were some territorial changes in Europe after World War I?
Answer:

1. Austria-Hungary became Austria, Hungary, and Czechoslovakia. Some land would eventually become Yugoslavia.

2. After dropping out of the war, Russia lost what would become Estonia, Ukraine, Finland, Latvia, and Lithuania.

3. Poland, which was not a nation when the war began, became independent.

4. What had been the Ottoman Empire became Turkey. Turkey's independence movement was led by *Mustafa Kemal Atatürk*. He became the first president of the Republic of Turkey in 1923, and transformed the country into a secular state (not controlled by Islam). He promoted increased legal rights for women, and encouraged them to give up their veils and dress in Western clothes. Women also received full political rights and could vote in national parliamentary elections in 1934.

5. The League of Nations came up with a Mandate System which allowed stronger Allied

nations to administer territories (once held by the Ottomans or Germans) they thought weren't yet fit for self-rule. Middle Eastern places such as Syria, Iraq, and Palestine were affected, as were some coastal African territories. Resistance to foreign control led to a **Pan-Arabism** nationalist movement which united people of a similar background in the Middle East.

Definition Armenian Massacres

Before World War I, the Christian Armenian population demanded rights within the Ottoman Empire. Their demands were put down with force. During the war, they were accused of supporting Russia, and were met with military resistance. Many Armenians were deported and endured starvation, forced marches, torture, and execution. An estimated 1-1.5 million people were killed in the atrocities. The killing ended in 1923. Though considered by many to be genocide, the Turkish government denied such claims.

Question: What do I need to know about the Mexican Revolution?

Answer: As World War I came and went, Mexico was involved in a decade of revolution from 1910-1920. The revolution resulted in a new constitution. You need to know:

1. Much like many Latin American countries of the late nineteenth century, Mexico was ruled by local dictators known as **caudillos**. One such caudillo was **Porfirio Díaz**, who used force against those who dissented with his rule. He kept firm control over Mexico c1900. Though he looked to modernize and industrialize Mexico, during his reign there was a large gap between the rich and the poor, as foreign industrialists became rich.

2. Calling for a revolution against Díaz, Francisco Madero emerged as the voice of the people. Revolutionaries such as Pancho Villa and Emiliano Zapata looked to take money from the rich and redistribute it to the poor. Díaz agreed to give up power, and Madero won an election in 1911. But, Madero was seen as an inefficient leader, was removed from power, and assassinated. From there, Mexico went through several presidents during years of civil war, including Victoriano Huerta and Venustiano Carranza.

3. In 1917, a new Mexican Constitution (still in effect today) was adopted during Carranza's reign. It favored commoners instead of the wealthy, allowed the government to seize private lands for public interest, gave rights to workers, and decreased the power of the Roman Catholic church in Mexico. Carranza believed the constitution was too radical. He was assassinated in 1920. Though 1920 is used as an end-date for the revolution, violence in Mexico continued long after the Constitution was adopted.

Le Petit journal. Supplément du dimanche: Paris (1898, Jan. 16)

1. The primary purpose of the above cartoon is to

A) show the importance of China as a military presence

B) illustrate European dominance in an unwelcome region

C) promote religious tolerance in China

D) call for an army to put down the Boxer Rebellion

2. The above situation was most similar to which of the following?

A) The Crusades and a Holy War

B) The Encounter and mercantilism

C) The Fall of the Roman Empire and fragmentation in Europe

D) The Peloponnesian War and emergence of philosophy

3. Compared to China, Japan's reaction to imperialism was to

A) learn from it, modernize, and become imperialists

B) fight several wars against western invaders of the mainland

C) strengthen the feudal structure under the samurai

D) rely on the daimyo for guidance during a resistance period

Review Questions for the SAT Subject Test

1. Which of the following was true of imperialism in China and Japan?
   A) Rebellions in Japan were successful and prevented European contact
   B) China quickly industrialized which led to the exit of imperial powers
   C) Japan's Meiji Restoration gradually turned them into an imperialistic threat
   D) The British could not capitalize on the opium and tea trade in China
   E) China took over parts of Japan with hopes of gaining valuable resources

2. Which of these African nations remained independent from European rule c1914?
   A) Sudan
   B) South Africa
   C) Congo
   D) Libya
   E) Ethiopia

3. What was one outcome of the Boer War?
   A) The end of British control in the western regions of Africa
   B) British domination in the Union of South Africa
   C) British control of the Congo River as an outlet to the Atlantic Ocean
   D) A decreased need for Britain to utilize Asian tea markets
   E) Indian nationalism and resistance

4. Which of the following saw a gradual loss of power from 1850 to World War I?
   A) Gupta Empire
   B) Ottoman Empire
   C) Second Reich
   D) Austro-Hungarian Empire
   E) British Empire

5. The "jewel in the crown" of the British Empire was
   A) Egypt
   B) Japan
   C) China
   D) India
   E) Iran

6. The outcome of the Opium Wars was
   A) decreased British imperialism in the eastern regions of China
   B) an elimination of American spheres of influence in China
   C) a transferring of Hong Kong to British hands
   D) the end of Chinese conversions to Christianity
   E) establishment of the British Raj

7. Which of the following was the spark that led to a chain reaction of war in 1914?
   A) The sinking of the *Lusitania*
   B) Assassination of Archduke Franz Ferdinand
   C) German militarization in a time of peace
   D) Unrestricted and ruthless submarine attacks in the Atlantic
   E) Interception of the Zimmermann Telegram

8. The Schlieffen Plan was
   A) a German war goal to quickly defeat France, and then shift attention to Russia
   B) an Allied strategy to gain land in the Balkans
   C) a proposed alliance between Germany and Mexico
   D) the transformation of World War I from a battle on land, to one in the air
   E) a framework for the Mexican Constitution

9. The Treaty of Versailles looked to do all of the following EXCEPT:
   A) Limit the manufacturing of weapons in Germany
   B) Remove Alsace-Lorraine from German hands
   C) Allow for an international army to enforce the Treaty
   D) Penalize Germany a large sum of money for their war guilt
   E) Limit German submarine capabilities

10. After World War I, which of the following countries was established from the former Austro-Hungarian Empire?
   A) Lithuania
   B) Estonia
   C) Latvia
   D) Turkey
   E) Czechoslovakia

Answers and Explanations

AP World History: Modern

1. **B**. China didn't have much of a say as they were reluctantly carved into spheres of influence by European powers.

2. **B**. Similarly, Native American empires couldn't stop European powers from taking resources and land.

3. **A**. Japan modernized, and then became imperialists. They needed raw materials to help fuel their industrializing nation.

SAT Subject Test

1. **C**. During the Meiji Era, Japan gradually industrialized. By 1900, they were an international force and started to imperialize neighboring countries.

2. **E**. After the Berlin Conference divided up Africa among European powers, Menelik II helped Ethiopia remain independent from imperial rule. Liberia also stayed independent.

3. **B**. The Boers were Dutch settlers in Southern Africa. The British defeated the Boers in a series of conflicts, and took control of what would become the Union of South Africa.

4. **B**. The Ottoman Empire was known as the "sick man of Europe," as it was slowly deteriorating by the twentieth century.

5. **D**. With a market containing millions of people, India was the most valuable of all of the British colonial treasures.

6. **C**. The Chinese handed over Hong Kong in the Treaty of Nanjing. They would not get it back until 1997.

7. **B**. The assassination of Archduke Franz Ferdinand was the spark that led to a chain reaction that erupted into World War I.

8. **A**. Strong German nationalism led to the belief that the Central Powers could quickly defeat France, and then focus their attention on Russia in the East. However, they were never able to defeat the Allies on the Western Front.

9. **C**. The League of Nations had no army. The United Nations would have one after World War II.

10. **E**. Czechoslovakia came out of the Austro-Hungarian Empire. The other choices were from Russia.

The Russian Revolution and Joseph Stalin

By the mid-twentieth century, the Soviet Union's importance in global affairs was immense. However in 1900, Russia was industrially backwards and ruled by czars incapable of providing for the welfare of the common people. The first two decades of the twentieth century led to the deaths of millions, as revolution, World War I, civil war, famine, and harsh living conditions took a toll on the Russian people. When the dust settled, a new nation emerged called the Soviet Union. Under the leadership of Vladimir Lenin, and later Joseph Stalin, the Soviet Union became the largest communist state in the world. Its emergence coincided with the sacrifice of individual rights and liberties.

HERE IS WHAT YOU NEED TO KNOW:
Definition: Pogroms

Under Czar Alexander III, there was a hope to unify Russian culture. This meant persecution of the many Jews who lived in the country. Pogroms were organized massacres that targeted them. Jews had long since been removed to an area of Russia known as the Pale of Settlement. *Anti-Semitism* caused many to emigrate from Russia in the early twentieth century.

Definition: Czar Nicholas II

Nicholas Romanov would be the last czar of Russia. During his reign there was massive industrialization. Specifically, the Trans-Siberian Railway became the longest rail project in the world. However, Nicholas fell out of favor with the people because of the following:

1. Russo-Japanese War, 1904-05. Besides giving up some land, the Russian people were embarrassed after losing a war to the small island of Japan.

2. *Bloody Sunday* – Protests and worker demonstrations took place in what's known as the Revolution of 1905. On January 22, 1905, thousands of workers protesting for labor rights in St. Petersburg were fired on by the Czar's Imperial Guard. The backlash to this event led to the creation of a Russian parliament known as the Duma. Though it was supposed to help legislate for more rights, it didn't have much power.

3. World War I misfortune – Russia suffered the most casualties in the war, with nearly 2 million soldiers killed. Russia proved ill-equipped for battle, as they lacked military supplies and sufficient food for its troops. Nicholas went to the front lines to try to boost morale.

Definition: Grigori Rasputin

Rasputin was a "holy man" who claimed to have mystical powers. The Czar's son suffered from hemophilia, a blood disease. When Rasputin appeared to ease the boy's symptoms, Czarina Alexandra rewarded him with political power. While Nicholas was away fighting the war, Rasputin had his hand in the government, and corruption became a large problem. Rasputin was ultimately murdered by aristocrats, and thrown into the Neva River in 1916.

Definition: March Revolution, 1917

The workers rose up to protest both their working conditions and the misfortunes of the Great War. The Czar was stripped of power, and a temporary *Provisional Government* was put in his place. Alexander Kerensky would later become its leader. This government proved weak. When they continued to press on fighting the war, it angered socialist groups of workers called *soviets*.

Definition: Vladimir Lenin and the Bolsheviks

Lenin was the leader of the *Bolsheviks*... revolutionaries who turned to the writings of Karl Marx. They believed that socialism was the answer to the poor living conditions and discontent of the Russian people. Lenin had previously fled Russia, but returned when the Czar abdicated the throne. He and the popular Bolsheviks had an opportunity to seize power.

Definition: November (Bolshevik) Revolution, 1917

Lenin hoped to bring the Russian people, *"Peace, Land, and Bread."* He and the Bolsheviks overthrew the Provisional Government to gain control of Russia. To make sure the Czar's supporters didn't restore him to the throne, the entire royal family was executed in 1918. The capital of Russia was soon moved from St. Petersburg to Moscow.

Question: How did Lenin deliver on his promise of Peace, Land, and Bread?

Answer:

Peace – The 1918 *Treaty of Brest-Litovsk* allowed Russia to drop out of World War I. They gave up western land to achieve this.

Land and Bread – Lenin began to divide up all of the farms and factories amongst the people. This upset the many *kulaks*, or wealthier Russians.

Definition: Russian Civil War, 1918-1921

Leon Trotsky led the Bolshevik Red Army against the anti-Bolshevik White Army. Between the fighting, famine, and disease, more Russians were killed in this war than in World War I. Estimates range from 10-15 million. The Red Army won the war and the Bolsheviks continued to rule Russia.

Definition: New Economic Policy, 1921

After the war, Lenin set up *NEP*. NEP permitted some capitalism, as shopkeepers were allowed to keep small profits. However, the government remained in control of most production in the factory system.

Definition: Communism in the USSR

The Bolshevik Party changed its name to the Communist Party. Communism was a system supported by the writer Karl Marx. This is a government that provides a classless society where the workers share the means of production. Communism became a dictatorship under Lenin. With Joseph Stalin, this dictatorship grew stronger.

In 1922, Russia and surrounding lands such as Ukraine and Belarus became the *Union of Soviet Socialist Republics* (USSR). It can also be called the *Soviet Union*. This enormous area extended into northern Asia. A movement called *Russification* attempted to expand the Russian culture and language to areas far away from Moscow.

Definition: Joseph Stalin and Totalitarianism

Joseph Stalin worked his way up the Communist Party and took control of it by 1928. Stalin was a harsh dictator who ruled through *totalitarianism*. Totalitarianism occurs when a government not only takes over the economic and political lives of the people, but their social rights as well. Stalin controlled production, the media, the economy, and everything else under the Soviet sun. Churches were destroyed, and *atheism* (rejection of a belief in God) was advised. Those who went against Stalin were either killed or sent to a labor camp known as a *gulag*. Many were worked to death in isolated Siberia.

Under Stalin's regime, women entered the

workplace. Communist law gave women equal rights. Despite working long days in the socialist economy, women were also instrumental in raising children and running the home.

Definition: Command Economy/First Five-Year Plan, 1928

Stalin commanded the economy, meaning he made all regulations for agriculture and industry. Regarding industry, Stalin made a series of *Five-Year Plans* which aimed to modernize the Soviet Union, as it lagged behind other European countries. The plan looked to produce raw materials such as coal and iron, and extend railway lines, electricity, and communication networks. Production from factories increased, but they never met the impossible quotas that Stalin set out to achieve. In addition, unlike in capitalist nations, there was a lack of consumer goods being produced in the Soviet Union.

In the command economy, Stalin seized all of the privately owned farms and made them *collective farms*. This obviously upset the landowners, known as kulaks. Many were executed during the collectivization process. In addition, collectivization led to a devastating famine in Ukraine (which was part of the USSR at the time, see pg. 102) from 1932-33. With the government taking much of the grain production, millions died of starvation. Many historians believe Stalin created this famine, known as the *Holodomor*, to quiet Ukrainian nationalists seeking independence.

Definition: The Great Purge of the 1930s

Stalin was very paranoid of his enemies… and his former friends. Because of this, he targeted any official whom he *thought* could be a traitor. To purge means to remove or kill. His secret police rounded up suspected enemies

Religious structures were destroyed in favor of statues celebrating Marx, Engels, Lenin, and Stalin

of the state, and they were either murdered or shipped to a gulag. The Great Purge targeted government officials in the Communist Party and peasants who were seen as enemies of the state. After unfair trials, most were executed. The killings peaked from 1937-38.

It is believed that Joseph Stalin killed more people than Adolf Hitler. Estimates are as high as 20 million. Through fear and immense *propaganda* (biased media coverage, posters, school curriculum, speeches, and parades), Stalin *indoctrinated* the people of Russia. This meant that his views were accepted as truth. All opposition was silenced.

Peace Treaty of Brest-Litovsk
Article 1

Germany, Austria-Hungary, Bulgaria and Turkey on the one hand and Russia on the other declare that the condition of war between them has ceased. They have decided to live in peace and accord in the future...

Article 3

The territories lying to the west of the line determined by the contracting powers and which formerly belonged to Russia will no longer be under her sovereignty…

Article 5

Russia will, without delay, proceed to demobilize her army, including those army units newly formed by her present government.

Moreover, Russia will either bring her warships into Russian ports and keep them there until general peace is concluded, or will disarm them at once…

1. What is the purpose of the above treaty?
   A) To escalate conflict on the Eastern Front of World War I
   B) To boost public confidence in the Czar
   C) To help Russia peacefully exit Word War I
   D) To increase the power of the Provisional Government of Russia

2. What was the short-term cause for the brokering of the above treaty?
   A) German aggression on the Western Front
   B) The assassination of Archduke Franz Ferdinand
   C) Decreased morale within Russia
   D) Japanese victory in the Russo-Japanese War

3. Which of the following would occur shortly after the Treaty?
   A) Russian Civil War
   B) March Revolution of 1917
   C) Bloody Sunday
   D) November Revolution of 1917

Review Questions for the SAT Subject Test

1. Under Czar Alexander's rule, Jews in Russia were
    A) given equal citizenship rights
    B) permitted religious tolerance
    C) targeted with organized violence
    D) forced to work as serfs on the Trans-Siberian Railway
    E) encouraged to play a key role in the Duma

2. Bloody Sunday was a violent response against Russians who wanted
    A) more rights for the working class
    B) religious toleration
    C) an end to Russification
    D) collectivization of private farms
    E) communism as a system of government

3. Vladimir Lenin's rise to power was related to all of the following EXCEPT:
    A) Discontent with czarist rule
    B) Dissatisfaction with labor conditions
    C) World War I's devastating effects on the Russian people
    D) Support from the Eastern Orthodox Church
    E) A low standard of living

4. The Bolshevik Revolutionaries supported the
    A) limiting of workers' rights
    B) Provisional Government of Alexander Kerensky
    C) Russian tradition of Czarist rule
    D) reign of Rasputin
    E) writings of Karl Marx

5. Vladimir Lenin's New Economic Policy
    A) eliminated all elements of capitalism
    B) advocated for full-scale capitalism
    C) denied peasants the ownership of livestock
    D) led to full scale unionization of workers
    E) permitted a few private businesses to profit

6. In a command economy
    A) unionization of workers is encouraged by the government
    B) the government can regulate prices, but not materials produced
    C) agricultural ventures are given preference over industry
    D) the leader of the nation-state determines what is produced
    E) state agencies independent of the leader control the economy

7. Which of the following was true of Joseph Stalin's Five-Year Plan of 1928?
    A) It was the only one of its kind during Stalin's reign as leader
    B) Stalin set quotas so high, that they could not be met
    C) The Soviet Union became the world leader in industrialization by 1933
    D) Major advances in consumer goods came out of the Soviet Union for the first time
    E) It proved fully successful in just five years

8. Kulaks were those who
   A) helped Stalin rise to the top of the Communist Party
   B) accumulated land and resisted the collectivization process
   C) policed the labor camps, or gulags
   D) advised Stalin on industrial measures
   E) fought for the Red Army

9. Joseph Stalin supported all of the following EXCEPT:
   A) Atheism
   B) Propaganda in schools
   C) Totalitarianism
   D) Free thought in literature
   E) Indoctrination

10. Women in the Soviet Union
   A) could not give birth to more than one child
   B) were forbidden to work industrial jobs
   C) gained education and entered the workforce
   D) were not permitted to work in the medical profession
   E) were encouraged to stop taking care of the home

Answers and Explanations

AP World History: Modern

1. **C.** The purpose of the treaty was to get Russia out of World War I.

2. **C.** Russia suffered the highest casualty rate of World War I. With morale suffering both militarily and among citizens, an exit from the war was desired.

3. **A.** Although Russia got out of World War I, a devastating civil war would follow.

SAT Subject Test

1. **C.** Jews suffered from the organized violence of the pogroms. They were also forced to live in a special area known as the pale of settlement.

2. **A.** Bloody Sunday was a violent reaction to a workers' protest in St. Petersburg. The Czar's Imperial Guard opened fire on the protesters.

3. **D.** Much like Stalin, Lenin did not support organized religion.

4. **E.** The writings of Karl Marx, notably the *Communist Manifesto*, helped inspire the Bolshevik Revolution.

5. **E.** Lenin's NEP allowed for a small amount of capitalism to take place.

6. **D.** In a command economy, the leader of the nation-state dictates the economy. In the case of the Soviet Union in 1928, that dictator was Joseph Stalin.

7. **B.** Stalin set quotas quite high. Many of the reported production numbers were embellished during the Five-Year Plans out of fear of upsetting Stalin. Stalin would put through a series of Five-Year plans as leader of the Soviet Union.

8. **B.** Kulaks were wealthy Russians who had nothing to gain from the collectivization effort. Kulaks lost their land, as it was redistributed to the peasants. Many were executed or sent to gulags.

9. **D.** Stalin was notorious for censoring any thought that criticized or undermined his totalitarian rule. He was in complete control of the media.

10. **C.** Similar to what would happen in China under Mao Zedong, women actually gained rights during communist rule. However, they were expected to not only work, but raise families as well.

Fascism, World War II, and the Holocaust

World War I was supposed to be the worst war in history. However, about twenty years after it ended, a second and more deadly war encompassed the globe. Reacting to discontent, nationalism, and economic depression, people rallied behind fascist dictators in Italy and Germany. When both nations aligned with the equally ambitious Japanese Emperor, the Axis Powers were formed. Their thirst for land and power led to invasions of their neighbors. World War II lasted in Europe from 1939-1945. As Germany was attempting to expand, they were committing horrific atrocities to the Jewish population of Europe. The tragedy of the Holocaust was made known to the world after the Allies defeated the Axis in World War II.

HERE IS WHAT YOU NEED TO KNOW:
• FASCISM
Definition: Fascism

Fascism became popular in certain European countries between the World Wars. It is a political ideology where a dictator promotes nationalism under the threat of extensive military force. A fascist dictator controls nearly all aspects of life within a nation. Fascism grew out of discontent and desperation in the years following World War I.

Question: What happened to the world economy after World War I?

Answer: A global depression developed in the 1920s, and the new governments formed after World War I struggled to cope with it. Specifically, in Germany, the new democratic *Weimar Republic* attempted to handle their economic problems by printing more money. This devalued the currency, as immense inflation occurred. This further made the economy spiral out of control. In Italy, there was also immense unemployment and high inflation.

Even in the United States there was a Great Depression by 1929, as farmers overproduced crops, banks failed, and the stock market crashed. Franklin Delano Roosevelt was elected President and attempted vast reform measures with his *New Deal*. His hope was to repair the banking system and create jobs through government-sponsored building projects.

Question: Why was Benito Mussolini able to rise to power in Italy?

Answer: Mussolini was a fascist dictator in Italy from 1922 through most of World War II. He was able to rise because:

1. There was extreme discontent that came with the economic depression following World War I. For years, Italian workers had been immigrating to places such as Argentina and the United States in great numbers looking for work.

2. There was a fear of a workers' communist revolt.

3. There was immense nationalism, as eventually Mussolini would play off of the history of the great Roman Empire. After seizing power, he would sometimes give speeches at monuments such as the Roman Colosseum.

Mussolini and his army of Blackshirts *marched on Rome* in 1922. King Emmanuel III gave Mussolini control of the government under the threat of violence. Mussolini took on a new title, *Il Duce* (The Leader).

Question: How did Mussolini control the government?

Answer: Like Stalin, Mussolini had a secret police which eliminated all opponents. He prohibited strikes, controlled the economy, and made Roman Catholicism the favored religion of Italy as per the *Lateran Pacts* (agreements with the Church). All opposition to the Fascist Party was controlled.

Question: Why was Adolf Hitler able to rise to power in Germany?

Answer: Adolf Hitler secured power under a fascist regime from 1933 through World War II. He was able to rise because:

1. There was economic discontent that came out of the depression.

2. The punishments of the Treaty of Versailles left many Germans angered. This sparked nationalism.

3. Regarding nationalism, people rallied behind the words of Hitler. He was arrested in 1923 for attempting a revolt in Munich, Germany. From prison he wrote *Mein Kampf* (My Struggle). In the book, he explained how he thought Germany should be governed. Furthermore, he spoke of the German *master race* of *Aryans*, whom he believed were superior to Jews and other minorities in Germany. His nationalistic tone, and his call for increasing the *living space (lebensraum)* of Germany, gave the book immense appeal among Germans.

4. The Weimar Republic was a weak and inefficient democracy. As stated earlier, the economy under the Weimar Republic was strangled with inflation after the government printed up too much money.

5. There was a fear of communism in Germany. Before a 1933 election, a fire broke out in the *Reichstag* (parliament) building. It was blamed on the communists. Many believe it was intentionally set by Hitler's *Nazi Party*. The fire helped the Nazis secure more seats in government.

Question: How did Hitler control the government?

Answer: In 1933, Hitler became Chancellor of Germany and took on the title of *Der Führer* (The Leader). Enemies were targeted through both Heinrich Himmler's military, the *SS* (Schutzstaffel), and the *Gestapo* (secret state police). Similar to other dictators, Hitler commanded the economy and increased the manufacture of industry and weapons. Also, like other leaders, Hitler encouraged a great deal of propaganda, which increased support for the Nazi Party. With the help of Propaganda Minister *Joseph Goebbels*, a "big lie" was created through radio, posters, school control, speeches, and parades. Everywhere, flags with the Nazi *swastika* symbol could be seen. Literature that went against Nazi ideals was banned or burned.

Hitler's *Third Reich* (name of his government) produced much nationalism. It was believed that the Aryans were the master race, and there should be racial purity and no intermingling of races. Jews were persecuted (explained later). The Nazis also relied on the nineteenth century philosophy of German *Friedrich Nietzsche*. They selectively quoted him to criticize democracy. Nietzsche was an *existentialist*, meaning he stressed that an individual's existence is based on self-determination and free-choice.

Definition: Francisco Franco, Spain

Spain became engaged in a civil war in 1936 when Francisco Franco's fascist Nationalist Army attempted to seize power. Hitler and Mussolini both supported Franco, and the Spanish government was overthrown in 1939. Franco was in office until 1975. Spain gradually moved to democracy after his death.

Question: What territories did Germany secure under Hitler?

Answer: Because the League of Nations had no army to stop him, Hitler disobeyed the Treaty of Versailles and increased the size of his army. Germany remilitarized the Rhineland on its western border (which was in violation of the Treaty). In addition, Hitler annexed (added to Germany) Austria through a process called *Anschluss*.

Hitler also wanted the *Sudetenland*, an area of Czechoslovakia where the people spoke German. He was given this territory at the 1938 *Munich Conference*. There, British Prime Minister Neville Chamberlain said that the transfer of land would give the world "peace in our time." He was wrong, as it only made Hitler hungry for more. The Munich Conference is an example of *appeasement*, or meeting the aggressor's demands to keep peace.

Definition: Nazi-Soviet Nonaggression Pact, 1939

Remember: Russia was once Napoleon's ally. Napoleon invaded Russia. Napoleon lost. The same would be true of Hitler. In 1939, the Soviets and Germans agreed not to attack each other. Because both powers were natural enemies, many were doubtful this agreement would last. It didn't.

Definition: Axis Powers

As Hitler and the Nazis were gaining territory, so too were Japan and Italy. Japan had been in Manchuria, (northern) China since 1931. Under *Emperor Hirohito*, Japan continued to gain land and commit atrocities on the Chinese people. In particular, the Nanjing Massacre of 1937 (also known as the Rape of Nanjing) involved the slaughtering of about 300,000 Chinese prisoners of war and civilians, and included the rape and execution of thousands of women.

Italy fought to gain control of Haile Selassie's Ethiopia. Although Ethiopia was able to remain free from Italian control during the Age of

Imperialism in the late nineteenth century, they fell to Mussolini in 1936. That same year, an alliance known as the *Axis Powers* was formed between Japan, Italy, and Germany.

• WORLD WAR II
Question: What important diplomacy occurred before and during the war?

Answer: In between the World Wars: The *Washington Naval Conference* of 1921-1922 saw the major powers agree to limit naval arms. The *Kellogg-Briand Pact* of 1928 renounced war as a form of national policy.

The United States and President Franklin Roosevelt remained *neutral* before the war. America's Neutrality Acts of 1935, 1937, and 1939 kept them neutral, mostly in terms of arms shipments to foreign countries. "Cash and Carry" was a 1939 policy proclaiming that America would aid Great Britain. This was only if the British came to the US on their own ships, paid in cash, and then left with the weapons. Finally, in the Destroyers for Bases Deal of 1940, Roosevelt *traded* older large ships (destroyers) in exchange for British bases in the Caribbean.

Of greater importance was the *Lend-Lease Act* of 1941. This act allowed the United States to sell unlimited weapons to the Allies. Much of the buying was done on credit. Over $50 billion in supplies were sent overseas (to Britain, Soviet Union, France, and China).

Definition: Invasion of Poland and Blitzkrieg

World War II in Europe began on September 1, 1939 when the Nazis invaded Poland. They did this in a surprise *blitzkrieg*, or "lightning war," that used immense air and land forces. Poland quickly fell. Great Britain and France declared war on Germany. Note: Many historians consider the beginning of the war to be in

1931 when Japan invaded Manchuria, China.

Question: What were the important events of World War II in Europe from 1940-1942?

Answer:

1. France fell to Germany quickly in 1940. *Charles de Gaulle*, a leader of the Free French Forces, evacuated to Britain. Other Allies escaped as well after the Battle of Dunkirk.

2. Germany bombed Britain in 1940, but stopped in 1941 after strong resistance from the RAF (Royal Air Force). Much of London's population, including Prime Minister *Winston Churchill*, fled underground to stay safe during the Battle of Britain.

3. In 1941, Hitler invaded the Soviet Union in *Operation Barbarossa*, thus breaking the nonaggression pact. The Germans never took Moscow. However, for 872 days they laid siege to Leningrad (formerly St. Petersburg). It is estimated that one million or more people died from starvation, bombing, disease, and a lack of provisions in the harsh Russian climate.

After the *Battle of Stalingrad* in 1942, the Soviets pushed back the German offensive. The harsh Russian winter played a great part in Germany's withdrawal. Like Napoleon over a century earlier, the German army had a hard time mobilizing.

Definition: Pearl Harbor, December 7, 1941

Reacting to a US oil embargo against Japan, the Japanese attacked Pearl Harbor, Hawaii by air. The sneak-attack resulted in 2,300 American soldiers killed, many of whom were aboard the USS *Arizona*.

After Franklin Roosevelt's "Day of Infamy" speech, Congress declared war on Japan. Shortly after, Germany declared war on the US. During the course of the war, the United States, Britain, France, and the Soviet Union were the major Allies who fought the Axis Powers.

Question: What military events in Europe should I know about from 1942-1945?

Answer:

1. The United States began fighting in northern Africa and then went further north to liberate Italy. Mussolini was executed by his own people after falling from power.

2. *D-Day* (June 6, 1944) was a major turning point of the war. The Invasion of Normandy created a second front for the Allies in Europe and led to the eventual liberation of France.

3. The Battle of the Bulge, which began in the Ardennes Forest of Belgium during the frigid winter of 1944-45, was the deadliest battle in Europe for the Americans. However, Germany could not permanently break Allied lines.

4. Adolf Hitler committed suicide in an underground bunker on April 30, 1945. V-E (Victory in Europe) Day would be on May 8th after Germany surrendered.

Definition: Yalta Conference, 1945

This was a meeting between Roosevelt, Churchill, and Stalin. The Conference gave the Soviet Union control over much of Eastern Europe. Though the Soviets promised free elections, these promises were empty, as the nations were turned into satellites. It can be said that Yalta was the start of the Cold War.

In the conference, it was also agreed that the Soviets would enter the war in Japan, and Germany would be divided into zones of occupation. This Conference, held in the Soviet Union, occurred in the final days of President Roosevelt's life. When he died soon after, Vice President Harry Truman took over.

Other conferences to know about:

1. Tehran, 1943 - Here, the Allies planned

the end of the war strategy to defeat the Nazis.

2. Potsdam, 1945 - The Allies discussed the fate of Germany after they surrendered.

Question: What do I need to know about the War in the Pacific (Japan)?

Answer:

1. American General Douglas MacArthur was the commander.

2. The United States followed a strategy of *island hopping* before reaching mainland Japan. Some of the islands attacked were Midway, Iwo Jima, and Okinawa.

3. President Truman decided a mainland invasion of Japan would be too costly in terms of casualties, so he put in the order for the *Enola Gay* to drop *Little Boy* (the Atomic Bomb). On August 6, 1945 Hiroshima was bombed resulting in the deaths of about 140,000 people. Nagasaki was bombed three days later leading to an estimated 70,000 deaths.

4. Japan surrendered on August 15, 1945. V-J (Victory in Japan) Day would be on September 2nd.

Question: What were the foreign policy results of World War II?

Answer: It is estimated that over 60 million people were killed in World War II, with about 1/3 of all casualties occurring among people in the Soviet Union. In the aftermath of the worst war in world history:

1. The US and Soviet Union became superpowers, and the Cold War began.

2. Germany was divided into occupational zones controlled by the Soviet Union in the East, and Allies (Britain, France, and the United States) in the West.

3. The **United Nations** was formed as an international peacekeeping organization that sought *collective security*. The US, Soviet Union, France, Britain, and China would be the Five Permanent Nations with veto power. The UN grew out of the **Atlantic Charter** of 1941, where Winston Churchill and Franklin Roosevelt agreed to stabilize the world with peace once the war ended. Unlike the League of Nations, the UN can assemble peacekeeping troops. Also, unlike the League, the US joined the UN.

4. The US demilitarized Japan and forced them to adopt a new constitution modeled after the American two-house legislature. Women over 20 were given suffrage (voting) rights. Japan was forbidden to wage offensive wars. The US occupied Japan until 1952. In the ensuing decades, Japan industrialized and became a worldwide economic power. They also became a firm ally of the United States.

• **THE HOLOCAUST**
Definition: Nuremberg Laws, 1935

These were German laws in the 1930s that labeled Jews as inferiors who could not hold government jobs, nor marry non-Jewish Germans. Therefore, Jews were second-class citi-

Jews were forced to wear yellow Stars of David during the War. Jüde is German for Jew.

112

The above sign at the concentration camp at Terezin translates to "work sets you free." This was an unfulfilled promise.

zens. When World War II began in Europe in 1939, they were forced to wear yellow badges in the shape of the Star of David.

To avoid persecution, many Jews fled to the United States and elsewhere abroad. However, nations began to close their doors to immigration. One who escaped Germany was physicist Albert Einstein. Creator of the ***Theory of Relativity*** that questioned the traditional laws of time and space, Einstein also recommended that the United States develop an atomic bomb. The Manhattan Project would become the code name for this operation.

Definition: Kristallnacht, 1938

Kristallnacht translates to "night of broken glass." On November 9, 1938 Nazi sol-

diers attacked Jews, their homes, and their synagogues. Thousands of Jewish establishments were burned and vandalized all over Germany and Austria. The violence was triggered when a Jewish man named Herschel Grynszpan assassinated a German government worker.

Definition: Ghettos

Like Russia's Pale of Settlement decades earlier, German Jews were forced to live in reserved areas (mostly in Poland). The Nazis sealed the borders of these ghettos leading to starvation and disease. Still, Jews were able to smuggle in necessities such as food, and religious materials.

Definition: Warsaw Uprising

Warsaw is the capital of Poland. The largest revolt of Jews during the Holocaust occurred in the Warsaw Ghetto in 1943. With limited weapons, Jews held off the Nazis for about one month before the Germans put down the uprising. The resistance became a symbol of Jewish solidarity and defiance.

Definition: The Final Solution

As the war progressed, the elimination of Jews became a priority for the Nazis. The Final Solution was *genocide*, or the methodical killing of an entire group of people. Those seen as undesirable or inferior to the master race of Aryans were targeted. Jews, Gypsies, homosexuals, the mentally ill, and others were murdered.

The killing was done in *concentration camps* and *extermination camps*. Many died in concentration camps through slave labor. Later in the war, extermination camps, such as Auschwitz in Poland, were used for the purpose of killing. A chemical named Zyklon B was used to murder Jews in showers. The bodies were then sent to crematoriums. An estimated 6 million Jews were killed in the Holocaust, and 11 million people overall. Most of the victims were from Poland and the Soviet Union.

The camps were liberated by the Allies in 1945. The reason why so many of the horrors of the Holocaust are known today is because of *primary sources,* or firsthand accounts. Survivors such as *Elie Wiesel*, who wrote *Night*, have made sure that the atrocities are still remembered in the twenty-first century.

Definition: Anne Frank

Anne Frank lived in Amsterdam in the Netherlands. Like many Jews, she and her family hid from Nazi officers. Anne kept a diary where she detailed the experiences of hiding out in an annex. The diary has become one of the most famous primary sources available on the Holocaust. Anne and her family were captured at the end of the war. Anne did not survive the Holocaust.

Definition: Nuremberg Trials and Tokyo Trials

After the war ended, the world looked for accountability regarding the Holocaust. In the first of a series of trials, 22 Nazis were charged with war crimes. 12 were sentenced to death. Hundreds of Nazi officers associated with concentration or extermination camps were never tried for crimes against humanity.

Japanese leaders were also put on trial for atrocities committed during World War II. At the Tokyo Trials of 1946-8, defendants were charged with war crimes and crimes against humanity. Seven were executed. Many Japanese officials were executed in other trials outside of Tokyo.

Following these trials, the UN (in a committee chaired by Eleanor Roosevelt) adopted the *Universal Declaration of Human Rights* which outlined specific liberties and rights that everyone should possess. In Article 1, it states that people are born free and equal in dignity and rights. Furthermore, the Declaration outlaws slavery and torture, while promoting public trials.

Review Questions for the AP World History: Modern Exam

Article 1.
All human beings are born free and equal in dignity and rights. They are endowed with reason and conscience and should act towards one another in a spirit of brotherhood.

Article 2.
Everyone is entitled to all the rights and freedoms set forth in this Declaration, without distinction of any kind, such as race, colour, sex, language, religion, political or other opinion, national or social origin, property, birth or other status. Furthermore, no distinction shall be made on the basis of the political, jurisdictional or international status of the country or territory to which a person belongs, whether it be independent, trust, non-self-governing or under any other limitation of sovereignty.

Article 3.
Everyone has the right to life, liberty and security of person.

— United Nations Universal Declaration of Human Rights

1. Which of the following philosophers expressed rhetoric most similar to the above Declaration?
  A) Baron de Montesquieu
  B) Plato
  C) Thomas Hobbes
  D) John Locke

2. Which of the following was the most contributing short-term cause for the adoption of the Declaration?
  A) Attack on Pearl Harbor
  B) The Final Solution
  C) Forming of the Axis Powers
  D) White Australia Policy

3. Whose actions would be most inconsistent with the above Declaration?
  A) Elie Wiesel
  B) Winston Churchill
  C) Joseph Goebbels
  D) Eleanor Roosevelt

Review Questions for the SAT Subject Test

1. Which decision by the Weimar Republic caused the greatest harm to the German economy?
   A) increasing taxes
   B) purchasing foreign bonds
   C) printing more money
   D) raising tariffs
   E) lowering taxes

2. A similarity between Adolf Hitler and Benito Mussolini was
   A) a strong belief in socialism
   B) support for unionization of workers
   C) use of propaganda techniques
   D) persecution of Roman Catholics
   E) increased power of the Church

3. In *Mein Kampf*, Adolf Hitler supported
   A) securing the Sudetenland through appeasement
   B) enforcing the provisions of the Treaty of Versailles
   C) the extermination of Russians and Poles
   D) a master race of Aryans superior to Jews
   E) an increased power of the Pope

4. Which nation is paired with the territory they took over in the 1930s?
   A) Germany - Ethiopia
   B) China - Austria
   C) Italy - Rhineland
   D) Austria - Turkey
   E) Japan - Manchuria

5. The United States ended their policies of neutrality in the 1940s when
   A) Japan invaded Manchuria
   B) Germany continued a policy of unrestricted submarine warfare
   C) Italy declared war on the United States
   D) United States boats were sunk in the Atlantic
   E) The Japanese attacked Pearl Harbor

6. Put the following events of World War II in chronological order
   1. German blitzkrieg of Poland
   2. Dropping of the Atomic Bomb on Hiroshima
   3. Japan attacks Pearl Harbor
   4. France falls to Hitler

   A) 1-2-4-3
   B) 4-1-3-2
   C) 4-1-2-3
   D) 1-4-3-2
   E) 1-3-4-2

7. The turning point of World War II in Western Europe occurred in the
   A) Invasion of Normandy
   B) Battle of Okinawa
   C) Battle of Stalingrad
   D) Battle of London
   E) Battle of Midway

8. The Yalta Conference presented which potential conflict for Europe?
   A) A struggle for land between Britain and the United States
   B) The resurgence of Adolf Hitler
   C) The unification of Germany
   D) A nuclear arms race between Western nations
   E) The spread of communism throughout Eastern Europe

9. The Nuremberg Laws of 1935 persecuted Jews by

A) denying basic freedoms

B) removing them to ghettos during World War II

C) ordering their removal to extermination camps in Poland

D) deporting them to the United States

E) forcing them into service for the Gestapo

10. Elie Wiesel's records of World War II have been important because they

A) give a clear picture of the Battle of Stalingrad

B) prove that Hitler died in an underground bunker

C) detail the atrocities of the Holocaust

D) display the importance of the airplane during World War II

E) give detailed testimony of the Tokyo Trials

Answers and Explanations

AP World History: Modern

1. **D**. John Locke's philosophy is most similar to Article 3, as he promoted rights to life, liberty, and property.

2. **B**. The Final Solution of the Holocaust had a great influence on the adoption of the Declaration, which outlawed slavery and torture, and promoted the rights of all people.

3. **C**. Joseph Goebbels was in charge of propaganda in the Third Reich, and promoted Anti-Semitic sentiment.

SAT Subject Test

1. **C**. To combat economic problems after World War I, the Weimar Republic of Germany printed up more money. When they did this, massive inflation occurred.

2. **C**. Both fascist leaders used elaborate parades, salutes, and speeches to promote nationalism among their people. Joseph Goebbels in Germany created a *big lie* using propaganda.

3. **D**. Hitler wrote *Mein Kampf* from a prison cell. In the book he detailed his plans for restoring Germany to glory. He believed the German Aryans were a master race of people. That master race did not include Jews.

4. **E**. Japan invaded Manchuria in northern China in 1931. Many historians consider this to be the beginning of World War II.

5. **E**. Pearl Harbor was attacked on December 7, 1941. The United States entered World War II in both Europe and the Pacific shortly after.

6. **D**. German blitzkrieg of Poland, 1939; France falls to Hitler, 1940; Japan attacks Pearl Harbor, 1941; Dropping of the Atomic Bomb on Hiroshima, 1945.

7. **A**. D-Day, or the Invasion of Normandy, was June 6, 1944. It led to the liberation of France, and the eventual surrender of the Nazis less than one year later.

8. **E**. Stalin received much of Eastern Europe at the Yalta Conference. Although he promised free elections, nations of Eastern Europe became satellites of the Soviet Union.

9. **A**. The Nuremberg laws were passed in 1935. They denied Jews basic rights within Germany.

10. **C**. Elie Wiesel wrote *Night*, in which he detailed his survival of the Holocaust. Primary sources from Wiesel, Anne Frank, and other victims and survivors have brought to light the tragedy of the Holocaust.

The Cold War, and Wars in Korea and Vietnam

After World War II, the United States and Soviet Union remained the only superpowers in the world. Although the two countries never directly fought, they antagonized each other throughout the Cold War. A space race, blockade of Berlin, spy plane controversy, and near nuclear war over Cuba were just some of the issues during these tense decades. America's policy to contain communism led them to conflicts in both Korea and Vietnam.

HERE IS WHAT YOU NEED TO KNOW:
• THE COLD WAR
Question: Why was it called a Cold War?

Answer: No, it's not because it's cold in Russia. The Cold War was fought (or not fought) between the US and the Soviet Union from 1945-1991. Although they never directly attacked one another, there were puppet wars at times, like Korea and Vietnam. One could argue that it's called a Cold War because bullets are hot and none were directly fired at each other. You might also say that the US and Soviet Union displayed cold feelings towards one another.

Question: What were the differences between the US and USSR (Soviet Union)?

Answer:

United States = Political system is democracy, and economic system is capitalism.

Soviet Union = Combined elements of a dictatorship, command economy, and socialism to establish power over the people.

The US wanted to: 1) contain communism, 2) strengthen Eastern European countries and open them up for trade, and 3) reunite Germany.

The Soviet Union wanted to: 1) spread communism, 2) control Eastern European satellite nations, and 3) keep Germany divided.

Definition: Containment

The foreign policy of the United States during the Cold War was containment. US diplomat George Kennan coined this term that meant preventing the spread of communism. This was typically done by forming alliances with weaker countries to fend off communist aggression. Containment is the opposite of appeasement (giving in to what the aggressor wants). Containment is also the most important term of the Cold War. Why did the US get involved in Korea? Containment. Why did the US send troops to Vietnam? Containment. Why did the US spend so much money on the military? Containment.

Definition: Truman Doctrine and Marshall Plan, 1947

The Doctrine gave military aid (no troops) to countries resisting communism. Greece and Turkey took advantage of the aid.

US Secretary of State George Marshall's plan was a strategy to give economic aid to countries that were not communist. The idea was to make countries stronger, and less susceptible to communist takeovers. About $12.5 billion was given to nations all over Europe. Remember: M for Money and Mar$hall.

Definition: Berlin Airlift, 1948

Soviet leader Joseph Stalin, wanting to keep Germany divided, blockaded the highway and rail resources coming into West Berlin (the non-communist side). He hoped this would make West Berlin dependent upon him and his satellites for supplies. However, the US and Great Britain sent 277,000 flights full of food and necessities for the German people. Many believed the airlift could lead to war between the US and Soviet Union. But,

119

as with everything else in the Cold War, direct conflict was avoided. The blockade was later lifted in 1949.

Definition: NATO vs. Warsaw Pact

Think of these two as the gangs of the Cold War. NATO (North Atlantic Treaty Organization) was founded in 1949 and supported democracy. The Warsaw Pact, consisting of the Soviet Union and their satellites, was founded in 1955 and was referred to more commonly as the Communist Bloc.

Some nations preferred to be non-aligned. India, a newly independent country, was against aggression and hoped to peacefully co-exist as to not disrupt their domestic development. Some countries remained neutral until world events made them support or condemn one side.

Definition: Sputnik, 1957

In 1957, the Soviets successfully launched a satellite named Sputnik into space. Not only did this make Americans nervous about Soviet technology, but it gave the US a feeling of inferiority. The result of Sputnik's launch was an American increase of spending on education and science. In 1969, the US would win the space race to the moon.

Definition: U-2, 1960

It's not the rock band. But, if you look at some of their cover art, you will see a plane. The U-2 was a spy plane that was shot out of the Soviet sky in 1960. Although the US initially denied a spy plane was flying behind the iron curtain (metaphor for Soviet border), the evidence was clear. Francis Gary Powers, the pilot, was held captive. The incident proved that distrust between the superpowers was real, and other spies were likely attempting to infiltrate both borders.

Definition: H-Bomb

The H-Bomb, or Hydrogen Bomb, worked on fusion. It was 1,000 times more powerful than the Atomic Bomb that worked on fission. The fear of a nuclear war was the underlying story of the Cold War, as it led to "duck and cover" drills in the US, as well as the creation of bomb shelters.

Definition: Military-Industrial Complex

When President Dwight Eisenhower left office, he warned of the military-industrial complex. The term refers to the money-relationships between legislators, the Pentagon (military), and industry. This web of money, weapons, and the people who make foreign policy could lead to corruption.

Definition: Brinkmanship

This meant going to the brink of war, but coming just short of fighting. The escalation of brinkmanship peaked from 1961-1962.

Definition: Berlin Wall

In 1961, Nikita Khrushchev's Soviet Union built the wall that would formally divide communist East Berlin from non-communist West Berlin. President John F. Kennedy traveled to the wall to deliver his famous *Ich Bin Ein Berliner* (I am a Berliner) speech. He told the people of Berlin that the rest of the world was behind them. It is disputed that what Kennedy said translated to "I am a doughnut" (a Berliner is also a jelly doughnut). In 1987 President Ronald Reagan traveled to Berlin to give his famous, "tear down this wall" speech as a challenge to Soviet leader Mikhail Gorbachev. The wall came down in 1989.

Definition: Bay of Pigs Invasion, April 17, 1961

Fidel Castro helped overthrow dictator Ful-

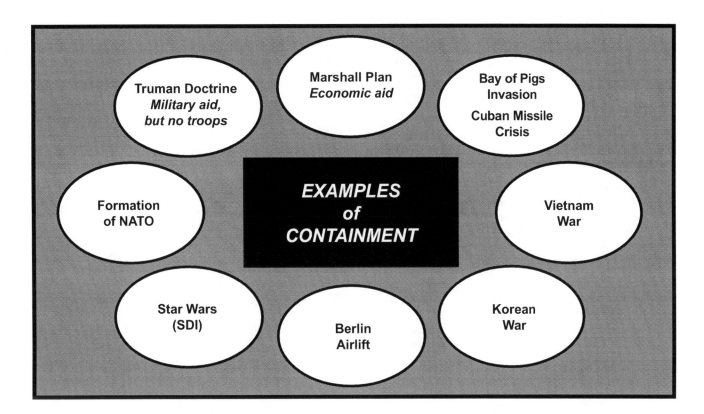

Examples of Containment:
- Truman Doctrine *Military aid, but no troops*
- Marshall Plan *Economic aid*
- Bay of Pigs Invasion / Cuban Missile Crisis
- Formation of NATO
- **EXAMPLES of CONTAINMENT**
- Vietnam War
- Star Wars (SDI)
- Berlin Airlift
- Korean War

gencio Batista at the end of the Cuban Revolution in 1959. Castro soon took over Cuba's economy and ruled firmly over the people. He eliminated all opposition. President John F. Kennedy saw Castro as a threat to political and economic security in the region. Therefore, the US supported a rebellion led by Cuban exiles. They were defeated at the Bay of Pigs in Cuba. Not only did the US sponsor the failed rebellion, but the event strengthened the legitimacy of Castro. Castro would soon become one of the Soviet Union's most important communist allies.

Definition: Cuban Missile Crisis, October of 1962

The closest the United States and Soviet Union ever came to nuclear war was during these two weeks of October. After the Bay of Pigs Invasion, Cuban and Soviet relations were quite good. So good, in fact, that the Soviets moved enough missiles to Cuba to destroy American cities. When US intelligence learned of this, Kennedy took it

as a threat of war. His solution was to:

1. Blockade (quarantine) Cuba by surrounding it with US naval ships. The goal was to prevent the delivery of Soviet weapons.

2. Threaten force if Khrushchev did not remove the missiles.

Ultimately, cooler heads prevailed, and Khrushchev removed the missiles. In return, the US agreed not to invade Cuba. Furthermore, the US removed missiles of their own from Turkey.

Definition: Détente

This means an easing of Cold War tensions. The Cuban Missile Crisis scared the heck out of everyone. The 1970s had friendlier diplomacy between the two superpowers. President Richard Nixon and Soviet leader Leonid Brezhnev were sometimes seen smiling together. You should know:

SALT – Strategic Arms Limitation Talks. This was a series of meetings that limited the number of nuclear weapons each country had

Soldiers step out of their tanks, signaling the end of communist rule in the Soviet Union

in their arsenal. Of course, this was all a charade, as no one knew for sure how many weapons each country had stockpiled.

In 1975, the Helsinki Accords were signed which promoted cooperation between 35 nations, and encouraged human rights.

Definition: Soviet-Afghanistan War

Afghanistan bordered the Soviet Union. In 1979, the Soviets invaded and attempted to take over the country. However, strong Afghan resistance, and United States aid to the Afghan people, prevented a permanent takeover. The Soviets withdrew in 1989.

Definition: Star Wars/Strategic Defense Initiative

President Ronald Reagan abandoned dé-

tente. Strategic Defense Initiative was an elaborate technological endeavor that looked to zap missiles out of the sky. The plan sounded like science fiction, so it was labeled *Star Wars*.

Question: How did communism ultimately fall?

Answer: With ***Mikhail Gorbachev's*** rule over the Soviet Union there was a new outlook. After he took office in 1985, the Soviet Union adopted two major policies:

1. ***Glasnost*** – this meant an *openness* that allowed people to voice their views on government.

2. ***Perestroika*** – this was a restructuring of economics, including some private business ownership.

By 1991, Communism was falling all over

Europe. Gorbachev lost his legitimacy, as the people supported a member of parliament named Boris Yeltsin to be their new president. In a desperate attempt to keep the Soviet Union in Communist Party hands, the conservative *State Committee* detained Gorbachev and ordered the military to attack the parliament. This *August Coup* (August 19-21, 1991) failed when soldiers stepped out of their tanks and refused to fight for the Communist conspirators. Gorbachev later resigned, and Yeltsin became president. The Soviet Union dissolved into the CIS, or Commonwealth of Independent States. Soon after, Russia became a country again.

Question: In what other European nations did communism fall?

Answer: Note: China, Cuba, and Vietnam continued to be communist. In Europe:

1. In 1990, East and West Germany came together in a process called *reunification*. The Berlin Wall came down in 1989.

2. With the economy weakening, Poland, with help from *Lech Walesa* and his labor union *Solidarity*, was able to get free elections in 1989. Soon after, Poland was free from communist rule.

3. In 1989, a rather peaceful student protest in Czechoslovakia, known as the *Velvet Revolution*, began in Prague and spread to the rest of the country. Years earlier in 1968, a movement for free speech and democratic reform was put down by Warsaw Pact troops in an event known as the *Prague Spring*. This action was justified by the Brezhnev Doctrine, which looked to protect the Soviet Union's socialist interests. However, the Velvet Revolution was successful in eliminating communist rule. In 1993, Czechoslovakia became two nations, The Czech Republic and Slovakia.

4. Yugoslavia experienced bloody conflict as it broke apart. With different ethnic groups in the area, there was a struggle for territory. In Bosnia-Herzegovina, *ethnic cleansing*, or the violent elimination of a group from an area, occurred as Serbian forces directed by President *Slobodan Milosevic* attempted to remove Muslim influences from Bosnia.

Ethnic cleansing involved executions and other human rights violations. The term "ethnic cleansing" is used because the atrocities were done as a war measure to remove people. Nonetheless, many consider the killings to be genocide. In 1995, NATO forces began a bombing campaign to control the conflict.

5. Kosovo, a region comprised mainly of people of Albanian descent, looked for independence from Serbia. Much violence occurred there in the decades following the Fall of Communism.

In 2008, Kosovo declared itself independent. However, Serbia disputed the claim and did not recognize them as a nation. Over the years, more nations have recognized Kosovo's independence.

6. The people of Chechnya looked for independence from Russia after the Fall of Communism. For centuries, there had already been a culture clash between Russia and the Chechens who are mostly Muslim. Despite Chechen hopes for independence, Russia did not recognize an independent Chechnya.

Two wars took place between 1994-2009 in the region. At the end of the latter, Russia took control over the area. Still, much violence and terrorism has taken place in this volatile area of Eastern Europe.

7. Most recently, Russia under President Vladimir Putin looked to expand into Ukraine. In 2014, Russian forces entered a Ukrainian area named Crimea. After a vote was held by the people, Crimea became part of Russia. The vote, or referendum, was highly criticized by some Western nations who accused Putin of annexing (taking) the territory.

123

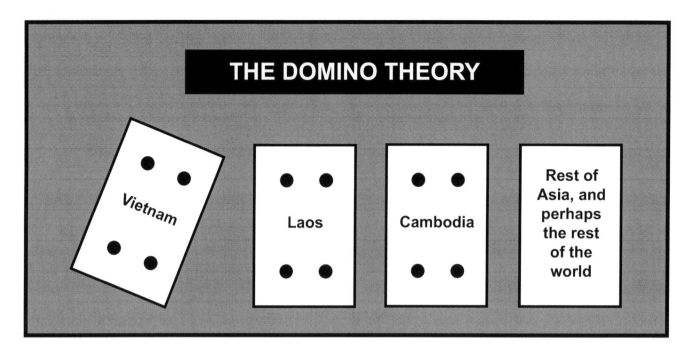

THE DOMINO THEORY

Vietnam

Laos

Cambodia

Rest of Asia, and perhaps the rest of the world

• **KOREAN AND VIETNAM WARS**

Question: What do I need to know about the Korean War?

Answer:

The UN voted to send troops into the area after communist North Korea crossed the 38th parallel and attacked non-communist South Korea in 1950. At that time, Taiwan (Republic of China), not the communist People's Republic of China, was recognized as a permanent nation of the UN. Communist China would have blocked the deployment of troops. The Soviet Union abstained from the vote. Therefore, no one vetoed the deployment of UN troops to stop the spread of communism in Korea.

The war ended in 1953 leaving an estimated death toll in the millions. In the aftermath, massive American aid poured into South Korea for decades. The 38th parallel is still the dividing line in Korea today, as the two countries are buffered by a demilitarized zone (DMZ).

South Korea has since emerged as one of the world's strongest economies and a major trading partner with the United States. South Korean exports such as cars, televisions, and smartphones have become popular all over the world. Indeed, since the war many South Koreans have assimilated to western culture in terms of music, social media, and sports. In 1988, Seoul (South Korea's capital) hosted the Summer Olympic Games. Meanwhile, North Korea has remained impoverished since the war, spending much money on military weaponry rather than necessities for its people.

Definition: Domino Theory

This was a belief in the US that if one nation in Asia fell to communism, then the rest of the nations would also fall...like dominos. It was important to stop that first country from becoming communist. (See above.)

Definition: Dien Bien Phu and Gulf of Tonkin Resolution

During the 19th century Age of Imperialism, France took over much of Indochina (peninsula south of China). French missionaries looked to spread Christianity, while business leaders saw economic opportunities

124

in cash crops such as rubber and rice. The French modernized roads and transportation. Still, nationalistic resistance to foreigners escalated in Vietnam. In 1954, the French saw the city of Dien Bien Phu fall to the communists and their leader, **Ho Chi Minh**. Minh used nationalism as a unifying force to drive out the French and spread communism. Under Presidents Dwight Eisenhower and John F. Kennedy, there was a gradual escalation of a US military presence in Southern Vietnam. When President Kennedy was assassinated in 1963, Vice President Lyndon B. Johnson became President.

In 1964, at the Gulf of Tonkin in Vietnam, American ships were fired on (many believe the severity of this was likely embellished). After the event, Congress approved the Resolution which gave Johnson a "blank check" to use the military as he saw fit in Vietnam. This meant a large escalation of American forces.

Definition: Vietcong

The Vietcong were communist guerrilla soldiers in *South* Vietnam. Vietnam was divided at the 17th parallel. As with Korea, the communists were supposed to be in the North...not the South.

Question: Militarily, what do I need to know about the Vietnam War?

Answer:

1. Much of the war was fought on dangerous terrain in a jungle.

2. Napalm was an explosive chemical that was used extensively in Vietnam. Agent Orange was a chemical used by the United States to remove leaves from the trees where guerrilla soldiers were positioned. Years later, this chemical was known to cause cancer to many American Vietnam veterans.

3. The Tet (lunar New Year) Offensive of 1968 was a massive thrust southward by the communists in the North. Although the United States pushed back the attack, the battle had a catastrophic effect on American morale, while increasing support for the communists within Vietnam.

4. In 1973, President Richard Nixon ended American involvement with the **Paris Peace Accords**. The country became communist shortly thereafter.

Definition: Vietnamization

Richard Nixon's plan to *gradually remove US troops* from Vietnam was called Vietnamization. He hoped to turn the war over to Vietnamese soldiers. As stated above, the US began pulling out for good in 1973.

Definition: Khmer Rouge

When the United States pulled out of Vietnam, the country turned communist. Communism spread to neighboring Cambodia. In 1975 a group called the Khmer Rouge set up a government under their leader **Pol Pot**. He hoped to create a collectivized agricultural state. Under Pol Pot's reign (1975-1979), genocide occurred, as an estimated 2 million Cambodians were killed through forced labor, or execution. The sites of the atrocities are commonly referred to as the *Killing Fields*.

Question: How did Southeast Asia gain autonomy?

Answer: After the Age of Imperialism, Southeast Asia was controlled by European nations. However, as imperialism became expensive and unpopular, countries gained their own rule (autonomy). Despite imperialist abandonment, many critics pointed to **neocolonialism** post World War II, whereby Western nations (sometimes in the countries they once controlled) and corporations utilized labor and resources in developing countries for capital gain.

1. The United States fought to control the Philippines in a bloody conflict c1900. The Philippines gained their independence in 1946. Ferdinand Marcos is a leader you should know. He stole from the people, and was exiled after he refused to accept the results of an election he lost in 1986. That election was won by **Corazon Aquino**. Under her rule the Philippines adopted a new constitution which limited Presidential powers and restored the power of a two-house (bicameral) Congress.

2. Indonesia is a complex network of islands in the Pacific. It is one of the most culturally diverse places in the world. Indonesia was controlled by the Dutch, and then the Japanese. Sukarno was the leader of the Indonesian independence movement. After World War II, he declared the region independent. Despite a Dutch attempt to regain the territory, Indonesia was officially granted independence by the Netherlands in 1949. Under the dictator Suharto, Indonesia was ruled by the military, and many suspected communists were executed.

In the twenty-first century, the most practiced religion in the area has become Islam.

Definition: Aung San Suu Kyi

In Myanmar (formerly called Burma), the military ruled as a dictatorship. Aung San Suu Kyi was instrumental in a nonviolent protest movement for democracy and human rights. Despite winning the 1991 Nobel Peace Prize, she spent over a decade as a political prisoner. After being freed in 2010, she won a parliament seat in 2012. In 2016, after being denied the presidency, she gained some executive power with the title of state counselor.

Question: How was Latin America affected by the Cold War?

Answer: After the Cuban Revolution, Fidel Castro established communism in Cuba. Castro was supported by another revolutionary ally named Che Guevara. Guevara looked to spread Marxist ideas to other places, such as Bolivia. However, he was captured and executed. In Nicaragua, civil war occurred between Daniel Ortega and the socialist Sandinistas, and anti-Communist forces known as Contras. After much fighting in the 1980s, a ceasefire gave way to elections in the region.

Non-communist dictatorships also emerged in the area. In 1946, Juan Perón took power in Argentina. Ruling alongside his wife, Eva, Perón established some rights for the people, but also restricted many freedoms.

With his popularity declining, Perón was forced into exile. Though he returned to power for a short time, after his death the military replaced him in a series of regimes. Most infamously, between 1976-1983, those who resisted the dictatorial government's wishes became targets of kidnappings and torture. Some 30,000 Argentinians were killed in what was called "The Dirty War."

In response to the state-sponsored violence, a nonviolent organization called the **Mothers of the Plaza de Mayo** emerged. They helped tell the story of their children who "disappeared," and also hoped to locate possible survivors. The organization has inspired fights for other human and civil rights issues.

In Chile, General **Augusto Pinochet** led a 1973 coup against Marxist Salvador Allende. Once in power, Pinochet oversaw a stronger free market economy. However, he also limited democracy and was accused of torturing and killing political opponents and Spanish citizens. He died before he could stand trial.

Review Questions for the AP World History: Modern Exam

"Aside from the demoralizing effect on the world at large and the possibilities of disturbances arising as a result of the desperation of the people concerned, the consequences to the economy of the United States should be apparent to all. It is logical that the United States should do whatever it is able to do to assist in the return of normal economic health in the world, without which there can be no political stability and no assured peace. Our policy is directed not against any country or doctrine but against hunger, poverty, desperation and chaos. Its purpose should be the revival of a working economy in the world so as to permit the emergence of political and social conditions in which free institutions can exist. Such assistance, I am convinced, must not be on a piecemeal basis as various crises develop. Any assistance that this Government may render in the future should provide a cure rather than a mere palliative. Any government that is willing to assist in the task of recovery will find full co-operation I am sure, on the part of the United States Government. Any government which maneuvers to block the recovery of other countries cannot expect help from us. Furthermore, governments, political parties, or groups which seek to perpetuate human misery in order to profit therefrom politically or otherwise will encounter the opposition of the United States."

— George Marshall, 1947

1. In this speech, George Marshall mostly advocates for which of the following?
   A) Donating troops to countries resisting communism
   B) Providing military supplies to developing nations
   C) Making European economies stronger and more stable
   D) Creating public works projects to relieve unemployment

2. Marshall's policy was associated with which foreign policy?
   A) Appeasement
   B) Neutrality
   C) Imperialism
   D) Containment

3. A year after Marshall's speech, which event would heighten tensions during the Cold War?
   A) Cuban Missile Crisis
   B) Berlin Airlift
   C) U-2 spy plane incident
   D) Launching of Sputnik

Review Questions for the SAT Subject Test

1. The United States policy of containment meant

   A) appeasement to the Soviet Union

   B) an attack on the Soviet Union and its satellites

   C) the division of Germany into zones controlled by the West and Soviet Union

   D) stopping both the spread of communism and Soviet Union interests

   E) a reliance on détente for diplomacy

2. The Truman Doctrine

   A) offered combat troops to help countries fighting communism

   B) gave economic aid to scientists developing the H-Bomb

   C) provided military aid, but not troops, to foreign countries threatened by communism

   D) looked to expand democracy to areas in the Middle East

   E) called for military aid to fight North Korea

3. What was John F. Kennedy's main course of action during the Cuban Missile Crisis?

   A) A threat of force and a strict quarantine of Cuba

   B) A calculated invasion of the Cuban mainland at the Bay of Pigs

   C) Diplomacy with Nikita Khrushchev which led to the disarmament of missiles in exchange for American bases in the Caribbean

   D) A treaty with the Cubans which transferred the missiles to Poland

   E) Reliance on NATO for military funding

4. Détente is most associated with

   A) The Marshall Plan

   B) The Truman Doctrine

   C) Strategic Arms Limitation Talks

   D) The Vietnam War

   E) The Berlin Airlift

5. After the Korean War, South Korea

   A) isolated itself to Western markets

   B) battled communist invaders from Vietnam

   C) suffered decades of oppressive rule

   D) became an adversary of NATO

   E) industrialized with the help of American aid

6. Why was the Tet Offensive significant?

   A) It led to a takeover of South Vietnam by the Vietcong

   B) When the Northern Vietnamese moved south, it decreased the morale of American forces

   C) It was the deciding battle in the American victory over the communists in Vietnam

   D) Ho Chi Minh's proclamation of victory led to an American withdrawal of troops

   E) It brought Pol Pot to power

7. The Gulf of Tonkin Resolution

   A) hastened the policy of Vietnamization

   B) allowed President Nixon to pull out of Vietnam

   C) led to the escalation of the War in Vietnam

   D) denied due process of law to Vietcong prisoners

   E) led to a formal declaration of war against Cambodia

8. All of the following occurred as part of the Fall of Communism in Europe EXCEPT:

A) Velvet Revolution

B) Reunification of Germany

C) August Coup

D) Prague Spring

E) Creation of the Commonwealth of Independent States

9. Glasnost and perestroika were policies that looked to

A) stop the spread of communism in Southeast Asia

B) open the Soviet Union to criticism and capitalism

C) spread communism to markets in Eastern Europe

D) send United Nations troops to South Vietnam

E) strengthen the grip of communism in Asia

10. Lech Walesa acted to

A) bring more rights to the workers of Poland

B) economically restructure the Soviet Union

C) replace Michael Gorbachev as the leader of the Soviet Union

D) advance communism in Eastern Europe

E) end human rights violations in Bosnia

Answers and Explanations

AP World History: Modern

1. **C**. The Marshall Plan looked to strengthen European nations susceptible to communist influence. To do this, massive economic aid was sent across the Atlantic.

2. **D**. Containment is a foreign policy that looks to stop the spread of communism.

3. **B**. In 1948, the Berlin Airlift occurred. This involved enormous amounts of supplies being dropped from airplanes in response to Joseph Stalin's blockade of West Berlin.

SAT Subject Test

1. **D**. Containment meant to stop the spread of communism. That was the main objective of American Cold War policies.

2. **C**. Greece and Turkey took advantage of the Truman Doctrine's military aid.

3. **A**. Kennedy threatened an invasion of Cuba after a strict quarantine. Khrushchev removed the missiles from Cuba, and the United States disarmed some weapons in Turkey.

4. **C**. Détente meant a lessening of Cold War tensions. SALT was a treaty that limited nuclear missiles in both the United States and Soviet Union.

5. **E**. After the Korean War, massive American aid helped South Korea industrialize. They became a strong trading partner, and a nation less susceptible to a communist takeover.

6. **B**. The Tet Offensive was when the North Vietnamese pushed South. This led to a decrease in American morale.

7. **C**. The Gulf of Tonkin Resolution gave President Johnson a "blank check" for dealing with the military crisis in Vietnam.

8. **D**. The Prague Spring was in 1968, well before the Fall of Communism. Although reforms were demanded, the movement was put down by the Warsaw Pact. The other choices reflect the Fall of Communism in modern-day Czech Republic, East Germany, and the Soviet Union.

9. **B**. Glasnost brought a feeling of openness to the historically rigid rule of the Communist Party in the Soviet Union. Perestroika looked to economically restructure the nation.

10. **A**. Lech Walesa was the leader of the Polish labor union, Solidarity. He helped weaken communist domination in Poland and gave workers more rights.

China and India After 1900

China and India were great imperial treasures of Britain in the nineteenth century. By the twentieth century, they both longed to expel foreigners and gain independence. In China, the overthrow of their Emperor was sparked by hopes for democracy. However, during the twentieth century China experienced Japanese imperialism, followed by the firm hand of dictatorship and communism. Despite civil war and adversity, China turned into an industrial giant at the brink of the twenty-first century. India also grew industrially after shaking off imperial rule. With hopes for independence, Mohandas Gandhi became an inspirational leader. Through passive resistance and civil disobedience, Gandhi and his followers gained support from around the world. However, after receiving independence in 1947, the region has experienced intense religious conflict and threats of war.

HERE IS WHAT YOU NEED TO KNOW:
• CHINA
Definition: Sun Yixian (Sun Yat-sen) and Qing Overthrow

The Qing (Manchu) was the last dynasty of China. In 1911, Dr. Sun Yixian of the Kuomintang (political party known as the Nationalist Party) helped overthrow the emperor. Yixian promised *Three Principles of the Chinese People*. They were:

1. Nationalism/People's Rule – This meant to bring unity and pride to the Chinese people who had been imperialized by foreign nations for almost a century.

2. Democracy – A goal of creating a government that met the needs of the people and ensured rights.

3. People's Livelihood – Making sure that everyone had a comfortable standard of living.

Though bold, Yixian never could unify the people, and civil unrest continued in China.

Definition: May Fourth Movement

After Japan received more land in China after World War I, young Chinese students took to the streets in protest. Demonstrations reached their peak on May 4, 1919, as a widespread nationalistic movement protested Japanese occupation. Many of these protesters would soon support a new form of government…communism.

Definition: Mao Zedong (Mao Tse-tung)

Mao Zedong took part in the demonstrations against Japan. He was also one of the founders of the Communist Party in China. Eventually, communists became influential in the Kuomintang. When Yixian died, *Jiang Jieshi (Chiang Kai-shek)* took over. He was anti-communist, and ordered the execution of many of their supporters. Despite their decrease in numbers within the government, communist popularity grew under Mao, and the seeds for a takeover were planted.

Question: Why did people turn to communism in China?

Answer:

1. Anti-imperialistic sentiment, notably against Japan. People wanted new leadership that could drive them out.

2. Communism seemed to be working in the Soviet Union. The Soviet Union had close ties to communists in China.

3. Communists promised land reform and equality to starving peasants.

4. By 1930, Jiang Jieshi's government was unpopular and abusing its power.

As seen in the Soviet Union, Mao offered

Mao's picture marks the spot in Tiananmen Square where he founded the People's Republic of China in 1949

an increase in women's rights. This meant marriage rights and an end to being publicly subservient. After he secured power, women gained these rights and were expected to provide for the state as well as their families.

Definition: Chinese Civil War 1927-1949

Jiang Jieshi's Nationalists fought *Mao Zedong's Communists*. You need to know:

1. It seemed that by 1934 the Communists were all but defeated. However, Mao Zedong went on a 6,000 mile trek known as the *Long March*. As he paraded around the country, he avoided capture and gathered supporters. The longer the war went on, the better it was for Mao.

2. The Japanese invaded Manchuria (northern China) in 1931, thereby starting World War II in Asia. They were attracted to the area because of an abundance of raw materials such as coal and iron. By the late 1930s, they had a stronghold in China. This forced Jieshi and Mao to agree on a ceasefire, thereby becoming reluctant allies against Japan.

3. After World War II, the civil war continued. The United States gave aid to the Nationalists, while the Soviets supported the Communists.

4. In 1949 the Communists claimed victory, and on October 1, 1949, Mao declared China's new name to be the *People's Republic of China*. The Nationalists and Jiang Jieshi fled to the island of Taiwan. The United Nations recognized Taiwan as the Republic of China until 1971. That year, the People's Republic of China was seated.

Definition: The Great Leap Forward, 1958-1961

This was Mao's plan to develop agriculture and industry. People were forced to live with other families on large plots of land called *communes*. Here, they collectively worked together. Citizens were encouraged to create furnaces in their backyards to make steel materials. Despite the increase in production, the Great Leap Forward was mostly a failure because bad weather and depleted agricultural workforces led to poor harvests and famines that killed millions. Furthermore, there was an overproduction of shoddy finished goods.

Definition: Cultural Revolution, 1966-1976

In the Cultural Revolution, Mao's government unleashed a massive censorship campaign that targeted intellectuals or any who dissented with the rule of the Communist Party. Chinese citizens were instructed to carry a Little Red Book entitled *Quotations from Chairman Mao*, which contained his famous speeches and thoughts.

Before the Cultural Revolution, Mao encouraged intellectuals to criticize his government when he said "let a hundred flowers bloom, let a hundred schools of thought contend." However, he didn't like the harsh criticism.

In the Cultural Revolution, many were killed or forced to do hard labor. The Cultural Revolution began in 1966, and ended with Mao Zedong's death in 1976.

Definition: Deng Xiaoping and the Four Modernizations

Today, China is one of the leading industrial powers in the world. However until about 1980, it lagged behind most other nations. Deng Xiaoping helped get the ball rolling on massive industrialization with a program called the *Four Modernizations*. Inheriting this policy from a decade before, he set new goals for agriculture, industry, national defense, and science/technology. Small businesses were permitted to operate, and with their profits, people began to purchase consumer goods. By the twenty-

China's modernization can be felt in every aspect of society... even in the bathrooms

first century, China became an industrial giant, and the fastest growing economy in the world c2000.

Definition: Tiananmen Square Massacre, 1989

Although China has welcomed industrialization and modified capitalism, they remain a communist nation. In 1989, students protested communist rule and peacefully campaigned for democracy in Beijing's Tiananmen Square. Deng Xiaoping's soldiers opened fire, killing many protesters. Although the massacre was condemned by nations around the world, demonstrations in China were quickly silenced. There's a famous photograph associated with the tragedy where a protester stands in front of a moving tank. The media labeled this person "Tank Man." Estimates of the dead and wounded exceed 2,000.

Definition: Tibet Independence Movement

Once an independent country and the center of Tibetan Buddhism, Tibet is a region in western China. The People's Republic of China took over the area in the early 1950s, but promised autonomy to the Tibetans and their religious leader, the Dalai Lama. However, Ti-

133

bet never gained self-rule. Through the years, several uprisings have led to deportations. The Tibetans cite human rights violations. The Chinese government denies these claims. Despite international pressure, Tibet remains part of China.

Definition: Pollution and One-Child Policy, 1978

China continues to grow at an incredible rate. Huge building projects, such as the *Three Gorges Dam* power plant (mostly operational by 2008) on the Yangtze River, surpassed other similar worldwide constructions. Because the dam elevated water levels on the Yangtze, many people were displaced from their homes and had to move inland. China's speedy industrialization has been accompanied by much pollution. It has led nations and scientists to criticize their environmental policies.

China's population is well over 1 billion. Fearful of running out of resources, the government instituted the One-Child Policy in 1978. This *family planning policy* limited much of the population (mostly city dwellers) to producing only one offspring. In 2013, China announced it was altering the policy to allow for a second child if one parent is an only child. In 2016, China ended the policy altogether, and permitted parents to have two children.

• INDIA
Question: How did World War I coincide with Indian demands for independence?

Answer: British Indian troops served proudly in World War I. However, this did not lead to India's independence from Britain. Outrage over imperial occupation in India grew by 1919, and protests emerged all over the country. Notably, a peaceful demonstration turned deadly in Amritsar, Punjab.

Definition: Rowlatt Act/Amritsar Massacre, 1919

The *Rowlatt Act* was passed at the end of World War I to control political unrest and potential terrorist threats to British rule in India. The law allowed British officials to round up suspected activists and imprison them without a trial. Furthermore, free speech and assembly were outlawed. When a group of Hindus and Muslims assembled in the city of Amritsar to give political speeches, British officer Reginald Dyer ordered his troops to fire. Hundreds were killed, and over one thousand were wounded. The massacre led to immense anti-British sentiment amongst the Indian people.

Definition: Mohandas K. Gandhi

Gandhi led a push for Indian independence from the British crown. His methods and education combined both Western and Eastern thought. Gandhi preached *civil disobedience* (disobeying laws seen as unjust) and *passive resistance* (peaceful protest). Resistance was achieved through powerful boycotts of British finished goods (specifically, Gandhi and others spun their own cloth), refusal to pay taxes, and lack of government participation. Known also for his hunger strikes, Gandhi's most famous act of disobedience involved salt (explained next).

Definition: Salt March, 1930

The Indian people were forced to purchase salt from the *British Raj* (name for British rule). This salt was taxed. Gandhi and his followers protested this British monopoly by marching 240 miles to the coastal city of Dandi to get their own salt. As the movement for salt escalated, British authorities violently beat the protesters, and many (including Gandhi) were arrested. When the Western media got wind of the British oppression, Gandhi gained international support. India received gradual gains for independence in the mid 1930s, and total independence in 1947.

Definition: Partition, 1947

India's fight for independence from Britain gave way to an internal struggle among religions. When Britain withdrew from India in 1947, the country was divided (partitioned) into the independent nations of:

1. India - Which was mostly comprised of Hindus who were supported by the Indian National Congress.

2. Pakistan - Which was mostly comprised of Muslims who were supported by the Muslim League. Their early leader was *Muhammad Ali Jinnah*.

Gandhi tried to bring peace between the region's Hindus, Muslims, and Sikhs (a monotheistic religion popular in Punjab, India). However in 1948, he was assassinated by a Hindu extremist who was upset that Gandhi was negotiating with Muslims. Violence after partition was fierce. There is still animosity between these two nuclear nations today, especially on the border in the disputed region of *Kashmir*.

Question: What later happened in this region?

Answer:

1. *Jawaharlal Nehru* became prime minster of India for two decades. He supported democracy and westernization. By 1950, women in India gained political rights such as suffrage. Nehru's daughter, *Indira Gandhi*, also became prime minister. Religious conflict and terrorism plagued the nation. Both Gandhi and her son Rajiv Gandhi were assassinated (1984, 1991).

2. Political strife also affected Pakistan. Originally, there was West and East Pakistan. However, the physical distance between the two regions created a split in culture and political decision-making. East Pakistan became *Bangladesh*.

3. In Pakistan, *Benazir Bhutto* became the first woman ever elected to lead a Muslim state. After facing corruption charges, she exiled herself in 1998. She returned in 2007, and was assassinated as she campaigned for public office.

4. A militant separatist group from Southern India, known as the *Tamil Tigers*, fought for a homeland in Buddhist Sri Lanka. From 1983-2009 there was a civil war. The Tamil Tigers engaged in guerrilla military and terror activities. They never gained a homeland in Sri Lanka.

5. Today, India is one of the fastest growing economies in the world. However, there is a wide gap between the rich and the poor. With its population over a billion, parts of India remain incredibly impoverished. The modern media showed many images of this poverty, and reported on *Mother Teresa*, who supported human rights for all and aimed to help the poor and sick. She founded the Missionaries of Charity in India, and was awarded the Nobel Peace Prize in 1979.

India has moved towards democracy over the last few decades. However, the presence of the caste system has challenged democracy. Over time, amendments have been added to India's Constitution. They look to alleviate oppression and discrimination based on caste, and reserve opportunities for all in areas such as government and education.

1. Which of the following can best be concluded from both of the above pictures?
   A) Rapid industrialization can have negative impacts on traditional society
   B) Pollution has been controlled by the Chinese government
   C) Deng Xiaoping's Four Modernizations were not successful
   D) Most structures in China have been built on waterways

2. What has been a short-term effect of the Three Gorges Dam construction project?
   A) Production of enough electricity to power all of China
   B) Elimination of the Chinese fishing industry
   C) Rising water and the relocation of many Chinese citizens
   D) A shift towards solar power and wind energy

3. Which of the following periods is most similar to China's rapid industrialization in the twenty-first century?
   A) Meiji Era
   B) Agricultural Revolution
   C) Ming Neo-Confucianism Era
   D) Scientific Revolution

Review Questions for the SAT Subject Test

1. Sun Yixian hoped to bring which of the following to China?
   A) Communist rule
   B) The beginnings of democracy
   C) Division of farmland amongst the peasants
   D) A restoration of the Emperor
   E) acceptance of Japanese rule

2. Mao Zedong's Long March resulted in which of the following in the 1930s?
   A) Recruitment of more communist allies from within China
   B) The disappearance of Japanese imperialism
   C) The deportation of Jiang Jieshi
   D) An unconditional surrender of communist forces
   E) Increased trade with foreign nations

3. The creation of communes and an increased production of finished goods by local families is most associated with the
   A) Cultural Revolution
   B) Four Modernizations
   C) Tibetan Independence Movement
   D) May Fourth Movement
   E) Great Leap Forward

4. The Four Modernizations could be considered an inspiration for the
   A) One-Child Policy
   B) Three Principles
   C) Cultural Revolution
   D) Great Leap Forward
   E) Three Gorges Dam

5. The Cultural Revolution attempted to
   A) incorporate Western thought and philosophy
   B) encourage free speech and expression
   C) bring great wealth to individual landlords
   D) contain opposition to the Communist Party
   E) change nearly every aspect of Chinese culture

6. The Tiananmen Square and Amritsar massacres directly resulted in
   A) more violent protests against China's Communist Party and the British Raj
   B) civil rights being bestowed on the peasants of China and India
   C) international outrage and pressures for reform
   D) the Fall of Communism in China, and end to British rule in India
   E) intervention on behalf of the United Nations

7. All of the following were tactics used by Mohandas Gandhi EXCEPT:
   A) Boycott of British taxes
   B) Hunger strikes
   C) Segregation of Hindus and Muslims
   D) Passive resistance
   E) Use of media support

8. An example of civil disobedience was the
   A) Salt March
   B) creation of the state of Bangladesh
   C) partition of India
   D) formation of the Muslim League
   E) purchasing of British textiles

9. After the British pulled out of the region, why was there still conflict in India?

A) There was anti-imperialistic sentiment against the United States

B) Religious strife escalated between Hindus and Muslims

C) There were political conflicts between India and China

D) The increased price of salt led to economic distress

E) More imperialistic nations assembled to take resources

10. The Tamil Tigers attempted to gain a homeland in Sri Lanka through

A) civil disobedience

B) guerrilla military tactics

C) passive resistance

D) an alliance with Pakistan

E) boycotts of goods

Answers and Explanations

AP World History: Modern

1. **A**. The picture on the left shows traditional architecture being overshadowed by a modern structure on the Yangtze River in China. The picture on the right shows a huge traffic jam in the city of Wuhan.

2. **C**. The Three Gorges Dam was one of the greatest building projects of the twenty-first century. Rising waters led to the displacement of people living close to the river.

3. **A**. Japan modernized and westernized at a great pace during the nineteenth century. That time of industrialization coincided with the Meiji Restoration.

SAT Subject Test

1. **B**. Sun Yixian's *Three Principles of the Chinese People* looked to bring democratic reforms, a fair standard of living, and the elimination of imperialism.

2. **A**. Mao Zedong went on a 6,000 mile march through China to avoid the Nationalist military and Jiang Jieshi. During the march, the communists recruited many supporters.

3. **E**. The Great Leap Forward is considered to be a failure by historians. It looked to increase production and agricultural output at local levels.

4. **E**. The Four Modernizations looked to increase industry and technology in China. When it became fully operational in 2008, the Three Gorges Dam became the largest hydro-electric dam in the world.

5. **D**. Mao ruled harshly during the Cultural Revolution. During this time, opposition to the Communist Party was severely punished.

6. **C**. Both incidents led to international outrage. Because it occurred more recently, images of the Tiananmen Square Massacre of 1989 were seen all over the world.

7. **C**. Although there was much religious strife between Hindus and Muslims within the region, Gandhi embraced all religions.

8. **A**. Gandhi led the Salt March in 1930 to defy the British salt monopoly. Gandhi and his followers hoped to secure their own salt.

9. **B**. The end of the British Raj led to new problems in the area between Hindus and Muslims. In 1947, the country was partitioned into Pakistan, a predominantly Muslim state, and India, a mostly Hindu one. Much violence took place on the border in the disputed region of Kashmir.

10. **B**. A militant separatist group from Southern India known as the Tamil Tigers fought for a homeland in Buddhist Sri Lanka. They engaged in guerrilla military and terror activities.

Post World War II Middle East, Africa, and the Modern World

Since World War II, the Middle East has been in constant conflict. After gaining independence, Israel fought wars in the first four decades of its existence. Despite attempts for diplomacy, violence in the Middle East continued into the twenty-first century. In Africa, some nations received independence after nearly a century of imperialism. However, conflict and violence still plagued the area, as feuding tribes and religions resulted in wars and massacres. In South Africa, decades of segregation and oppression finally ended in the 1990s, as apartheid dissolved. The world has changed a lot since the Neolithic Revolution. Today, interdependent nations deal with problems such as pollution, economic crashes, and environmental destruction. All of these issues have left many concerned about the future.

HERE IS WHAT YOU NEED TO KNOW:
• THE MIDDLE EAST
Definition: Zionism

Led by *Theodor Herzl*, this was a movement in the late nineteenth century to find a permanent homeland for Jews in the Holy Land of the Middle East. In 1917, a letter (known as the *Balfour Declaration*) written by British Foreign Secretary Arthur James Balfour called for the creation of a Jewish state within Palestine of the Middle East.

After suffering through the Holocaust, Jews received a homeland when the United Nations recommended the creation of a Jewish state in 1947. Israel gained independence on May 14, 1948. Almost immediately, Arab nations invaded in what would become the first of four Arab-Israeli wars. Israel pushed back this early threat. David Ben-Gurion became the first Prime Minister of Israel.

Question: What wars were fought between Israel and other Middle East nations from 1956-1973?

Answer: After the initial 1948 conflict, the following occurred:

1. Suez Crisis, 1956 – The Suez Canal was completed in 1869, and controlled by European nations as a means to connect the Red Sea to the Mediterranean Sea. Egypt's leader, *Gamal Abdel Nasser*, took control of the canal in 1956. This angered Britain and France, who aligned with Israel to take it back. Despite their military victory, international pressure from the US and Soviet Union led to the withdrawal of troops from the area.

2. Six-Day War, 1967 – Egypt threatened war with Israel. In response, Israel made pre-emptive strikes against Egypt and neighboring Arab nations. After the war, Israel controlled Jerusalem, the Sinai Peninsula, and the West Bank.

3. Yom Kippur War, 1973 – Led by Egypt and Syria, Arab nations surprised Israel on the holiest day of the Jewish calendar, Yom Kippur. They caused heavy losses and gained some land. Israel took back much of it before a ceasefire. During the 1970s, Israel received much aid from the United States through the diplomacy of their Prime Minister, *Golda Meir*. She was one of the Zionists influential in the creation of the State of Israel.

Definition: Camp David Accords, 1978

This was one of the rare peace agreements in the Middle East. Menachem Begin of Israel, Anwar Sadat of Egypt, and President Jimmy Carter of the United States met at Camp David in Maryland. There, it was agreed that Egypt would recognize Israel as a nation-state, and Israel would give back the Sinai Peninsula. Diplomacy with Israel angered many Muslims, and Sadat (like Gandhi) was assassinated by an extremist of his own faith.

Definition: Iranian Revolution, 1979

Great Britain and Russia had a strong presence in Persia before World War I. However, Persian officials gained control. In 1935, the nation was renamed Iran and went through a period of modernization and industrialization. However, corruption and resentment to Westernization prevailed.

Iran's leader, the **Shah of Iran** (Mohammad Reza Pahlavi), looked to solidify power by instituting reforms in 1963 known as the **White Revolution**. The reforms looked to improve education, give women voting rights, and redistribute land to the peasants. The Shah was viewed as an unpopular Western ally by adversaries, especially religious traditionalists. In 1978, anti-Western riots spread throughout Iran. To control order, **martial law** (emergency military rule) was established by the Shah. Still, opposition mounted. As his popularity decreased, the Shah fled Iran and **Ayatollah Khomeini** took power in 1979. Khomeini supported an Islamic state, not a westernized one. That same year, Iranian students stormed the US Embassy in Tehran. For 444 days, Americans were held hostage.

Question: What other violence occurred in the area?

Answer: Israel, Jordan, and Egypt coexisted rather peacefully in the late twentieth and early twenty-first centuries. However, violence between Israelis and Palestinians continued. In the 1970s, the **PLO** (Palestine Liberation Organization) was led by **Yasser Arafat**. Arafat hoped to get self-determination for a Palestinian State. Much violence occurred in the area. Many Palestinians displayed their unrest through what's known as the *intifada*, or public demonstration. Protesters threw rocks at Israeli soldiers and used boycotts to demonstrate against occupation.

In the 1993 Oslo Peace Accords, US President Bill Clinton attempted to bring peace between Arafat and Israeli Prime Minister **Yitzhak Rabin**. Israel agreed to withdraw some troops and permit Palestinians to self-govern the territories of the Gaza Strip and West Bank. Rabin, like Sadat, was killed by an extremist of his own faith who thought the Prime Minister negotiated too much.

In 2007, the political group Hamas (classified by the US as a terror organization) took power in Gaza. In 2008, Israel blockaded the Gaza Strip when rockets were being fired at them. This escalated into the Gaza War. Israel issued a ceasefire less than a month after invading, as worldwide criticism of occupation increased. A similar war took place a year before, as rockets came from the north from an organization called Hezbollah in Lebanon. After 34 days of fighting, the UN negotiated a ceasefire.

Violent altercations between Gaza and Israel returned in the summer of 2014, leading to another Israeli offensive into Gaza.

In the **Arab Spring** of 2011, the Middle East saw a wave of democratic protests and reforms. The first successful uprising was in Tunisia. Most notably, in Egypt, President Hosni Mubarak was removed from power. Beginning in 2011, violent protests spread to Syria as well, where President Bashar al-Assad responded with military force. He was accused of crimes against humanity. The conflict escalated into a civil war between Assad's government and various rebel groups.

In 2015, a refugee crisis escalated as thousands of people fled war-torn Syria looking to find safety in places such as Europe. The conflict sparked debates regarding the ability of nations to admit and afford large populations of refugees.

In 2014, a US-led coalition began airstrikes against the extremist Islamic State of Iraq and Syria, or ISIS. Amidst the war-torn background of Syria and Iraq, ISIS gained control over large areas in the region. They became associated with violence, human rights violations, and terror threats in both the Middle East and Western World.

Definition: OPEC

The Organization of the Petroleum Exporting Countries is a very influential union of the world's largest oil producing nations such as Iran, Saudi Arabia, Nigeria, and Venezuela. Many consider OPEC to be a *cartel* because they are a powerful association that controls much of the world's oil supply. Therefore, they have great influence over the worldwide prices of oil and gasoline products.

Definition: Taliban

The Taliban controlled a *fundamentalist* (strict adherence to religious principles) Islamic government in Afghanistan c2000. They isolated themselves from most of the Western World. Women were restricted rights to education, labor, medical care, and movement throughout cities. The Taliban supported the terrorist organization al-Qaeda, which was behind the attacks on the United States on September 11, 2001. Osama bin Laden organized the crashing of hijacked planes into New York's World Trade Center, and the Pentagon in Washington, DC. A final plane crashed in an open field in Pennsylvania after heroic actions by passengers. Nearly 3,000 died in the attacks.

The United States went to war with the Taliban in 2001, and quickly removed them from power. In 2003, the US invaded Saddam Hussein's Iraq. Hussein was captured in 2003, and

later tried for crimes against humanity. He was executed in 2006. The United States continued its involvement in the war-torn region for more than a decade.

A decade earlier, the US was engaged in military conflict. In the Persian Gulf War in Iraq, American forces liberated Kuwait from Saddam Hussein. The US looked to protect oil interests in the area.

• AFRICA
Definition: Apartheid in South Africa, 1948-1994

Given self-rule from Great Britain, the Republic of South Africa's white National Party members and Afrikaners (Dutch descendants) discriminated against black Africans. *Apartheid* (notice the word apart) was a legal separation of the *majority* black population from the *minority* white race in South Africa. The entire country was segregated for nearly 50 years.

Definition: Nelson Mandela

Black South Africans protested apartheid, and formed the *African National Congress*. The ANC supported boycotts and strikes to bring attention to apartheid. The government cracked down on this organization's activities and imprisoned many followers. One man arrested was Nelson Mandela. Mandela became a symbol of the resistance movement, as he sat in a prison cell from 1962-1990. Explained next, he was instrumental in bringing an end to apartheid. He was awarded the Nobel Peace Prize in 1993.

Question: How did apartheid end?

Answer: Sympathizing with protests in South Africa, the world rallied against apartheid. A bishop named *Desmond Tutu* helped bring attention to the injustice, and gathered support against it. Countries leveled sanctions (economic punishments) and trade embargos on South Africa. In 1990 F.W. de Klerk, the new President of South Africa, released Mandela. Soon after, apartheid ended. When all people were allowed to vote in 1994, the African National Congress gained control of the Parliament and Mandela became President. In 1996, a new democratic constitution was adopted for the Republic of South Africa.

Question: What African names were associated with independence movements?

Answer: After World War II, European nations loosened their grip over their African colonies. Economic concerns as well as new beliefs in expanding liberties were influential in African independence. Still, much violence accompanied *decolonization* (withdrawing from colonies). You need to know the following:

1. Kwame Nkrumah – Conflict in Ghana existed for decades under British rule. The Asante rebelled in 1900 when the British demanded the respected "Golden Stool" of the kings. However, **Queen Yaa Asantewaa** urged her people to fight back. Despite maintaining the stool and having the British recognize Asante tradition in the aftermath, Great Britain continued to control the area. It wasn't until the middle of the century that Ghana would have more success. This time, under Kwame Nkrumah, organized boycotts economically stung the British. The British Gold Coast became an independent Ghana in 1957 under Nkrumah's leadership.

2. Kenya looked to gain independence from Britain. The **Mau Mau Uprising** involved violent actions of the Kikuyu people against the local imperialist government. They attacked both government operations and the farms of white settlers. **Jomo Kenyatta** eventually emerged as the nationalist leader in the area, and voice of the people. Kenya received independence in 1963.

3. Mobutu Sese Seko – He became leader of Zaire (name of Congo from 1971-1997) several years after the nation received independence from Belgium in 1960. Belgium had controlled the Congo since the days of imperialism, where King Leopold II looked to spread Christianity while forcing millions to work collecting rubber. World pressure led the Belgium government to take the territory from the king.

Mobutu ruled through military force. He took wealth for himself and attempted to eliminate colonial and communist influences from the country. He was removed from power in 1997, and the country became the Democratic Republic of Congo. Years of civil war and instability followed.

4. Ahmed Ben Bella – He was a leader of the FLN (Algerian National Liberation Front) which fought for independence from France (the French would not relinquish power after World War II). Despite deployment of French troops, Algeria received independence in 1962, and Ben Bella later became the first elected president. In Algeria, an Islamic fundamentalist resistance grew as the government could not meet the economic needs of its people. This sparked civil war in the 1990s.

The Sokoto Caliphate was a Muslim Empire in modern-day Nigeria. The Caliphate fell in 1903 to the British, who continued to recognize the sultan as a cultural leader. The coastal region became split among Britain, France, and Germany. Although Nigeria received a peaceful independence from Britain in 1960, it would be plagued by civil war and ethnic turmoil, as three ethnic factions (Hausa-Fulani, Yoruba, and Igbo) coexisted in separate states. Ethnic tension and military rule followed. A state called **Biafra** seceded from Nigeria in 1967. Although Nigeria would reunite, an estimated one million died from violence or famine.

During this time, the idea of **Pan-African-**

ism began to spread throughout the region and world. This is a belief in solidarity between those of African descent (both within Africa and elsewhere around the world). The movement celebrates culture while supporting individual rights and independence. For example, the Organization of African Unity aimed to defend sovereignty and find cooperation between African nations from 1963-2002.

Like ending apartheid, movements for rights and celebrations of culture for those of African descent took place around the world during the 20th century. In the United States during the 1920s, a movement in African American culture took place in New York known as the *Harlem Renaissance*. During the next few decades, in Paris, the *Negritude Movement* protested assimilation to French colonial rule in Africa and the Caribbean.

Definition: Rwandan Genocide, 1994

Two rival ethnic groups exist in Rwanda… Hutus (the majority) and Tutsis. For centuries, there has been conflict. In 1994, violence was triggered after Rwandan President Juvénal Habyarimana, a Hutu, died in a plane crash. Hutus accused the Tutsis of shooting down the plane. In reaction, genocide occurred. For about 100 days an estimated 800,000 Tutsis were killed, mostly by Hutus. Many Tutsis fled the country until the Rwandan Patriotic Front (RPF) restored order.

Definition: War in Darfur

Darfur is a region of Sudan that borders neighboring Chad. In 2003, the government was accused of oppressing non-Arab Africans. The Sudan Liberation Army (SLA) and Justice and Equality Movement (JEM) took to arms in protest. The Sudanese government fought back, thus creating a civil war. A group loyal to the government, the Janjaweed, forcefully re-moved non-Arab Africans to the border, killing many in the process.

Over the next decade, 3-5 million Sudanese people were brought to camps patrolled by the Janjaweed. Statistics on the killings are difficult to obtain, but the UN estimated that over 300,000 people died from starvation or killing in the first five years of relocation.

• THE MODERN WORLD
Definition: Developing/Developed Nations

Developing nations are those who are slowly becoming industrialized. Access to clean water, raw materials, energy, and food are vital for this development. As nations have developed, they have increased social services such as health care and education. Still, in places such as Brazil (see below) there is a gap between the rich and the poor. Developed nations have established themselves with manufacturing centers and more advanced economies. The fastest industrializing nations since 2000 have been Asian countries like China and India, and Latin American ones such as Brazil.

As for Brazil, manufacturing greatly increased in the first decade of the twenty-first century. Farm goods such as coffee and soybeans created much economic growth. Brazil has also become a great producer of oil. Although the economy grew at a fast pace, so did debt. Whereas some gained great wealth, there is still vast poverty and crime. The government has looked to institute social programs to alleviate this wealth gap, but prevailing inequality has been a media focus as Brazil hosted both the 2014 World Cup and the 2016 Summer Olympic Games. Industrial Brazil has also seen an increase in deforestation (see pg. 146). In neighboring Venezuela, although great wealth was accumulated by oil, steep declines in oil prices c2017 were a strong contributor to economic decline, inflation, and difficulties obtaining imported items such as food and medicine.

The term **Third World** was associated with poorer, or developing nations. The term was used during the Cold War to identify countries not aligned with either the United States or the Soviet Union. However, this term can be misleading, as in a large nonaligned country such as India, the western state of *Kerala* experienced a series of land reforms for peasants and echoed other socialist undertones of the Cold War. In addition, whereas most of Africa wasn't aligned, Ethiopia turned to communist thought and received military supplies from communists under **Mengistu Haile Mariam**, who took over in 1977. Under Mariam's *Red Terror*, thousands of intellectual opponents to socialism were targeted, famine ensued, and over one million people died.

Definition: Green Revolution, c1950-1970

The world population has been growing quickly since World War II, and has become increasingly harder to feed. Inequality of resources such as food, water, education, health care, and energy prevail, with developed countries more abundant. The Green Revolution saw new farming techniques, chemical pesticides, and fertilizers used to increase crop yields in the twentieth century. More food for consumption meant less world hunger. Think: Lettuce is green, and so was this revolution.

Definition: European Union, 1992

The Maastricht Treaty of 1992 established the European Union a year later. The EU is a political union between certain European Nations. The EU allows people to travel freely through member nations, creates common legislation, and operates on the currency of the Euro. In 2009, Greece and other nations began to have severe economic problems which threatened the stability of the EU. This led to a series of bailouts from economically stronger members, specifically Germany.

In 2016, the United Kingdom voted nationally to leave the EU. This "Brexit" involved much campaigning and organizing over social media, as the internet helped to persuade many voters on both sides of the issue.

North American nations looked to bring less restrictive trade to its continent. In 1993, the North American Free Trade Agreement (**NAFTA**) eased restrictions such as taxes on imports (or tariffs) between Canada, Mexico, and the United States.

Definition: Global Interdependence

In recent years, nations have become dependent on each other. They also can have their livelihood affected by events thousands of miles away. When the 2004 tsunami hit Indonesia, or the 2010 earthquake devastated Haiti, the rest of the world helped out. With information readily available on television and the internet, the entire world has become a network of dependent nations.

The world has come together to condemn terrorism as well. After al-Qaeda attacked the United States on September 11, 2001, other nations helped the United States fight the **War on Terror** by supplying intelligence and land for military bases.

Definition: G8 (G7), G20

A great example of global interdependence is the Group of Eight, which became a Group of Seven after Russia left in 2014. The group consists of some of the strongest industrial nations in the world, including the United States, Germany, the United Kingdom, and Japan. Every year they hold a summit meeting to discuss the state of the world, and ways to solve global problems.

There's also a Group of Twenty (G20) which is a summit composed of finance leaders from twenty major economic world powers. They meet to discuss the stability of the world's economy.

Question: What should I know about the modern global economy?

The term *globalization* has been used to describe the interconnected trade and communication networks that have linked the world together. Besides the EU and NAFTA (see pg. 145), much development in globalization has taken place in the last few decades. *Free trade*, or the ability to trade without restrictions outside of one's borders, has been a key component regarding globalization. In the 1980s, leaders such as Ronald Reagan of the United States and Margaret Thatcher of the United Kingdom supported free trade as essential to economic growth.

Those who support globalization look at the benefits of having a world community. They hope to improve lives in developing countries with increased industry and jobs, and the spread of new products. In addition, prices tend to decrease with freer trade and overseas labor. Those against globalization point to the loss of their nation's factories and jobs (freer migration laws can create an influx of workers), which they believe has weakened the domestic economy. For example, many *multinational corporations* (those who have major operations in multiple countries) have outsourced jobs to India and China, thereby leading to the closing of factories in developed nations such as the United States. Also, much of the world has lost some of its ethnic diversity, as *homogenization* (sameness) of Western culture, such as malls, fast food chains, and other popular culture, can be seen dotting the landscape of foreign countries. Also relevant to the world economy:

1. World Trade Organization - Global entity that looks to establish fair rules of trade between countries. It also helps to settle disputes that could hinder trade.

2. World Bank - Global entity which is concerned with battling poverty by helping out developing countries through low-interest loans and grants.

3. International Monetary Fund - The IMF looks to sponsor financial stability through global cooperation. It promotes economic growth and employment while aiming to decrease world poverty.

4. On a smaller scale, *microfinance institutions* look to help poorer populations in developing countries by offering loans to entrepreneurs, or others hoping to lift themselves out of poverty.

5. In 2008, when the stock market took a dive in the United States, markets around the world were affected. This *financial crisis* deeply affected markets and employment opportunities in Europe, Asia, and Latin America as well. Export dependent countries such as China saw steep declines in overseas demand.

6. Certain developed countries such as the United States, Japan, and Finland are considered *knowledge economies*, or those that value both the skills and the gathering of information necessary to succeed in the global economy. Other countries tend to focus on production and manufacturing of materials such as Bangladesh and Vietnam in Asia, and Mexico and Honduras in Latin America.

Question: What are some of the environmental and technological issues threatening the Earth today?

Answer:

1. Deforestation - Destruction of trees, notably near the Amazon River in South America. Fewer trees not only means more carbon dioxide in the atmosphere, but also the destruction of animal habitats. One non-government

organization (NGO), called the World Wildlife Fund, looks to protect the future of nature, including conservation of the world's most important forests.

2. Desertification – The expanding of deserts, as seen in the Sahel of the Sahara.

3. Climate Change - There has been an increase in average world temperatures. Many scientists believe this is influenced by pollution, and that increases in temperature can affect crop yields, water depletion, and could increase the strength of violent storms. Coastal areas in the Pacific such as Papua New Guinea are vulnerable to a rise in sea levels.

An international agreement in 1997, called the *Kyoto Protocol*, aimed to get countries to reduce greenhouse gas emissions under the premise that man-made carbon emissions contribute to global warming. The Protocol's first reduction commitment period expired in 2012.

4. Ozone Depletion – The ozone layer protects people from the sun's ultraviolet rays. Chemical pollution released into the atmosphere could deplete this barrier. In 1962, American Rachel Carson wrote a book called *Silent Spring* in which she helped spark an environmental movement to ban certain chemical pesticides that could harm the environment. The world community has addressed environmental concerns. The Green Belt Movement was founded in 1977 to encourage Kenyans, mostly women, to conserve land, plant trees, and nurture the soil. One NGO called Greenpeace was created in 1971 and looks to limit nuclear testing, prevent commercial whaling, and protect the ecosystem of Antarctica. In 1970, the first Earth Day celebrated clean land, air, and water.

5. *Nuclear Proliferation* – This means the spread of nuclear weapons around the world. Neighboring nations with unfriendly relations, such as India and Pakistan, have nuclear weapons that could do serious harm to the environment if deployed.

In addition to nuclear weapons, there's a threat of biological weapons which could spread dangerous bacteria and viruses, and chemical weapons such as the poison gas used during World War I. Such materials could be traded across international lines.

6. Cyber Warfare – Nations must confront the threat of having their classified files hacked. Some cyber warfare is sponsored by governments. Nations must also protect their computer systems in electrical grids and other infrastructure.

7. Spread of disease through continents - Throughout history, there have been terrible outbreaks such as the plague of the Middle Ages and the 1918 Spanish Flu pandemic, both of which killed millions of people. The World Health Organization was established by the United Nations in 1948 to promote a healthier world. They aid in research and treatment of worldwide diseases. Globalization and interactions have spread disease across cultures. From the 1980s to the present, the HIV and AIDS epidemic led to increased worldwide awareness and medical research. In recent years, other deadly viruses such as SARS, H1N1, and Zika have spread throughout the world causing alarm, international research, and response. Other diseases have been associated with changing lifestyles such as the abundance of food and alcohol in developed countries. For example, heart disease, has become the leading cause of death in the United States. Lifestyle is believed to play a part in certain diagnoses of diabetes. Increased life expectancy due to advanced medicine has had the shortcoming of an increase in the diagnosis of Alzheimer's disease.

Review Questions for the AP World History: Modern Exam

"Convinced that the so-called "new constitution" endorsed on 2 November 1983 by the exclusively white electorate in South Africa would continue the process of denationalization of the indigenous African majority, depriving it of all fundamental rights, and further entrench apartheid, transforming South Africa into a country for "whites only",

"Aware that the inclusion in the "new constitution" of the so-called "coloured" people and people of Asian origin is aimed at dividing the unity of the oppressed people of South Africa and fomenting internal conflict, ….

"Declares that the so-called "new constitution" is contrary to the principles of the Charter of the United Nations, that the results of the referendum of 2 November 1983 are of no validity whatsoever and that the enforcement of the "new constitution" will further aggravate the already explosive situation prevailing inside apartheid South Africa."

— United Nations Security Council Resolution 554, August 17, 1984

1. What is the primary purpose of the above Resolution?

A) To put pressure on South Africa to change their social policies
B) To call for troops to be deployed to South Africa
C) To banish South Africa from the United Nations
D) To further support segregation laws

2. Which of the following would the UN most likely consider the new constitution to be a violation of?

A) Treaty of Versailles
B) Universal Declaration of Human Rights
C) Charter of NATO
D) Kyoto Protocol

3. Which of the following can be considered a continuity of the above Resolution?

A) Weakening of support for the African National Congress
B) Imprisonment of Nelson Mandela
C) Sanctions and worldwide condemnation of apartheid
D) The end of the Boer War

Review Questions for the SAT Subject Test

1. Gamal Abdel Nasser's actions in 1956 caused controversy along the
   A) Indian Ocean
   B) Suez Canal
   C) Dead Sea
   D) Atlantic Ocean
   E) Pacific Ocean

2. A goal of the 1979 Iranian Revolution was to
   A) establish a state based on capitalism and economic growth
   B) remove Western influences from the country
   C) create a secular society
   D) give more rights to Iranian women
   E) bring the Shah back to power

3. The Camp David Accords brought peace mostly between Israel and
   A) Egypt
   B) the PLO
   C) Iran
   D) Syria
   E) Iraq

4. OPEC influences the world in the twenty-first century because they
   A) have great control over oil prices
   B) encourage revolution in the Middle East
   C) provide new ways to control global warming
   D) make sure trees are replanted after deforestation
   E) are at the forefront of cyber security

5. Which was true of apartheid in South Africa in the twentieth century?
   A) It always had the support of Great Britain and the United States
   B) Minority whites limited rights of the majority black population
   C) Hindus and Muslims lived in a state of segregation
   D) The African National Congress and Afrikaners historically supported one another
   E) A new constitution was never adopted

6. Kwame Nkrumah and Jomo Kenyatta were associated with
   A) establishing a constitution in South Africa
   B) bringing peace to Darfur
   C) resistance to apartheid
   D) African independence movements
   E) ending conflict in Rwanda

7. Regarding Rwanda in 1994, most of the people killed were
   A) Sudanese
   B) South African
   C) Tutsi
   D) Hutu
   E) Nigerian

8. Which of the following South American countries has seen the most amount of industrial growth in the twenty-first century?
   A) Peru
   B) Ecuador
   C) Brazil
   D) Bolivia
   E) Uruguay

9. Which of the following is an example of global interdependence?

A) International support in the War on Terror
B) Massive industrialization in India creating a booming economy
C) Forests being destroyed near the Amazon River disturbing the local ecosystem
D) Protests for change in Tunisia lead to the overthrow of the government
E) North Korean missile tests into international waters

10. The Green Revolution was most associated with

A) limiting the amount of crude oil extracted from Middle Eastern countries
B) the elimination of pesticides and chemicals from certain household products
C) reducing the effects of man-made global warming
D) ending deforestation in South America
E) increasing the amount of food suitable for consumption around the planet

Answers and Explanations

AP World History: Modern

1. **A**. The United Nations is firmly condemning apartheid in the Resolution, and doing their best to get South Africa to stop the policy.

2. **B**. After World War II, the UN adopted the Universal Declaration of Human Rights which looked to ensure and protect fundamental rights.

3. **C**. To protest apartheid, nations began to administer sanctions, or penalties, against South Africa.

SAT Subject Test

1. **B**. Egypt took control of the Suez Canal, thereby creating the Suez Crisis. After international forces took it back, the United Nations pressured for its return to Egypt.

2. **B**. In the Iranian Revolution, the pro-West Shah was taken out of power. Ayatollah Khomeini and his followers looked to establish a state based on Islamic law.

3. **A**. In the agreement, Israel was recognized as a nation and the Sinai Peninsula was returned to Egypt.

4. **A**. OPEC is the Organization of the Petroleum Exporting Countries. They control the supply of much of the world's oil.

5. **B**. Apartheid segregated and limited the rights of black Africans. Apartheid was administrated by South Africa's minority white population.

6. **D**. Both leaders helped bring about independence…Kenyatta for Kenya, and Nkrumah for Ghana.

7. **C**. The Hutus targeted the Tutsis with violence. The tribes had been adversaries for centuries.

8. **C**. Brazil has been industrializing at an enormous speed. Rio de Janeiro was chosen to host the 2016 Summer Olympic Games.

9. **A**. Global interdependence occurs when countries thousands of miles away become dependent upon one another. Nations can share intelligence and air space to help stop terrorist threats.

10. **E**. The Green Revolution increased the amount of food available for world consumption. Try to remember that lettuce is green, as was this revolution.

Format of the AP World History: Modern Exam

The format of the AP World History: Modern exam changed in the 2019-2020 school year. The new test begins c1200 and carries to the present. <u>The contents of this book cover all of World History as to serve as a guide for the SAT Subject Test as well</u>. The AP World History: Modern Exam features document analysis and the connection of themes throughout World History. There are two sections, which include four separate tasks which you need to address. The following pages contain rubrics and tips.

Section I, Part A — 55 multiple choice questions in 55 minutes.
Unlike the SAT Subject Test, there are only four choices, and the questions are based on documents. This section will count for 40% of your grade. See the document style multiple choice within No Bull Review.

Section I, Part B — Three Short Answer questions in 40 minutes.
These require brief written answers, not in full essay format. The following pages contain 20 examples of this type of question. The short answers might challenge you to select ONE, or TWO of the things you know the most about regarding the major themes of the course. Short answers could include primary and secondary sources, graphs or images. This section will count for 20% of your grade.

Section II, DBQ and Long Essay in 1 hour 40 minutes (60 minute DBQ, and 40 minute Long Essay).

You will be given a Document Based Question essay and a standard Long Essay. Both will be explained in the following pages. The DBQ makes up 25% of your grade, and the Long Essay is worth 15%. Here is a breakdown of what is tested. The exam covers concepts that are divided into nine different periods and date ranges. These include:

Unit 1: The Global Tapestry – c1200 to c1450 = 8-10% of the exam
Unit 2: Networks of Exchange – c1200 to c1450 = 8-10 % of the exam
Unit 3: Land-Based Empires – c1450 to c1750 = 12-15% of the exam
Unit 4: Transoceanic Interconnections – c1450 to c1750 = 12-15% of the exam
Unit 5: Revolutions – c1750-c1900 = 12-15% of the exam
Unit 6: Consequences of Industrialization – c1750-c1900 = 12-15% of the exam
Unit 7: Global Conflict – c1900-present = 8-10% of the exam
Unit 8: Cold War and Decolonization – c1900-present = 8-10% of the exam
Unit 9: Globalization – c1900-present = 8-10% of the exam

Some of the topics which are covered in the above time periods include:

Unit 1, The Global Tapestry – Religion and philosophy in Asia and the Muslim world, and state building among Native American and African empires.
Unit 2, Networks of Exchange – Silk Roads, Indian Ocean, Trans-Saharan trade routes, and the spread of religion throughout the world.
Unit 3, Land-Based Empires – Expansion of empires, how empires administrate over such a vast area, and the clashes that can occur within the close proximity of others.

152

Unit 4, Transoceanic Interconnections – Motivations and effects of exploration, Columbian Exchange, and the strength and developments of maritime empires.

Unit 5, Revolutions – The effects of Enlightenment around the world, Industrial Revolution, nationalism, and worldwide revolutions.

Unit 6, Consequences of Industrialization – Motivations for imperialism, expansion of states, effect on indigenous people, and causes of migration in an interconnected world.

Unit 7, Global Conflict – World War I causes and effects, World War II causes and effects, and human rights violations.

Unit 8, Cold War and Decolonization – Spread and fall of communism, independence for once imperialized countries, and conflicts in the aftermath of decolonization.

Unit 9, Globalization – Technological advances, economic changes, globalized culture, and resistance to globalization.

All of the questions on the test will reflect one of the following themes:

Humans and the Environment (ENV) – Understanding the interaction between people and their environment. People have been affected by, and have altered their environments. Examples include terrace farming, climate affecting trade routes, global migration and pollution, expansion of empires, Little Ice Age, urbanization, and spread of disease.

Cultural Developments and Interactions (CDI) – Understanding the origins of culture such as belief systems, philosophy, art, technology, and how one views themselves against others. Also, an understanding of cultural diffusion is key. Examples include religious beliefs, Social Darwinism, Enlightenment, nationalism, communism, globalization, and migration spreading culture and religion.

Governance (GOV) – Understanding the formation, expansion, and decline of states. In addition, understanding how governments administrate and maintain order while exercising power is key. Examples include emergence of states, taxation, strength through trade, Meiji Era, Gunpowder Empires, governing over colonies, social hierarchies, nationalism, Cold War geopolitics, anti-imperialist movements, architecture and belief systems spreading, ethnic clashes, global war, and global interdependence.

Economic Systems (ECN) – Understanding how societies can affect or be affected by the production, exchange, and utilization of products. Examples include traditional economy, industrialization, capitalism, socialism, the global economy, encomienda, slavery, Marxism, transnational banks, mercantilism, Columbian Exchange, oil and nuclear power, and the Green Revolution.

Social Interactions and Organization (SIO) – Understanding the ways that societies organize their social structure, status, and interactions between individuals. Also, comprehending how social stratification has changed over time. Examples include gender hierarchy, caste system, Enlightenment ideals, nationalism, post-imperialism independence, migration, religious beliefs sustaining or challenging class, abolition of slavery, and suffrage rights.

Technology and Innovation (TEC) – Understanding how humans have innovated throughout history by creating products and ideas that have enhanced comfort, efficiency, and security. In addition, one should understand how technology has had both intended and unintended results. Technology examples include the caravel, radio, television, and atomic bomb.

AP Historical Thinking Skills and Reasoning Processes

The exam focuses on 6 AP Historical Thinking Skills and 3 important AP History Reasoning Processes. How they are applied to your DBQ and Long Essay will be explained later. The AP Historical Thinking Skills are:

Developments and Processes – You must be able to identify and explain historical developments, processes, and concepts that have occurred in the nine units mentioned earlier.

Sourcing and Situation – You must be able to describe and evaluate relevant evidence from both primary and secondary sources. On primary sources, you should describe arguments and explain how the source helps emulate the larger historical setting. As will be seen in the DBQ, you should be aware of the source's credibility, context, situation, purpose, point of view, and audience. For example, the writings of Mao Zedong had a nationalistic and communist bias, with the purpose of gaining support during the Chinese Civil War and beyond. His audience might have been poor peasants who he was looking to persuade into support. On secondary sources, you must understand arguments and use of evidence, explain and analyze patterns or trends in data, comprehend argument construction and effectiveness, and explain how context could influence claims. Understanding the arguments and evidence used by historians is important.

Claims and Evidence in Sources – You need to be able to analyze arguments in both primary and secondary sources whether it is text-based or non-text based. Comparing arguments is key, as is explaining how evidence supports, modifies, or refutes a source's argument.

Contextualization – It is important to connect history to the bigger picture by describing historical context accurately, and explaining how that context influenced the development or process of history. Furthermore, you should grasp the significance of such historical development. For instance, socialist movements coincided with rapid industrialization. So too did the increasing gap between the rich and the poor and prolific child labor. Hitler was able to rise in the 1930s because the League of Nations, which stemmed from World War I, could not stop him.

Making Connections – It is important to use the historical reasoning processes mentioned next (comparison, causation, and continuity and change) and analyze connections, patterns, and relationships regarding historical developments and processes.

Argumentation – As will be explained with the essay writing, you must construct an argument using specific and relevant information. You must show the relationships between the historical evidence, and analyze to support a convincing thesis. You should be able to find diverse information that could modify the argument. Indeed, it's also helpful to know both sides of an argument. What were the pros and cons of dropping the atomic bomb? Why is globalization viewed as positive or negative? You can argue either side if you have enough evidence.

Reasoning Processes ... it is critical to identify these!

Reasoning Process #1: Comparison - You need to find similarities and/or differences between specific developments or processes and explain the relative significance. For instance, you might compare the similarities and differences of the Japanese samurai warrior and Middle Ages knight, yet also see how their roles changed throughout time. *Get concrete examples of this process on the following pages.*

Reasoning Process #2: Causation - You need to be able to understand and analyze the complex causes and effects of history (both long-term and short-term, and primary and secondary). For instance, the assassination of Archduke Franz Ferdinand was a short-term cause for World War I, while nationalism, imperialism, alliances, and militarism were long-term causes. A short-term effect of the French Revolution was the removal of the king. A long-term effect was the rise and fall of Napoleon. One might argue a different primary cause for certain events. Of course, that will depend on how extensive your historical evidence is. *Get concrete examples of this process on the following pages.*

Reasoning Process #3: Patterns of Continuity and Change Over Time - Sometimes issues of history continue down the same path. Other times, there is change over time. For instance, decades before the Berlin Conference and imperialism, European countries were already establishing colonies in North and South America. However, anti-imperialist movements of the twentieth century led to great change, and eventual independence of nations. However still, the word neocolonialism was used, as Western nations and corporations continued to utilize labor and resources in developing countries for capital gain. *Get concrete examples of this process on the following pages.*

Concrete Examples of Comparison, Causation, and Continuity/Change

Understanding Comparison, a few examples:

The Industrial Revolution and modern-day globalization are *similar* in that both periods saw corporations and finance emerge, as capitalism affected multiple continents. In addition, both utilized workers on different continents. However, they are *different*, as modern-day globalization has created homogenization throughout the world, and seen a greater degree of interdependence between nations.

Enlightenment thinkers such as Jean-Jacques Rousseau were *similar* to Gandhi in terms of believing one should not obey an unjust law. In addition, both inspired revolution whether in Europe or India. However, Gandhi was *different* in that he used hunger strikes, openly led activities such as the Salt March, and was assassinated by an extremist as he attempted to bring peace to a conflicted region.

Militarily speaking, Napoleon and Nazi Germany were *similar* in that both attempted to invade Russia, and both suffered great losses. In addition, Napoleon was once an ally with Russia, and Germany had a non-aggression pact. They were *different* in that Hitler didn't survive the war, while Napoleon was exiled. In addition, although France would lose power, Germany would be divided into two separate countries after World War II. Furthermore, the Nazis were held responsible for human rights violations at the Nuremberg Trials.

Both the Mughals and Ottomans were *similar*, as they used gunpowder and military strength to achieve an empire. Furthermore, Suleiman the Magnificent and Akbar the Great offered religious tolerance. However, there were *differences*, because whereas the Ottomans weakened as diverse populations experienced nationalism, the Mughals fell when Europeans expanded their trade, as Britain turned India into the "jewel in the crown."

The massacres in Tiananmen Square and at Amritsar were *similar* in that both began as protests against the government. Both led to deaths and casualties. Both also received media attention, as sympathy spread around the world. However, they were *different*, as Amritsar was a protest against imperialism, while Tiananmen Square was against the Chinese government. Amritsar also led to more protests, such as the rise of Gandhi. The Tiananmen Square incident saw limited resistance in its aftermath.

The French, Russian, and Glorious Revolutions were *similar* in that all led to important changes in the political structure of Europe for decades to come. All three also looked to help out classes of people who had been denied success under previous leadership. The Glorious Revolution was *different* in that it was bloodless. The Russian Revolution was *different*, as its long-term effect strengthened dictatorship for over 70 years.

156

Judaism, Christianity, and Islam are *similar* in that they emerged in the Middle East and are monotheistic. However, many *differences* exist, such as dietary restrictions, holiday observance, and core beliefs.

The Renaissance and Enlightenment were *similar* in that both experienced philosophical, artistic, and literary achievements. However, they were *different*, as the Enlightenment affected political revolution around the globe, while the Renaissance was mostly cultural and confined to Europe.

Gold-salt in Africa, the Silk Roads, and Hanseatic League were *similar* systems which created prosperous trade that connected cultures. However, they were *different*, because whereas gold-salt and the Hanseatic League were confined to regional areas, the Silk Roads connected continents thousands of miles apart.

Mansa Musa and Akbar the Great were *similar* in that both were strong leaders who gained much wealth and territory. However, they were *different*, because whereas Mansa Musa encouraged conversion to Islam in Mali, Akbar expressed religious tolerance in the Mughal Empire.

Japan and the New World experienced a *similar* isolation for centuries. During this time, both places developed unique and advanced cultures. However, though isolated, Japan had much interaction with the Eastern World. The Western Hemisphere was quite *different*, as they had no connection with the East. Furthermore, once Japan was opened, they became a strong imperialist nation within a few decades. Native American civilizations such as the Aztec, Maya, and Inca, collapsed within decades of European contact.

The Aztecs and Incas were *similar* in that they were both conquered by conquistadors, and modified their environments for agriculture (floating gardens and terrace farming). Furthermore, religion was affected by a sun god, and pyramids were built. They were *different*, as the Incas had to adapt to the Andes Mountains and utilized a communal public works program for roads. The Aztecs had a complex system of writing. The Inca used quipu to record information on stringed knots.

Zheng He and Columbus were *similar* in that both utilized maritime travel to gain fame and strength. However, they *differed*, as Zheng He's fleet of ships was greater, and he was gaining tribute whereas Columbus was exploring. Furthermore, the travels of Columbus affected both hemispheres, while Zheng He was confined to the east.

Understanding Causation, a few examples
The long-term, and secondary, causes of World War I were militarism, alliance formations, nationalism, and imperialism. The *short-term*, and *primary*, cause was the assassination of Archduke Franz Ferdinand. The *short-term* effects of the war were devastation to the political, economic, and social fabric of Europe. The *long-term* effects included the rise of Adolf Hitler and

defiance of the Treaty of Versailles. Hence, many historians consider the weaknesses of the Treaty of Versailles (and inefficient League of Nations) to be causes for World War II.

The *short* and *long-term* causes of the Enlightenment included centuries of absolute despotism throughout Europe. The short-term effect was the establishment of a limited monarchy, and the American and French Revolutions. The *long-term* effects included revolutions that reached other places such as Latin America.

Two *short-term* causes of the Cold War were Yalta and superpowers emerging from World War II. However, a *long-term* cause was a disdain for communism in the United States that dated back to the Bolshevik Revolution. The *short-term* effects included an arms race, and worldwide strategic positioning. The *long-term* effects included the establishment of NATO, nuclear proliferation, and increased South Korean industry resulting from American aid.

Imperialism had many *short-term* causes, including a desire for resources and markets. However, there was still a *long-term* goal of bringing Christianity to other parts of the world. The *short-term* effects included the Berlin Conference, and carving of China into spheres of influence. The *long-term* effects included Apartheid, the Boxer Rebellion, and the Meiji Era which led to Japan becoming imperialists themselves.

The Russian Revolution was caused by *short-term* dissatisfaction regarding World War I struggles, and *long-term* events such as Bloody Sunday and the Russo-Japanese War. The *short-term* effects were the establishment of a Provisional Government, and rise of Lenin. The *long-term* effects were about 70 years of firm communist rule in the soon-to-be established Soviet Union.

The *short-term* cause (and *primary cause*) of the Protestant Reformation was the posting of Martin Luther's 95 Theses. However, *long-term* causes were prevalent, such as corruption in the Church and the selling of indulgences. The *short-term* effect was the establishment of new sects of Christianity. However, in the *long-term*, religious wars occurred in Europe.

The Chinese Civil War began in the *short-term* when Mao Zedong and the communists gained popularity. However, there had been *long-term* causes such as a desire to end foreign rule, and a hope to bring land reform to peasants. In the *short term*, the People's Republic of China was formed, and the Nationalists retreated to Taiwan. However, *long-term* effects included the spread of communism during the Cold War, and wars relating to communism in Asia.

The *short-term* causes of the Age of Exploration included technological innovations such as the caravel and astrolabe, and *long-term* causes included a desire for new trade routes, a search for wealth and glory, and the spread of Christianity. *Short-term* effects saw conflict between Conquistadors and Native Americans, and the establishment of new colonies. *Long-term* effects were the Columbian Exchange, mercantilism, and the *encomienda* system.

As for the Columbian Exchange mentioned above, that led to **short-term** effects such as the improving of diets, and spread of disease. A **long-term** effect of such a spread of disease was a population shift in the Americas, as European colonists increased in terms of population percentage.

The short-term causes for the Fall of Communism included glasnost, perestroika, and the August Coup. However, **long-term** problems included a lack of economic incentive, oppression under leaders such as Stalin, and a desire for more freedom. The **short-term** effects included the rise of Boris Yeltsin in Russia and Solidarity in Poland. However, **long-term** strife was seen in Bosnia with ethnic cleansing.

The **short-term** pressure for Indian independence included Gandhi's civil disobedience and Salt March. However, **long-term** pressure came from the Amritsar Massacre, and resentment of the British Raj. After India received independence, a **short-term** effect was violence and the Partition of India. A **long-term** effect of conflict between India and Pakistan (both nuclear nations) continued into the twenty-first century.

Understanding Continuity and Change Over Time, a few examples:
The Renaissance displayed a *continuity* of Greek and Roman influence in art, architecture, and literature. The move toward secular themes was a great *change* from the religious themes of the Middle Ages.

The Korean and Vietnam Wars can be seen as a *continuity* of containment, which was experienced in Europe with the Truman Doctrine and the Marshall Plan. The Korean War was a *change* regarding collective security, as the United Nations was involved (unlike the League of Nations, which had no military before World War II).

Nineteenth century imperialism was a *change*, as European nations sought world empires by establishing colonies in Africa and Asia. However, this could also be seen as a *continuity* of colonization in the New World which began with the Encounter c1500.

There has been a *continuity* in terms of communication technology that has evolved from the telegraph, to the telephone, radio, television, and internet. Mostly fueled by technology, a *change* in globalization and global interdependence has occurred in recent decades.

The crop rotation of the Agricultural Revolution can be seen as a *continuation* of the Three-Field System of the Middle Ages. The Agricultural Revolution accompanied the great *change* of the Industrial Revolution which had created labor's high demand for food.

The Industrial Revolution *continued* to spread…starting in England, then going to Europe, the

United States, and the rest of the world. At this time, *change* occurred, as factories, production, and urbanization increased. All the while, there had been a *continuity* of corporations, capital, labor forces, union activity, and problems such as child labor and pollution.

Japan's isolation *continued* for centuries until the middle of the nineteenth century. They had a feudal system which included samurai warriors. However, great *change* came in the Meiji Era as factories, railroads, and production emerged. This change highlighted a *continual* problem, that of a fierce demand for raw materials. Hence, a *change* in foreign policy occurred as Japan imperialized China to secure those materials.

There was a *continuity* of Anti-Semitism in Europe for centuries. The Roman Empire dispersed Jews throughout the Eastern Hemisphere. The Dreyfus Affair in France and programs in Russia happened decades before Adolf Hitler wrote *Mein Kampf*. However, Hitler's continuity of Anti-Semitism was a *change* from earlier methods, as genocide and the Final Solution became a more extreme human rights violation.

Peter the Great *continued* the practice of a strong monarch ruling absolutely over Russia. However, he brought great *change* through westernization. Catherine the Great later *continued* such changes in modernization, and became an enlightened despot who embraced some Enlightenment ideas.

For thousands of years, nomads *continued* to chase food sources such as agriculture and migrating animals. However, a great *change* occurred with the Neolithic Revolution, as new agriculture and animal domestication techniques led to permanent settlements and complex civilizations.

For centuries, China saw great *changes* in its leadership, as dynasties such as the Han, Tang, and Song emerged. As these great political changes occurred, there was still a *continuity* in that the dynastic cycle of leadership was embraced, which explained why dynasties emerged and declined.

Short Answer Practice for the AP World History: Modern Exam

   You need to answer three short answer questions on the test. You might have to analyze historians' interpretations, sources, and propositions regarding history. Questions could include text, images, graphs, or maps. Question 1 is required, and includes one secondary source, and focuses on historical developments or processes between c1200-2001. Question 2 is required, and includes 1 primary source. It focuses on historical developments or processes between c1200-2001. You will then have to choose between Question 3 (1200-1750) and Question 4 (1750-2001). There are no sources included for these questions.

1.   a) Briefly explain TWO arguments which support globalization efforts post-1945.

   b) Briefly contrast and explain TWO arguments which reject globalization efforts post-1945.

   c) Identify and explain TWO organizations, treaties, and/or agreements made post-1945 that fostered globalization efforts.

2.   "The old Roman Empire, which in its decay had divided into an Eastern and a Western Empire (in the fourth century), had by the fifth century succumbed to the new forces which assailed it, leaving only a glittering remnant at Byzantium. The Eastern or Byzantine Empire, rich in pride and pretension, but poor in power, was destined to stand for one thousand years more, the shining conservator of the Christian religion and of Greek culture. It is impossible to imagine what our civilization would be today if this splendid fragment of the Roman Empire had not stood in shining petrification during the ages of darkness, guarding the treasures of a dead past. While these tremendous changes were occurring in the West, unconscious as toiling insects the various peoples in Russia were preparing for an unknown future."

   — Parmele, Mary Platt. *A Short History of Russia*. New York: Charles Scribner's Sons, 1900. 12.

   a) Briefly explain the author's argument concerning the significance of Western Culture.

   b) Briefly explain how ONE nation westernized after 1750.

   c) Briefly explain ONE geographic, religious, or political reason which prevented a specific country from westernizing after 1750.

3.   a) Identify ONE change to a country or region brought upon by a specific economic system c1750-2001.

   b) Explain ONE challenge to an established economic system that took place during this time period.

   c) Briefly explain how an economic system fostered political instability and/or policy change during this time period.

4.   a) Briefly explain the point of view of the artist concerning the political cartoon.

b) Identify TWO events in Africa during the nineteenth century which support the point of view of the cartoon.

c) Identify ONE way the situation in the cartoon continued after 1945, or ONE way it changed.

— Cartoon by Edward Linley Sawbourne, Illus. in: *Punch*, (December 10,1892)

5.   a) Briefly explain how ONE trade network linked the world from c1450 to 1750.

b) Explain how ONE specific item traded in a network mentioned above affected the history of a nation, empire, or dynasty.

c) Briefly explain how ONE region of the world promoted isolation c1450-1750.

6.   a) Briefly explain ONE way in which collective security was utilized in a global conflict between 1945-2001.

b) Identify ONE worldwide cause of a specific global conflict between 1945-2001.

c) Briefly ONE worldwide effect of a specific global conflict between 1945-2001.

7.   a) Identify and explain ONE continuity regarding absolute rule in Europe from 1450 to 1679.

b) Briefly explain ONE change that occurred regarding absolute rule in Europe from 1679-1750.

c) Briefly explain ONE specific change regarding the expansion of labor, political, or social rights in Europe before 1750.

8. Article 1 of the Treaty of Versailles

...Any fully self-governing State, Dominion, or Colony not named in the Annex may become a Member of the League if its admission is agreed to by two-thirds of the Assembly provided that it shall give effective guarantees of its sincere intention to observe its international obligations, and shall accept such regulations as may be prescribed by the League in regard to its military, naval, and air forces and armaments.

Any Member of the League may, after two years' notice of its intention so to do, withdraw from the League, provided that all its international obligations and all its obligations under this Covenant shall have been fulfilled at the time of its withdrawal.

Article 125 of the Treaty of Versailles

Germany renounces all rights under the Conventions and Agreements with France of November 4, 1911, and September 28, 1912, relating to Equatorial Africa. She undertakes to pay to the French Government, in accordance with the estimate to be presented by that Government and approved by the Reparation Commission, all the deposits, credits, advances, etc. ...

Article 165 of the Treaty of Versailles

The maximum number of guns, machine guns, trench-mortars, rifles and the amount of ammunition and equipment which Germany is allowed to maintain during the period between the coming into force of the present Treaty and the date of March 31, 1920...

  a) Briefly explain the purpose of Article 1.

  b) Identify ONE reason a nation would support, or ONE reason a nation would object to any of the above articles.

  c) Evaluate the degree of success for TWO of the above provisions when considering the time period of 1920-1939.

9.   a) Explain ONE similarity concerning the gap between the rich and the poor in both developing and developed nations from 1945-2001.

  b) Describe ONE difference concerning how developed and developing nations have dealt with the widening gap between the rich and the poor.

  c) Briefly explain ONE globalization effort that has improved wealth distribution in developing nations.

10.   "The mob began to get a taste of blood (July 14, 1789)…

"The insensate conduct of the court, which called the Assembly together and then wished to get rid of it, which threatened but dared not act, which provoked yet knew neither how to intimidate nor to coerce, which cherished childish hatreds and had no resolution, in only two months had caused the reformation to deviate from its pacific methods. That fourteenth of July is explained by circumstances and by the state of men's minds. It was, nevertheless, the first of those revolutionary days, which were destined to demoralize the people by habituating them to regard the power and the law as a target against which they could always fire."

— Duruy, Victor. *A General History of the World*. New York: Thomas Y. Crowell & Company, 1898. 415.

a) Explain the author's argument regarding the character of the revolutionaries of France.

b) Briefly explain ONE revolutionary action of the people of France from 1789-1793.

c) Briefly explain ONE short-term or long-term effect of the actions mentioned above.

11.   a) Explain ONE human rights violation which occurred from c1750 to 1941.

b) Explain ONE human rights violation which occurred after 1941.

c) Explain ONE similarity and ONE difference concerning both human rights violations explained above.

12.   a) Explain TWO examples of gender inequality in an empire, dynasty, and/or nation from c1750 to 2001.

b) Provide ONE specific example of change which led to an increase in women's rights in Europe, North America, or South America from c1750 to 2001.

c) Provide ONE specific example of change which led to an increase in women's rights in Asia, Africa, Australia, or the Middle East from c1750 to 2001.

13.   a) Identify and explain ONE method which led to the spread of religion c1750-2001.

b) Identify and explain TWO ways in which assimilation occurred throughout the world during this time.

c) Briefly explain ONE conflict that resulted from a clash between belief systems after 1750.

14. "…The crimes to be punished. The criminality of the German leaders and their associates does not consist solely of individual outrages, but represents the result of a systematic and planned reign of terror within Germany, in the satellite Axis countries, and in the occupied countries of Europe. This conduct goes back at least as far as 1933, when Hitler was first appointed Chancellor of the Reich. It has been marked by mass murders, imprisonments, expulsions and deportations of populations; the starvation, torture and inhuman treatment of civilians; the wholesale looting of public and private property on a scale unparalleled in history; and, after initiation of "total" war, its prosecution with utter and ruthless disregard for the laws and customs of war.

We are satisfied that these atrocities were perpetrated in pursuance of a premeditated criminal plan or enterprise which either contemplated or necessarily involved their commission."
— Report of Robert H. Jackson, United States Representative to the International Conference on Military Trials (London, 1945)

a) Provide TWO specific examples of atrocities from 1933-1945 which support the author's claims.

b) Briefly explain ONE change the world embraced after World War II to end such atrocities.

c) Briefly explain ONE example of a human rights violation continuing after World War II.

15.   a) Provide ONE similarity between mercantilism c1750, and imperialism c1880.

b) Provide ONE difference between mercantilism c1750, and imperialism c1880.

c) Provide ONE example of local resistance to either mercantilism or imperialism in the above time periods.

16.

The Plumb-pudding in danger
— Engraved by James Gillray. London : H. Humphrey, 1805 Feb. 26 [1851 printing]

a) Briefly explain the point of view of the artist concerning world affairs.

b) Briefly explain the historical context for the above cartoon.

c) Briefly explain ONE similarity or difference between Napoleon's Empire and the British Empire in the early nineteenth century.

17.   a) Identify and explain ONE similarity between any two Native American civilizations c1200-c1450.

b) Identify and explain ONE difference between any two Native American civilizations c1200-c1450.

c) Briefly explain ONE cultural, scientific, or architectural achievement of a Native American civilization before 1450.

18.   a) Provide ONE similarity regarding any two movements in the arts from 1750-present.

b) Provide ONE difference regarding any two movements in the arts from 1750-present.

c) Briefly explain how ONE movement in the arts affected a political or social movement in world history.

19.   "Life was so beset with peril that independence or freedom became impossible, and there was developed a society which has lasted almost down to the present time, and which we call Feudalism. The free but weak man gave up his freedom and his lands to some stronger man, who became his lord. He swore obedience to this lord, while the lord engaged to furnish him protection and gave him back his lands to hold as a "fief," both sharing in the product. This lord swore allegiance to some still more powerful man, or "overlord," and became his "vassal," …   Thus were men united into large groups or nations for help or protection. There was little understanding of love of country. Patriotism, as we feel it, was replaced by the passion of fidelity or allegiance to one's feudal superior."
— Barrows, David Prescott. *A History of the Philippines*. New York. American Book Company, 1905. 43.

a) Explain the author's argument concerning the relationship between feudalism and patriotism.

b) Provide ONE piece of historical evidence which helps support the author's argument.

c) Briefly explain ONE reason why feudalism began to disappear in Europe.

20.   a) Provide TWO reasons as to why pollution has continued to increase in South America or Asia since 1970.

b) Briefly explain ONE change the world has looked to implement to decrease global pollution since 1970.

c) Provide ONE obstacle which prevents worldwide reduction of greenhouse gas emissions.

166

Writing a DBQ and a Long Essay

Section II will consist of a DBQ and a Long Essay. First, let's talk about the Document Based Question (DBQ) essay, where you will be given a question followed by a series of seven documents. The topics tend to be general and the question looks to address the *AP Historical Thinking Skills and Reasoning Processes* (see earlier). The DBQ will be on a topic from 1450-2001.

You can succeed on the DBQ if you answer "yes" to the following:
1. Do I have a detailed **thesis**?
2. Did I put the documents into **historical context**?
3. Did I utilize at least six of the documents to **support the argument**?
4. Is my **outside information** impressive?
5. On at least three documents, did I explain the relevance towards the argument regarding the **audience, purpose, historical situation, or author's point of view**?
6. Did I demonstrate a **complex understanding** of what the question is looking for? Did I use evidence to corroborate, modify, or qualify an argument?

Let's assume we have a DBQ that offers the following question:
1. Compare and contrast the major social, economic, and political issues of the nineteenth and twentieth centuries, and evaluate the extent to which they caused conflict.

Grouping Documents

Every DBQ sets up a task that will divide documents into different groups. Read the question first, and then make a grid that looks like this:

Document Number

Social	
Economic	
Political	

As you go through each document, put its number in the proper place on the grid. Let's assume that your documents are as follows:

1. Primary source from a Chinese Boxer rebel expressing anger for the spread of Christianity in China.
2. Austrian newspaper article detailing the assassination of Archduke Franz Ferdinand.
3. Speech from British official embracing the Berlin Conference.
4. Map of the world showing the transfer of opium throughout the British Empire.

5. An appeal to the United Nations to end apartheid.
6. Map showing the raw materials available to Japan after their invasion of Manchuria in 1931.
7. An Armenian family's story about escaping persecution after World War I.

After flipping through the documents, you have determined that your grid now looks like this:

Document Number

Social	1, 5, 7
Economic	4, 6
Political	2, 3

Thesis = 1 Point (The Essay is Worth 7 Points in Total)

The exam wants you to make a defensible thesis or claim which responds to all parts of the question. Be warned! ***Do not just use the sentence they give you as the thesis.*** We know that there are economic, political, and social causes for conflict. If you get a little creative, it will help your grade.

Average Thesis: The economic, political, and social issues of the nineteenth and twentieth centuries created division and conflict around the world.

Better Thesis: Although economic, political, and social divisions were similar in that they brought about increased tensions and global conflict, economic motivations were more powerful in that they ultimately caused immense political and social strife.

The second thesis shows a greater level of creative and critical thinking. Often, starting your thesis with a word like "although" will send you on the right path to comparing *and* contrasting, or showing continuity *and* change. Your thesis doesn't have to be as elaborate as above, but this example should help you understand critical thinking.

Evidence from the Documents = 2 Points

Mark up those documents in the 15 minute reading period! Include only the vital bits and pieces from them. Use the clock or bring a noiseless watch to the testing site, and keep an eye out on the time! You should be able to write down in the margin of each document the answers to the following:
1. What are the important and relevant details of this document?
2. Where does it fit into my essay, and how does it relate to the history reasoning process targeted?
3. How can I use this information to support the argument?

Don't just quote…analyze and utilize the documents to support that all-important thesis! *For both points,* you must support the argument by accurately describing at least *six* of the documents. Accurately describing three documents will help you only get one point.

Evidence Beyond the Documents = 1 Point; Contextualization = 1 Point

No Bull, you need to have a lot of evidence beyond the documents, or outside information. *You will not get credit for only providing a phrase!* As you go through each document, jot down notes in the margins.

I don't see anything about the Treaty of Nanjing. That's political outside information.
I don't see anything about resistance to apartheid. That's social outside information.
I don't see anything about diamonds in South Africa. That's economic outside information.

Throw it in. Show *impressive detail,* or a great scope of knowledge, to get this point. *It must relate to the prompt and argument. A phrase won't cut it!*

Impressive Detail: On June 28, 1914, Austrian Archduke Franz Ferdinand was assassinated in Sarajevo by a Serbian nationalist named Gavrilo Princip. The assassination set off a chain reaction that caused World War I.

Impressive Detail: After European nations divided up Africa at the Berlin Conference, there was still conflict in South Africa, as the superior British military fought the Second Boer War c1900.

Do you see the difference? Throw in a fact here, a year there. That's impressive detail!

Similar to your outside knowledge, you must show *contextualization*. In other words, you must connect the documents to the larger picture of events, processes, and developments occurring before, during, or after. *You can't use the same outside knowledge for your contextualization.* So, if the document is about the rise of fascism, connect it to the Treaty of Versailles. If it's on Japanese imperialism, link it to the Meiji Era and modernization of Japan. But like above, be in-depth, as a phrase just won't cut it.

Analysis and Reasoning = 2 Points

For at least **three** documents, you should point out the Historical *Situation, Audience, Point of View, and/or Purpose* and explain why it is relevant to the argument. For instance, in Document 2, the *Historical Situation* would be the uneasy calm before World War I. The *Audience* would be the Austrian public who would see the event as a national tragedy. The *Purpose* would be to inform about hostilities and conflict. The *Point of View* would be sympathetic, angry, and perhaps suggest retribution. This effort is worth one point.

Now for the final point: Complex Understanding. This question is looking for you to *compare and contrast*. Don't just show similarities…show differences as well! If they ask for *continuity and change*, **SHOW BOTH!** If they ask a question about *causation*, show short-term and long-term causes, as well as short-term and long-term effects. This will display a higher level of understanding. **You get one point** for this type of complex understanding. For the point, you could also analyze multiple variables, qualify or modify an argument by looking at alternative views or evidence, explain relevant connections across different time periods, or confirm an argument's truth by looking at perspectives in different themes.

The Long Essay

The Long Essay is what you might consider a standard essay. You will be given a question, and might have to consider how history changed, or remained the same over time. Or, perhaps it's an essay targeting the skill of comparison, or causation. Nonetheless, this essay will need a thesis and historical evidence to support that thesis. Your goal is to persuade the reader that your thesis is sound and well-supported by historical facts. Introduction and conclusion paragraphs are required. You will write one of three choices (1200-1750, 1450-1900, or 1750-2001). Each choice will address both the same skill and reasoning process.

Point 1 - Thesis

Similar to the DBQ, you must have an original thesis that reflects all parts of the task and the reasoning process being targeted. If you just copy the statement they give you then ... SORRY!

NOTE: They may ask you to "Support, Modify, or Refute" a question. If this happens, on say, a "turning point" question:

Support Thesis: The Russian Revolution was a turning point because...

Modify Thesis: Although the Russian Revolution was a turning point because..., it also cannot be considered one, as...

Refute Thesis: The Russian Revolution was not a turning point because...

NOTE: You can do any of three. If you choose to "Modify," this might give you an opportunity to write more and show you can understand both sides of the argument!

Point 2 - Contextualization

Similar to what was seen with the DBQ, you must show *contextualization*.

Points 3-4 - Evidence

You must *argue* your thesis. The degree to which you *argue the thesis with specific and relevant evidence* will determine if you get 0, 1, or 2 points. The more analysis, explanation, and linkage between evidence and thesis, the more likely you are to succeed. Therefore, it is recommended that you write a lot! Show all you know! This is where studying comes in. For the long essay, you should be examining major concepts and time periods more so than the miniscule facts. Although you shouldn't get an essay devoted only to Shah Jahan, you might get one that is relevant to Gunpowder Empires and state building.

Points 5-6 – Analysis and Reasoning

You need to dig deep to get both points. You could use evidence to corroborate, modify, or qualify the argument addressed by the question. You should have a deep and complex understanding of the history and skill in the prompt. **See the DBQ information for more on Analysis and Reasoning, and Complex Understanding.**

Be sure to read our concrete examples of continuity and change over time, causation, and comparison. They are critical for understanding connections throughout history.

For the long essay, you will have three options: 1200-1750, 1450-1900, and 1750-2001. Here are some practice long essay prompts to consider:

1. Evaluate the extent to which the spread of Hinduism, Buddhism, and Christianity can be considered a turning point in world history, while analyzing the effects of one religion from 1200-1750.

2. Develop an argument that describes continuities and changes concerning European-African connections from 1200-1750.

3. Analyze the continuities and changes regarding global relationships between nations from Europe and Asia c1945-2001.

4. Explain similarities and differences when comparing the causes and effects of the French and Russian revolutions.

5. Evaluate the extent to which technological innovation and environmental alteration helped transform societies between 1700 and 1900.

6. Explain similarities and differences concerning global interactions of trade when considering the time period of 1500 to 1750.

7. Develop an argument that analyzes the important short-term and long-term causes and effects regarding industrialization from 1700-1900.

8. Evaluate continuities and changes concerning the presence of human rights in Europe and Africa from 1850 to 2001.

9. Develop an argument that analyzes the short-term and long-term causes and effects concerning global adaptations to geography from 1200-1750.

10. Evaluate the extent to which the fall of communism can be considered a turning point in world history while analyzing both its causes and effects.

No Bull Tips for the SAT Subject Test

On the SAT Subject Test you will have 60 minutes to complete 95 questions. There are no essays.

Time Periods:
Prehistory and civilizations to the year 500 CE - 25%
500 to 1500 CE – 20%
1500 to 1900 – 25%
Post 1900 – 20%
Cross-chronological – 10%

Geographical Material:
Global or comparative – 25%
Europe – 25%
Africa – 10%
Southwest Asia – 10%
South and Southeast Asia – 10%
East Asia – 10%
The Americas (excluding the United States) – 10%

Each question has five choices. The test is graded out of 800 points.

No Bull Disclaimer: Students are always looking for an edge. But sometimes, they do very well just by their own abilities. We don't recommend changing your style drastically if you are scoring well. In this section, we will give advice to those who have trouble finishing the test on time. **Here are five tips to help you finish your test strongly in the allotted time constraint:**

No Bull Tip #1, You're on the Clock

Wear a noiseless watch, look at the clock. When you have 95 questions to answer in an hour, things can get tough. That's why you don't have to just know your stuff, but you have to be able to answer multiple choice questions with some degree of speed. *On the SAT Subject Test, you will find some questions noticeably easier than others.* Specifically, give yourself enough time for **EXCEPT** or **"not"** questions. These tend to take a longer time to answer. If you are too leisurely with your time, you might not finish your test.

No Bull Tip #2, Be Careful on Centuries

"Nineteenth century"...Cross it out! People don't think in terms of centuries, they think in terms of years. Some of the questions might say: *In the early nineteenth century...* Cross out "early nineteenth century," and write down 1800-1820...Make "mid-twentieth century" 1950-1960. Oftentimes, students get confused as to which time-period the question is referring to. This eats up precious time! As honor students, you are very smart. But, you are still human. Don't be 100 years off because of a simple mistake. Cross it out.

No Bull Tip #3, Know When to Omit

If you are stuck on a question, don't stare it at for an eternity. Here's our guide for guessing: On the SAT Subject Test, we suggest you consider ***playing the probability***. If you can eliminate two of the five choices, you might want to answer the question.

For every question you get wrong, you lose 1/4 of a point. So, if you have 3 choices to choose from, your odds are now 1 in 3...if you can get down to two choices, it's 1 in 2. If you are correct 1 out of every 3 guesses, you come out ahead. If you get just 1 out of every 4 guesses right, you break even. If you are looking to get a high score, then you cannot afford to omit too many questions. If you get a question about someone who you've never heard of, that's when you probably should omit. There's a list of some people you may never have heard of on the No Bull Review Sheet. ***But if you are looking to get a grade higher than 700, you shouldn't omit too many.***

No Bull Tip #4, For Those Who Struggle With Time: Skip the Long Passages, For Now

We recommend this tip for people who struggle with the time constraint. If questions have difficult graphs or long passages to read, then answer them last. They are time consuming, and are only worth one question. You could do five questions in the same time it takes to read one long passage.

If you follow this strategy, and you do run out of time, it's as if you only omitted a few questions...rather than half of the test.

BEWARE though: Make sure you skip the choice on your answer sheet, as to not mess up your answer order. If time is ***not*** a factor for you, then we recommend answering the test in normal sequence.

No Bull Tip #5, Bubble in Your Answers NOW!

On most tests, it is recommended to circle an answer on the test, and then go back over each question before bubbling in your answer-sheet. This could be risky on the SAT Subject Test.

This again depends on how you are as a test taker. It could take you over 5 minutes to bubble in an answer sheet during a test. You might not have that much time to spare.

100 More SAT Subject Test Practice Questions

1. The Neolithic Revolution was important because it
   A) established new writing systems in Mesopotamia
   B) paved the way for independent nation states
   C) provided agricultural techniques necessary for permanent settlements
   D) led people to question natural rights for the first time
   E) led to the migration of people into Asia

2. Civilizations tend to develop near
   A) rivers
   B) mountain ranges
   C) equatorial latitudes
   D) the center of land masses
   E) dense forests

3. Christianity and Judaism have similarities in their
   A) high holy day observances
   B) beliefs in monotheism
   C) acceptance of reincarnation
   D) teachings that all living creatures have souls
   E) origins in the Roman Empire

4. All of the following were associated with writing systems EXCEPT:
   A) ziggurats
   B) glyphs
   C) cuneiform
   D) hieroglyphics
   E) papyrus

5. The Silk Roads linked all of the following cultures EXCEPT:
   A) Rome
   B) China
   C) India
   D) Mesoamerica
   E) Eastern Europe

6. *"If a man destroys the eye of another man, they shall destroy his eye."*
   The above quote could be found in
   A) Justinian's Code
   B) The Old Testament
   C) Twelve Tables of Law
   D) Pericles' Direct Democracy Decree
   E) Hammurabi's Code

Use the following for Questions 7 and 8:

"Table IX. (From the Twelve Tables)
   "4. The penalty shall be capital for a judge or arbiter legally appointed who has been found guilty of receiving a bribe for giving a decision.
   "5. Treason: he who shall have roused up a public enemy or handed over a citizen to a public enemy must suffer capital punishment.
   "6. Putting to death of any man, whosoever he might be unconvicted is forbidden."

7. The above excerpt from the Twelve Tables is attributed to which city?
   A) Athens
   B) Sparta
   C) Rome
   D) Byzantium
   E) Mesopotamia

8. Which is true according to the excerpt?
   A) capital punishment was illegal
   B) betraying the state and judicial system was a fate worthy of death
   C) trials were not used to determine guilt
   D) the accused benefitted from great mercy
   E) women's equality was held sacred

9. All of the following leaders preached religious tolerance EXCEPT:
   A) King Nebuchadnezzar II
   B) Akbar the Great
   C) Ashoka
   D) Suleiman the Magnificent
   E) Mohandas Gandhi

10. The Tang and the Song were associated with the development of all of the following EXCEPT:
   A) paper currency
   B) porcelain
   C) movable type printing
   D) caravel ships
   E) mechanical clock

11. Chivalry of the knight in feudal European culture was similar to what Japanese code?
   A) Kabuki
   B) Haiku
   C) Bushido
   D) Shintoism
   E) Animism

12. The above architecture is considered
   A) Classical
   B) Baroque
   C) Gothic
   D) Romanesque
   E) Rococo

13. Direct democracy in Greece during the Age of Pericles involved
   A) electing representatives to a life-term in the Senate
   B) equality of women in the legislating process
   C) the election of both men and women to judicial offices
   D) two kings ruling on behalf of the people
   E) allowing citizens to create laws as an assembly

14. Which agricultural technique was used first?
   A) Slash-and-burn farming
   B) Three-Field System
   C) Use of the Seed Drill
   D) Wheelbarrow farming
   E) Crop Rotation

15.   • Gupta Empire
      • Deccan Plateau
      • Ganges River
All of the above are associated with which modern-day country?
   A) India
   B) Mongolia
   C) China
   D) Afghanistan
   E) Iraq

16. Hellenistic Culture can best be described as
    A) an Egyptian religious movement
    B) a combination of cultures within Alexander the Great's Empire
    C) the breaking away of the Byzantine Empire from Rome
    D) the abandonment of Confucianism in the Qin Dynasty
    E) a schism in religious adherence

17. Legalism of the Chinese was similar to the writings of Niccolò Machiavelli in that both
    A) celebrated freedom of speech as a guaranteed right
    B) emphasized the importance of private property
    C) celebrated the concept of a limited monarchy
    D) believed that citizens had to be ruled by strict and powerful governments
    E) were documented during the Middle Ages

Use the following map for Questions 18 and 19.

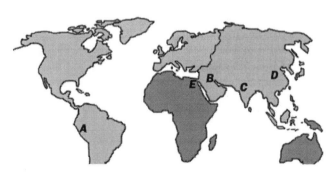

18. In which of the above would one find the ancient civilizations of Harappa and Mohenjo-daro?
    A) A
    B) B
    C) C
    D) D
    E) E

19. Which area would be in the Andes Mountain Range?
    A) A
    B) B
    C) C
    D) D
    E) E

20. Who was at the bottom of the social hierarchy of European feudalism?
    A) Lords
    B) Vassals
    C) Knights
    D) Kings
    E) Serfs

21. The development of the Russian language was most dependent on which alphabet?
    A) Bantu
    B) Greek
    C) Latin
    D) Arabic
    E) Cyrillic

22. The schism of the Church that occurred in 1054 led to
    A) new Protestant sects in Eastern Europe
    B) Roman Catholicism in the West and Eastern Orthodox in the Byzantine Empire
    C) England becoming Anglican
    D) a Pope in Rome, and a Pope in France
    E) religious wars in France

23. The Crusades were fought over
    A) a controversy involving the selling of sacraments
    B) control of the Holy Land
    C) land disputes within the feudal system
    D) a split in the Catholic Church
    E) claims to trading rights on the Silk Roads

24. Thomas Aquinas and Averroës were similar in that both
    A) were scholars of Islam
    B) used Greek philosophy in their study of religion
    C) were excommunicated for their beliefs
    D) expressed a devotion to polytheism
    E) supported religious scholarship from the Far East

25. A direct result of the Crusades was
    A) a split in the Catholic Church
    B) European control of Jerusalem
    C) an increase in cultural diffusion
    D) the fall of the Ottoman Empire
    E) the rise of Henry VIII

26. What impact did the bubonic plague have on the Catholic Church in the fourteenth century?
    A) There was a decreased faith in the Church as prayers went unanswered
    B) Because of the need for prayer, the Church's power grew by the end of the plague
    C) Many Catholics converted to Judaism and Islam
    D) The plague directly caused the Protestant Reformation
    E) New religious sects prospered in Germany

27. Terrace farming was used extensively by which Empire of the Andes Mountains?
    A) Mayan
    B) Toltec
    C) Aztec
    D) Incan
    E) Olmec

28. Today, there is an incomplete history of the Mayan Empire because the
    A) wars between the Aztecs and Mayans wiped out most written records
    B) Mayans did not have a written form of record-keeping
    C) Spanish burned or destroyed much of the historical record
    D) language can't be interpreted
    E) Mayans erased their historical records at the onset of the Encounter

29. Pyramids in Egypt and structures like the one above from Native America both
    A) were made out of clay
    B) look similar despite a lack of cultural contact
    C) had no mortar to hold the stones in place
    D) were used for human sacrifice
    E) were damaged by Ottoman invaders

30. Besides the Indus, which river was most associated with early civilizations in India?
    A) Nile
    B) Yangtze
    C) Tigris
    D) Ganges
    E) Huang He

31. Bantu migrations were most important in Africa because they
A) led to the development of languages still used today
B) opened Africa to trade with European nations
C) eliminated reliance on hunting and gathering
D) blended both Arabic and African cultures
E) led directly to a thriving Zimbabwe

32. Marco Polo's world travels were most similar to those of
A) Suleiman the Magnificent
B) Mansa Musa
C) Shah Abbas
D) Ibn Battuta
E) Akbar the Great

33. All of the following empires were associated with the subcontinent of India EXCEPT:
A) Mughal Empire
B) Gupta Empire
C) Mauryan Empire
D) Delhi Sultanate
E) Umayyad Empire

34. Mansa Musa was influential, as he
A) helped spread Islam to the African Kingdom of Mali
B) was a great traveler who went from Africa to Asia
C) was the first African king to sell his people into slavery
D) ended the gold-salt trade and isolated western Africa
E) pushed back advances of the Roman Empire

35. Which of the following reflects the most influential religious teachings of John Calvin?
A) Divine right was not protected by the Bible
B) The use of icons was necessary for successful prayer
C) A person's salvation was predetermined by God
D) The Pope was the highest authority in Christianity
E) The sale of indulgences should be protected

36. Pope Alexander VI hoped to bring peace between Spain and Portugal in 1493 by
A) instituting a line of demarcation for exploration
B) taking land from both nations and adding it to the Church
C) outlawing all further conquests in the New World
D) making Catholic nations share gold taken from their colonies
E) dividing the spoils of the Mayan Empire between them

37. Shortly before 1500, Portugal took advantage of the East Coast of Africa because of its
A) proximity to Mesoamerica
B) riches of gold, ivory, animal skins, and other resources
C) market for selling finished textile goods
D) location near Australian markets
E) proximity to the Atlantic Ocean

38. The Peace of Augsburg and the Thirty Years' War both reflected the
A) severity of religious division in Europe
B) need for the Pope to intervene during the Age of Exploration
C) popularity of Enlightenment philosophy
D) splits within the Anglican Church of England
E) instablity of Spain's monarch succession

39.   1. Black Plague
      2. Fall of Rome
      3. Protestant Reformation
      4. Elizabethan Age

Put the above in their proper chronological order.
  A) 1 - 2 - 3 - 4
  B) 2 - 1 - 4 - 3
  C) 1 - 3 - 2 - 4
  D) 1 - 3 - 4 - 2
  E) 2 - 1 - 3 - 4

40. Classical ideas regarding humanism and Western Heritage came from
  A) Greece and Rome
  B) Byzantium and Constantinople
  C) England and France
  D) Ancient Mesopotamia
  E) Chinese river valleys

41. Algebra, astronomy, calligraphy and the Abbasid Empire were all associated with which region?
  A) Asia
  B) Middle East
  C) Europe
  D) Native America
  E) Ghana

42. The Khmer Empire in the year 1200 was similar to the ancient Phoenicians in that both
  A) established dominance through sea travel
  B) produced alphabets adopted by the west
  C) traded extensively in the Mediterranean
  D) constructed magnificent Hindu temples
  E) influenced settlement in mountain regions

43. Though many years apart, the Han and Tang dynasties of China both fell partly because of
  A) economic instability and famine
  B) warfare with invading Germanic tribes
  C) overexpansion into parts of India
  D) discontent over a lack of civil liberties
  E) religious persecution of the people

44. Traditional African and Native American cultures c1000 CE were based on
  A) fascism
  B) industrialization
  C) a command economy
  D) agriculture
  E) laissez-faire capitalism

45. Which of the following Empires controlled the most territory at the peak of their rule?
  A) Mongol Empire
  B) Byzantine Empire
  C) Alexander the Great
  D) Holy Roman Empire
  E) Mughal Empire

46. Of the following, the one with the greatest fleet of ships was
  A) Vasco da Gama
  B) Christopher Columbus
  C) Zheng He
  D) Ferdinand Magellan
  E) Hernán Cortés

47. The system of mercantilism involved
  A) developing large standing armies
  B) acquiring raw materials from colonies
  C) gaining military bases in the Pacific
  D) seeking alliances with nations within Central Europe
  E) development of social connections

48. Louis XIV's absolute rule in France, and Joseph Stalin's totalitarian government in the Soviet Union both
    A) commanded all economic production
    B) divided all land among the peasants
    C) preached atheism
    D) expanded power of the rich
    E) limited political civil liberties

49. Which of the following is paired with his proper writing?
    A) Charles Darwin - *The Communist Manifesto*
    B) Mao Zedong - *The Social Contract*
    C) Simón Bolívar - *Little Red Book of Quotations*
    D) Maximilien Robespierre - *The Prince*
    E) John Locke - *Two Treatises of Government*

50. *"Man is born free, and everywhere he is in chains."*
The intention of this quote by Jean-Jacques Rousseau was to
    A) defend absolutism and divine right
    B) call to arms the peasants of Russia
    C) limit the power of the Roman Catholic Church in everyday affairs
    D) bring more rights to workers in labor unions
    E) encourage the disobeying of unjust laws

51. In the seventeenth and eighteenth centuries, Enlightenment thinkers wanted a society where
    A) the factors of production could be owned by the people
    B) natural rights would be protected
    C) the government would take its *hands off* the economy
    D) absolute monarchs could rule with divine right
    E) private property would be divided amongst the peasants

52. The theocracy of Egypt and the Mandate of Heaven of China were similar to European ideas regarding
    A) The Protestant Reformation
    B) Divine Right
    C) Enlightened Despotism
    D) Imperialism
    E) agricultural reform

53. Which style was a reaction to baroque architecture of the early eighteenth century?
    A) Classical
    B) Impressionism
    C) Realism
    D) Gothic
    E) Neoclassical

54. Which was true of the punishments of Galileo and Socrates?
    A) Socrates admitted his methods were flawed and was released
    B) Galileo was put to death for his claims
    C) Socrates died for his beliefs while Galileo did not
    D) Both men were set free after protests of the people
    E) Socrates was punished after Galileo was

55.   • Humanism
      • *The David*
      • The Medici Family

All of the above were associated with
    A) The Dark Ages
    B) The Enlightenment
    C) The Renaissance
    D) The Scientific Revolution
    E) The Glorious Revolution

56. Which was a goal of Peter the Great in his westernization of Russia in the early eighteenth century?

A) Ridding the country of Mongol influence
B) Taking part in the Industrial Revolution
C) Securing overseas colonies in Africa
D) Adopting the teachings of Karl Marx
E) Establishing communes for the peasants

57. Those of Spanish descent that could hold high office in the New World were called

A) Peninsulares
B) Creoles
C) Mestizos
D) Mulattos
E) Native Americans

58. José San Martin and Simón Bolívar were mostly associated with

A) philosophical writings of the Enlightenment
B) Latin American independence movements
C) the divine right theory of government
D) slave revolts in the Caribbean
E) Communist activities in Latin America

59. In the nineteenth century, demands in the Western Hemisphere for self-rule were inspired by

A) European Enlightenment thought
B) promises of economic supremacy
C) a desire for religious freedoms
D) support for absolutism
E) resistance against the *encomienda* system

60. Maximilien Robespierre's Reign of Terror aimed to

A) assassinate Enlightenment thinkers such as John Locke
B) eliminate all opposition to the French Revolution
C) destroy the Committee of Public Safety
D) restore the Bourbon family to the throne
E) esablish an Estates General for the first time

61. All of the following were examples of cultural diffusion EXCEPT:

A) Columbian Exchange
B) Silk Roads
C) Westernization of Russia
D) Continental System
E) Globalization

62. Which of the following was true of the Napoleonic Code?

A) It reflected mostly all of Justinian's Code
B) Women's rights were limited, as was freedom of speech
C) The Code severely limited the ruler's power
D) It was written to increase Jacobin authority
E) It was based almost entirely on the earlier codes of the Byzantine Empire

63. A coup d'état was accomplished by

A) Simón Bolívar
B) John Locke
C) Mao Zedong
D) Napoleon Bonaparte
E) Winston Churchill

64. All of the following were associated with the Industrial Revolution in England in the late eighteenth century EXCEPT:
A) Steam powered vessels
B) Urbanization
C) Entrepreneur opportunities
D) Socialism
E) Agricultural improvements

65. The Sepoy Mutiny and the Boxer Rebellion were similar in that both
A) began in western China
B) led to the development of industrialization in Asia
C) failed to put an end to European imperialism
D) ended the practice of spheres of influence
E) resisted the Open Door Policy

66. How did the Meiji Era of the nineteenth century affect Japan in the twentieth century?
A) A return to isolation continued into the twentieth century
B) A lasting peace led to the development of new religious practices
C) There was an increase in European spheres of influence within Japan in the twentieth century
D) Revolutions in Japan led to the removal of the Emperor
E) Massive industrialization transformed Japan into an imperial power

67. Which of the following artists was associated with the impressionism and post-impressionism movements of the nineteenth century?
A) Rembrandt van Rijn
B) Jan van Eyck
C) Leonardo da Vinci
D) Jan Vermeer
E) Vincent Van Gogh

68. In laissez-faire economics, Adam Smith argued that governments should
A) provide the greatest good for the greatest amount of people
B) abandon capitalism in favor of socialism
C) heavily tax the biggest businesses
D) regulate the stock market to prevent unfair trading practices
E) allow for free markets to trade without government intervention

69. Which of the following is matched up with the territory they conquered?
A) Hernán Cortés – Aztec Empire
B) Adolf Hitler - Soviet Union
C) Napoleon Bonaparte - Britain
D) Kublai Khan - Japan
E) Alexander the Great - Mesoamerica

70.   1. Age of Enlightenment
      2. French Revolution
      3. American Revolution
      4. Latin American Independence Movements

Put the above in their proper chronological order
A) 1 - 4 - 3 - 2
B) 3 - 1 - 4 - 2
C) 1 - 3 - 2 - 4
D) 2 - 4 - 1 - 3
E) 3 - 1 - 2 - 4

71. Otto von Bismarck's newly unified Germany gained territory
A) from the Pope
B) through international conflict
C) from the Eastern Orthodox Church
D) after a land purchase from Russia
E) which was annexed from Spain

72. The major cause for massive emigration from Ireland c1845 was
   A) war with the British mainland
   B) failure of the potato crop
   C) Napoleon's invasion
   D) religious wars in Northern Ireland
   E) heavy taxation and inflation

73. By 1900, which country gained the most land from the Berlin Conference and the Age of Asian Imperialism?
   A) Britain
   B) France
   C) Netherlands
   D) Germany
   E) Spain

74. Whose scientific theories were used to justify imperialist activity in the late nineteenth century?
   A) Albert Einstein
   B) Guglielmo Marconi
   C) Sigmund Freud
   D) Charles Darwin
   E) Nicolaus Copernicus

75. The Treaty of Versailles provided for
   A) an international peace-keeping organization
   B) aid to Germany to help rebuild defense plants
   C) the restoration of monarchs to Spain and France
   D) an official surrender of the Allied Powers
   E) Alsace-Lorraine to be ceded to the Germans

76. Protests in Amritsar, India and St. Petersburg, Russia in the early twentieth century ended when
   A) citizens received reforms from the government
   B) the military killed many demonstrators
   C) new elections were scheduled
   D) communist demands were met
   E) imperialist nations agreed to treaty negotiations

77. Which of the following locations would the above monument of the Khmer Empire be located?
   A) Cambodia
   B) India
   C) Iraq
   D) Mesoamerica
   E) Persia

78. Joseph Stalin's Five Year Plan in the Soviet Union and Mao Zedong's Great Leap Forward in China were similar in that both
A) attempted to dramatically increase production
B) had universal support among the people
C) were considered successful by historians
D) allowed unions to collectively bargain for wages and reforms
E) relied on capitalistic principles

79. All of the following were supporters of the Allied powers in World War II EXCEPT:
A) France
B) Great Britain
C) Japan
D) China
E) United States

80. Which of the following was used by Joseph Stalin, but NOT Adolf Hitler?
A) A secret police
B) Immense propaganda campaigns
C) Division of land among the people
D) Use of work camps for those considered enemies of the state
E) Reliance on free enterprise

81. Which of the following was true of *glasnost* in the late twentieth century?
A) Mao Zedong welcomed criticism from the people
B) There was strict enforcement of communism in the Soviet Union
C) The Cultural Revolution brought Roman Catholicism to China
D) New ideas from the Soviet people were welcomed
E) Aggressive industrialization was encouraged

82. Dr. Martin Luther King, Jr. and Mohandas Gandhi were similar in that
A) the writings of Machiavelli were influential to their beliefs
B) both helped gain independence for their nations
C) violence was used to achieve civil rights
D) both disobeyed government laws seen as unjust
E) neither were imprisoned for their acts of protest

83. Mohandas Gandhi's Salt March was most similar to the actions taken by which organization in the twentieth century?
A) ISIS
B) Tamil Tigers
C) NATO
D) Taliban
E) African National Congress

84. Which of the following can be traced to the Achaemenid Empire ?
A) Grand Canal
B) Three Gorges Dam
C) Great Royal Road
D) Suez Canal
E) Silk Roads

85. All of the following were examples of Anti-Semitism EXCEPT:
A) Kristallnacht
B) Camp David Accords
C) Pogroms
D) Dreyfus Affair
E) Final Solution

86. How did the partition of India in 1947 compare to the reunification of Germany in 1990?

A) Both events were originally prevented by a UN resolution

B) Germany unified under communism, whereas India did not

C) Both processes were accompanied by war

D) India remained one country, while Germany's reunification was short-lived

E) Unlike Germany, India's partition was accompanied by religious conflict

87. The policy of détente was used during the Cold War to

A) provoke North Korea into invading South Korea

B) increase the manufacturing of nuclear weapons

C) help return Cuba to its pre-communist state

D) stop the spread of communism to Korea and Vietnam

E) decrease the level of political tension

88. Which of the following human rights violations took place in Southeast Asia?

A) Pol Pot's massacre of opponents to the Khmer Rouge

B) Hitler's Final Solution

C) Hutu killings of the Tutsis

D) Armenian massacres during and after World War I

E) Anti-Semitic pogroms

89. Which of the following civilizations had the greatest impact on Roman religious rituals, art, and architecture?

A) Celts

B) Etruscans

C) Hittites

D) Persians

E) Sumerians

90. The Tamil Tigers were concerned with obtaining

A) freedoms of speech and assembly

B) a permanent homeland

C) women's rights

D) elimination of the caste system

E) a secular state in Eastern Africa

91. Who of the following gave significant rights to women?

A) Napoleon Bonaparte

B) Mao Zedong

C) Louis XIV

D) Genghis Khan

E) Philip II

92. Westernization was an objective of all of the following EXCEPT:

A) Reza Pahlavi, the Shah of Iran

B) Peter the Great of Russia

C) Emperor Mutsohito of Japan

D) The Taliban of Afghanistan

E) Jawaharlal Nehru of India

93. In 1989, the government of Deng Xiaoping responded to protests in Tiananmen Square by

A) displaying a strong military presence

B) passing the Four Modernizations

C) eliminating the One-Child Policy

D) extending rights to freedom of assembly

E) calling in UN troops to diffuse the situation

94. Mikhail Gorbachev's perestroika was most similar to which other communist policy?

A) Lenin's NEP

B) Stalin's totalitarian rule

C) Mao's Great Leap Forward

D) The Cultural Revolution of China

E) Stalin's Five-Year Plan

95. Which of the following was an example of Zionism?
   A) Six-Day War
   B) Yom Kippur War
   C) Russian pogroms
   D) Dreyfus Affair
   E) Balfour Declaration

96. Which statement is true of the twenty-first century when compared to the fifteenth century?
   A) There were many more religious sects in the fifteenth century than there are today
   B) The world in the twenty-first century has a greater degree of globalization
   C) There is less pollution today because of legislation looking to decrease carbon emissions
   D) The fifteenth century presented a greater degree of democratic reforms
   E) Both time periods experienced a "Little Ice Age"

97. The Neolithic Revolution and the Green Revolution were similar in that both
   A) were limited to Europe and Asia
   B) decreased the need to settle into permanent civilizations
   C) increased the life expectancy of certain populations
   D) led to divisions among religious sects
   E) spread disease to both hemispheres of the globe

———————

"Albeit, the King's Majesty justly and rightfully is and oweth to be the supreme head of the Church of England, and so is recognised by the clergy of this realm in their Convocations; yet nevertheless for corroboration and confirmation thereof, and for increase of virtue in Christ's religion within this realm of England, and to repress and extirpate all errors, heresies and other enormities and abuses heretofore used in the same, Be it enacted by authority of this present Parliament that the King our sovereign lord, his heirs and successors kings of this realm, shall be taken, accepted and reputed the only supreme head in earth of the Church of England ..."
   – Act of Supremacy, 1534

98. The above Act resulted in
   A) the spread of Roman Catholicism to England
   B) an increase in power for Henry VIII
   C) the end of Anglicanism in England
   D) an increase in power for the Pope
   E) the beginning of the Enlightenment

99. A major factor that helped lead to the above legislation was
   A) the condemnation of simony
   B) a desire for England to acquire papal land in Rome
   C) the King's desire to divorce his wife
   D) a hope to weaken French religious authority in the region
   E) the selling of indulgences

100. Which statement comparing the eighteenth century Industrial Revolution to industrialization in the Modern Era is true?
   A) Unlike the first Industrial Revolution, today's industrialization is more of an urban phenomenon
   B) The earlier Industrial Revolution used a factory system to produce finished goods, whereas modern-day nations have abandoned using factories for production
   C) Only recent industrialization has created pollution
   D) Industrialization in recent years is not as dependent on energy resources found nearby
   E) Both periods experienced communist alternatives to capitalism in developed nations in Asia

Answers and Explanations

1. **C.** The Neolithic Revolution's new agricultural techniques led to permanent settlements and a decreased dependence on nomadic lifestyle. All over the world civilizations emerged.

2. **A.** Civilizations develop near water because of farming and trading opportunities. In Mesopotamia, the rivers are the Tigris and Euphrates. In China, you should know the Huang He (Yellow) and Yangtze. In India, the Ganges and Indus are vital for survival.

3. **B.** Both religions believe in one God. This is called monotheism. A belief in multiple gods is called polytheism.

4. **A.** Ziggurats were religious structures built in Sumer of ancient Mesopotamia. Glyphs were symbols used by the Mayan Empire. Hieroglyphics were written in Egypt. Cuneiform was from ancient Sumer.

5. **D.** Mesoamerica is in the New World, and therefore isolated from the Silk Roads. The New World would be isolated from all foreign cultures until the Age of Exploration. .

6. **E.** "An eye for an eye" is from Hammurabi's Code. The code applied to everyone, but remember...it punished the poor and gave women a lower status.

7. **C.** These are excerpts from the collection of laws known as the Twelve Tables of Rome.

8. **B.** In the excerpt, one can see that capital punishment (death) is a penalty for treason and for judges taking bribes.

9. **A.** King Nebuchadnezzar II put Jews into captivity in ancient times. The other leaders displayed acts of religious tolerance during their reigns.

10. **D.** Caravel ships were designed by the Portuguese as a means for exploration in the fifteenth century.

11. **C.** Like chivalry, the bushido code of Japan stressed a similar importance on bravery. The samurai warrior was expected to honor all obligations.

12. **A.** The Parthenon is a well-known classical structure. Classical buildings are symmetrical, and many also contain columns. Classical architecture was copied all over the Western World.

13. **E.** The Greek direct democracy allowed average male citizens to take part in lawmaking. Women and slaves were denied such participation in government.

14. **A.** Slash-and-burn farming was associated with early human settlements. Trees were burned to create open fields. Then, the ashes from the fire would be used to fertilize the farmland.

15. **D.** India. Try to remember DIG...Deccan, India, Ganges (Gupta)

16. **B.** Alexander the Great amassed an impressive Empire which created Hellenistic Culture. A blending of Egyptian, Persian, Greek, and Indian ideals was accomplished through trade.

17. **D.** Both Legalism and Machiavelli's *The Prince* emphasized the importance of strict rule and order. The belief was that if the ruler gave too many rights to their citizens, the people would strip them of their power.

18. **C.** Harappa and Mohenjo-daro were in the Indus River Valley in modern-day India.

19. **A.** The Andes Mountains can be found on the western coast of South America.

20. **E.** Serfs were bound to the land in European feudalism. Czar Alexander II did not emancipate (free) Russian serfs until the middle of the nineteenth century.

21. **E.** The Cyrillic alphabet of Russia has Slavic roots and was influenced by Saint Cyril.

22. **B**. There was too great of a distance between the Byzantine Empire in the East, and the Roman Catholic Church of Rome. There were arguments over religious practices, notably the use of icons. The religion in the East became Eastern Orthodox. Be careful with choice D...that refers to the Great Schism of the Middle Ages where two Popes claimed legitimacy.

23. **B**. Christians and Muslims fought a Holy War after Pope Urban II called for a Crusade in 1095. The objective was to control the Holy Land in and around Jerusalem.

24. **B**. Both philosophers combined the philosophy of Aristotle with theology (study of religious faith). Aquinas wrote the *Summa Theologica*. Averroës wrote *The Incoherence of the Incoherence*.

25. **C**. Although violent, the Crusades led to an increase of trade between Europe and the Middle East.

26. **A**. Although one would expect more people to attend Church services during the plague, there was an overall decrease in faith because prayers went unanswered.

27. **D**. Terrace farming is an agricultural technique used to level off the slopes of mountains and hills. This was done all over the world and notably in the Andes Mountains by the Incan Empire.

28. **C**. The Conquistadors believed that Mayan religious writings were pagan and dangerous. They burned most of the written record.

29. **B**. Although from different ends of the globe, both structures have wide bases that narrow towards the top.

30. **D**. The Ganges River has great significance to the people of India.

31. **A**. The Bantu-speaking people migrated all over sub-Saharan Africa (south of the Sahara Desert). Today, many African languages have roots in Bantu.

Swahili is also big in Africa, but it came much later after Arabic contact.

32. **D**. Ibn Battuta was the great traveler of Africa in the middle of the fourteenth century. He visited many of the thriving cultures of the world.

33. **E**. The Umayyads built one of the early Muslim Empires that existed west of the subcontinent of modern-day India.

34. **A**. King Mansa Musa of Mali went on the hajj (pilgrimage to Mecca), and helped spread Islam to his African Kingdom.

35. **C**. Calvinism was a sect of Christianity that emerged during the Protestant Reformation. John Calvin preached predestination, or the belief that one's path to salvation had already been determined.

36. **A**. The Pope's Line of Demarcation divided land in the New World between the Spanish and Portuguese. Spain received the land to the west of the line. Portugal received what was east (in modern-day Brazil). The Treaty of Tordesillas of 1794 moved the line a bit to the west to give Portugal more territory.

37. **B**. Eastern Africa offered many valuable resources to the Portuguese before 1500.

38. **A**. The 1555 Peace of Augsburg allowed princes of Germany to determine if their regions would be Catholic or Protestant. The Thirty Years' War began as a religious conflict in 1618.

39. **E**. Fall of Rome, 476 CE; Black Plague, c1350; Protestant Reformation, c1517; Elizabethan Age, c1580.

40. **A**. Greco-Roman culture influenced humanism and the development of Renaissance culture.

41. **B**. Although some other cultures had calligraphy and astronomical advances, algebra and the Abbasids were relevant to the Middle East.

42. **A**. The Khmer Empire of Southeast Asia established maritime trade connections with China and India. The ancient Phoenicians were sea travelers as well, spreading their culture around the Mediterranean.

43. **A**. The Han and the Tang imposed high taxes and their people suffered from famine. As per the Dynastic Cycle, both dynasties fell.

44. **D**. Both Africa and Native America were predominantly agricultural societies.

45. **A**. Genghis and Kublai Khan proved to be strong leaders, and amassed an Empire that stretched from Asia to Eastern Europe. It even extended into parts of the Middle East. However within a century of Kublai's death, the Mongol Empire lost its strength.

46. **C**. Zheng He traveled the Eastern World on behalf of the Ming Dynasty of China. The size of his fleet of ships far exceeded what the Europeans would send out a century later.

47. **B**. Mercantilism involved European countries acting as a Mother Country and extracting resources from their colonies. They sold finished goods to the colonies as well.

48. **E**. Both had absolute, or total control of the country. Many civil liberties were limited, including free speech and fair trials.

49. **E**. Locke's *Two Treatises of Government* was a strong contribution to the Enlightenment. He believed in natural rights such as life, liberty, and property.

50. **E**. Jean-Jacques Rousseau wrote the *Social Contract*. He believed that freedom was important, and people should not obey unjust laws.

51. **B**. Enlightenment thinkers wanted monarchies to limit their power to ensure the protection of natural rights.

52. **B**. Divine Right meant that the absolute ruler was a representative of God. In both Egypt (theocracy) and China (Mandate of Heaven), there was a relationship between the ruler and religion.

53. **E**. Neoclassical styles were less ornate than the impressive baroque architecture used in castles like Versailles.

54. **C**. Unlike Socrates who died for his beliefs, Galileo "admitted" his research was flawed. He spent the rest of his life under house-arrest.

55. **C**. All of the terms were from the Renaissance period. Humanism was the spirit of human achievement, and the *David* was sculpted by Michelangelo. The Medici Family of Florence helped sponsor impressive artistic endeavors.

56. **A**. Peter the Great wanted to imitate Western European nations. To become modern, or Western, Russia needed to remove Mongol influences upon their culture. If you said choice B, you are a little early. The Industrial Revolution came decades later.

57. **A**. Peninsulares were atop the pyramid of social power in the New World. They were born in Spain, and then ventured over for political and economic gain.

58. **B**. José San Martin and Simón Bolívar were influential leaders of nineteenth century Latin American independence movements against Spain.

59. **A**. Revolutions in Latin America were inspired by Enlightenment thought and the French Revolution. Countries such as Venezuela, Chile, Brazil, Mexico, and Haiti all fought for independence in the nineteenth century.

60. **B**. Robespierre was a Jacobin whose Committee of Public Safety looked to rid France of traitors to the Revolution, such as supporters of the King.

61. **D.** Napoleon's Continental System was a blockade that looked to isolate Britain from its trading neighbors in Europe. It was unsuccessful.

62. **B.** The Napoleonic Code was a body of law written after the French Revolution. The code limited certain rights of women, as well as freedom of speech.

63. **D.** Napoleon suddenly seized power with a bloodless overthrow of the government. This action is known as a coup d'état.

64. **D.** Although socialist ideas were a response to the Industrial Revolution, socialism never took hold in England.

65. **C.** Both of these violent insurrections were unsuccessful at removing imperialists from India (Sepoy Mutiny) and China (Boxer Rebellion).

66. **E.** After the Meiji Restoration, Japan massively industrialized and modernized. In the twentieth century, they became a major power that fought wars and imperialized other countries.

67. **E.** Vincent Van Gogh was an impressionist/post-impressionist painter who captured the emotion of a moment.

68. **E.** Laissez-faire means that the government should take its hands off the economy and allow for natural forces to take over.

69. **A.** Hernán Cortés conquered the Aztecs. Hitler, Napoleon, and Kublai Khan were all unsuccessful in taking over the places they were paired up with.

70. **C.** Age of Enlightenment, c1700-1740; American Revolution, c1776; French Revolution, c1789; Latin American Independence Movements, c1810.

71. **B.** Germany unified through "blood and iron." In a short Seven Weeks' War they took land from Austria. In the Franco-Prussian War of 1870-71, they received the territories of Alsace and Lorraine from France.

72. **B.** The potato famine in Ireland led to the death of an estimated one million people. Many immigrated to places around the world, notably the United States.

73. **A.** Great Britain acquired a great number of colonies, specifically in Africa, India, and China.

74. **D.** Darwin's theory of evolution led to beliefs in Social Darwinism, or survival of the fittest. Social Darwinism was used to rationalize the domination of weaker societies during the Age of Imperialism.

75. **A.** The Treaty of Versailles punished Germany greatly. It also created an international peace-keeping organization called the League of Nations. Because the League could not raise troops to fight in international conflicts, Germany was able to ignore the provisions of the treaty, and remilitarize.

76. **B.** In 1919, the British fired on demonstrators in the Amritsar Massacre. The Czar did the same in 1905 in St. Petersburg on Bloody Sunday.

77. **A.** The monument is in Cambodia. The Khmer Empire dominated Southeast Asia c1200 in what is present-day Cambodia. The capital of the Empire was Angkor.

78. **A.** Both were attempts at modernization. Stalin set quotas so high, that he never achieved his goals. Mao's Great Leap Forward is considered by historians to be a failure.

79. **C.** Alongside Germany and Italy, Japan was part of the Axis Powers.

80. **C.** Hitler was against communism. Dividing land amongst the people was a communist reform.

81. **D.** Glasnost means openness. The Soviet Union was not historically associated with openness, but under Mikhail Gorbachev there were reforms to change that.

82. **D**. Civil disobedience means to disobey unjust laws. Gandhi and King were also advocates of passive resistance, or nonviolent protests.

83. **E**. The African National Congress used boycotts to try to bring about an end to apartheid in South Africa.

84. **C**. One of the achievements of the Persians was the Great Royal Road which stretched over 1,500 miles and enhanced communication throughout the empire.

85. **B**. The Camp David Accords brought some stability to the Middle East. Egypt recognized Israel as a nation, and Israel returned the Sinai Peninsula.

86. **E**. India's predominantly Hindu population feuded with Muslims in Pakistan. Violence has occurred since partition, especially in the disputed region of Kashmir.

87. **E**. Détente means a lessoning of Cold War tensions between the United States and the Soviet Union. This occurred in the 1970s after a very tense 1960s that included the potentially catastrophic Cuban Missile Crisis.

88. **A**. The Khmer Rouge killed an estimated 2 million Cambodians who were seen as threats to their power. The genocide was led by Pol Pot.

89. **B**. The Etruscans (768 BCE-264 BCE) controlled much of northern and western Italy, and influenced Roman religious rituals, art, architecture (arches), use of iron, and even their system of writing.

90. **B**. The Tamil Tigers used military and terror tactics. They failed to establish a separate state in Sri Lanka.

91. **B**. Communist leaders like Mao Zedong and Joseph Stalin granted more rights to women. However, this generally meant that women would work longer hours, yet still be expected to care for the family.

92. **D**. The Taliban in Afghanistan is fundamentalist (relying on religion) and opposed to westernization.

93. **A**. The Tiananmen Square Massacre was a government response to a protest for democracy in Beijing. Xiaoping's military violently ended the protest. Estimates of the dead and wounded exceeded 2,000.

94. **A**. Both perestroika and Lenin's New Economic Policy created capitalist opportunities in the communist Soviet Union.

95. **E**. The Balfour Declaration came from a British official who spoke in favor of creating a Jewish State. Zionism is the support for such a creation.

96. **B**. Globalization in the twenty-first century is at an all-time high, as developed and developing countries around the world affect the global economy. In addition, the internet has made communication between nations incredibly easy.

97. **C**. Both revolutions were associated with increasing the amount of food available for consumption. Both increased life expectancy.

98. **B**. In 1534, Parliament (the legislature of England) passed the Act of Supremacy. This made Henry the head of the Church of England, and thereby increased his authority.

99. **C**. The Church did not allow Henry to annul, or declare invalid his marriage. He decided to break away from the Church. Because he was now independent of Rome, Henry could divorce his wife Catherine.

100. **D**. In the first Industrial Revolution that started in England, the energy resources were more often found nearby. By the nineteenth century, that would change. Today, oil from the Middle East is exported to all over the world

SAT Subject Test Scoring Guide

Note: This is not scientific, and remember that the SAT Subject Test has 95 questions on it.

Get your raw score by first adding the total questions correct. Then for every four wrong, subtract a point off of your raw score.

90-100	-	800	52-53	-	600
88-89	-	790	50-51	-	590
86-87	-	780	48-49	-	580
84-85	-	770	46-47	-	570
82-83	-	760	44-45	-	560
81	-	750	42-43	-	550
79-80	-	740	40-41	-	540
77-78	-	730	38-39	-	530
75-76	-	720	36-37	-	520
73-74	-	710	35	-	510
71-72	-	700	33-34	-	500
69-70	-	690	31-32	-	490
67-68	-	680	30	-	480
65-66	-	670	29	-	470
63-64	-	660	28	-	460
62	-	650	27	-	450
60-61	-	640	25-26	-	440
58-59	-	630	23-24	-	430
56-57	-	620	21-22	-	420
54-55	-	610	20	-	410

Now we're ready to begin!

NO BULL NOBLE REVIEW SHEET

Here are my Review Sheets. Use them often to help you study.

You will notice numbers in brackets after a word or sentence. These are the pages where you can find more detailed information.

Good luck!

Your friend,

Nobley

Most Important Terms of the Course (Numbers in brackets are reference pages in text)

1. Neolithic Revolution [13]
2. Nomads, and Hunters & Gatherers [13]
3. Ziggurat [14]
4. Cultural Diffusion [14]
5. Cuneiform [14]
6. Theocracy [16]
7. Hieroglyphics [16]
8. Mandate of Heaven/Dynastic Cycle [20]
9. Tokugawa Shogunate [24]
10. Haiku and Kabuki [24]
11. Harappa and Mohenjo-daro [25]
12. Caliph [26]
13. Twelve Tables of Law [36]
14. Pax Romana [37]
15. Feudalism [42]
16. Chivalry [43]
17. Three-Field System [43]
18. Spanish Inquisition [44]
19. Great Schism [45]
20. Bubonic Plague [45]
21. Humanism [45]
22. Printing Press [46]
23. 95 Theses [47]
24. Predestination [48]
25. Bantu-speaking People [53]
26. Ibn Battuta [54]
27. Terrace Farming [56]
28. Conquistadors [57]
29. *Encomienda* [58]
30. Middle Passage [58]
31. Mercantilism and Commercial Revolution [59]
32. Absolutism [63]
33. Spanish Armada [63-64]
34. Limited Monarchy [65]
35. Scientific Method [65]
36. Heliocentric Model [65]
37. Enlightenment [65-66]

38. Baroque [66]
39. Enlightened Despots [67]
40. Bourgeoisie [73]
41. Tennis Court Oath [73]
42. Declaration of the Rights of Man [74]
43. Political Spectrum [74]
44. Jacobins [74]
45. Coup d'état [75]
46. Napoleonic Code [75]
47. Congress of Vienna [76]
48. Urbanization [81]
49. Agricultural Revolution [81]
50. Capitalism [82]
51. Socialism [82]
52. Potato Famine [84]
53. Berlin Conference [90]
54. Spheres of Influence [92]
55. Open Door Policy [92]
56. Meiji Era [93]
57. *Lusitania* and Zimmermann Telegram [94]
58. League of Nations [95]
59. Treaty of Versailles [95]
60. Mexican Revolution [96]
61. Pogroms [101]
62. Russia's Bloody Sunday [101]
63. NEP [102]
64. USSR/Soviet Union [102]
65. Totalitarianism [102]
66. Command Economy/Five-Year Plan [103]
67. Fascism [108]
68. Weimar Republic [108]
69. *Mein Kampf* [109]
70. Appeasement [110]
71. Axis Powers [110]
72. Blitzkrieg [110]
73. Yalta Conference [111]
74. Atomic Bomb [112]

75. United Nations [112]

76. Ghettos [113]

77. Final Solution (Genocide) [114]

78. Nuremberg Trials and Tokyo Trials [114]

79. Universal Declaration of Human Rights [114]

80. Containment [119, 121]

81. Truman Doctrine and Marshall Plan [119]

82. Berlin Airlift [119-120]

83. NATO and Warsaw Pact [120]

84. Sputnik [120]

85. Berlin Wall [120]

86. Bay of Pigs Invasion [120-121]

87. Cuban Missile Crisis [121]

88. Détente [121-122]

89. Glasnost and Perestroika [122]

90. Domino Theory [124]

91. Dien Bien Phu [124-125]

92. Vietcong [125]

93. Khmer Rouge [125]

94. Long March [132]

95. Great Leap Forward [132-133]

96. Cultural Revolution [133]

97. Four Modernizations [133]

98. Tiananmen Square Massacre [133]

99. Three Gorges Dam [134]

100. One-Child Policy [134]

101. Amritsar Massacre [134]

102. Salt March [134-135]

103. Partition [135]

104. Zionism [140]

105. Balfour Declaration [140]

106. Camp David Accords [140-141]

107. OPEC [142]

108. Taliban [142]

109. 9-11-2001 [142]

110. Apartheid [142]

111. Developing Nations [144]

112. Green Revolution [145]

113. European Union [145]

114. Mothers of the Plaza de Mayo [126]

115. Arab Spring [141]

116. Global Interdependence [145]

These terms are important to know!

Key Questions

1. What do I need to know about the history at the beginning of my textbook? [13]

2. How did the Han Dynasty govern such a large area? [21-22]

3. What were the contributions of the early Muslim world? [27-28]

4. What were the differences between Athens and Sparta? [34]

5. What were the contributions of the ancient Greeks? [34-35]

6. How did the Roman Republic function? [36]

7. What were the contributions of Rome? [37]

8. What led to the Fall of Rome? [38]

9. What happened in the schism of 1054? [38]

10. What were the important aspects of the Church during the Middle Ages? [43]

11. What were the causes, events, and results of the Crusades? [44]

12. What should I know about Renaissance art and literature? [46-47]

13. What were the causes and results of the Protestant Reformation? [47-48]

14. What motivated Europeans in the Age of Exploration? [57]

15. What was the social hierarchy of the New World under Spanish rule? [59]

16. How did the Enlightenment affect the arts? [66-67]

17. What were the three Estates of France's Old Regime? [73]

18. What were Napoleon's three mistakes that led to his downfall? [75]

19. Why has nationalism been a major force in World History? [80]

20. Why did the Industrial Revolution begin in England? [82-83]

21. What were some innovations of the Industrial Revolution? [81-82]

22. Why did countries want to imperialize? [90]

23. What were the causes, results, and technological innovations of World War I? [93-95]

24. What were the foreign policy results of World War II? [112]

25. What were the major examples of containment during the Cold War? [121]

26. How did Communism ultimately fall in the Soviet Union and Eastern Europe? [122-123]

27. What happened to India during the Partition? [135]

28. What wars were fought between Israel and other Middle East nations from 1956-1973? [140]

29. What led to the end of apartheid? [142-143]

30. What should I know about the modern global economy? [146]

People to Know

1. King Hammurabi [14]
2. Hatshepsut [16]
3. Shi Huangdi [20-21]
4. Genghis and Kublai Khan [23]
5. Zheng He [22]
6. Akbar the Great [25-26]
7. Socrates, Plato, and Aristotle [35]
8. Julius Caesar [37]
9. Justinian and Theodora [38]
10. Thomas Aquinas; Margery Kempe [44-45]
11. Leonardo da Vinci [46]
12. Niccolò Machiavelli [46]
13. Martin Luther [47]
14. Queen Elizabeth I [46, 48]
15. Mansa Musa [54]
16. Louis XIV [63]
17. Maria Theresa [64]
18. Ivan the Terrible [64]
19. Peter the Great [64]
20. Copernicus and Galileo [65]
21. Enlightenment Thinkers (Hobbes, Rousseau, Locke, Voltaire, Montesquieu) [66]
22. Napoleon Bonaparte [75-76]
23. Simón Bolívar [76]
24. Toussaint L'Ouverture [76]
25. Benito Juárez [76]
26. Adam Smith [82]
27. Karl Marx [82]
28. John Stuart Mill, Thomas Malthus [83]
29. Queen Victoria [83]
30. William Wilberforce [83]
31. Charles Darwin [84]
32. Mustafa Kemal Atatürk [95]
33. Porfirio Díaz [96]
34. Nicholas II [101]
35. Grigori Rasputin [101]
36. Vladimir Lenin [102]
37. Joseph Stalin [102-103]
38. Benito Mussolini [108-109]
39. Adolf Hitler [109-110]
40. Friedrich Nietzsche [109]
41. Joseph Goebbels [109]
42. Francisco Franco [109]
43. Elie Wiesel [114]
44. Anne Frank [114]
45. Fidel Castro [120-121, 126]
46. Mikhail Gorbachev [122-123]
47. Lech Walesa [123]
48. Ho Chi Minh [125]
49. Pol Pot [125]
50. Aung San Suu Kyi [126]
51. Augusto Pinochet [126]
52. Sun Yixian [131]
53. Mao Zedong [132-133]
54. Deng Xiaoping [133]
55. Mohandas Gandhi [134-135]
56. Benazir Bhutto [135]
57. Mother Teresa [135]
58. Theodor Herzl; Golda Meir [140]
59. Nelson Mandela [142]
60. Jomo Kenyatta [143]

Religion and Philosophy...What You Need to Know

1. Animism [5]
2. Shintoism [5]
3. Hinduism [5-6]
4. Buddhism [6]
5. Jainism [6]
6. Confucianism [6]

7. Daoism [6]
8. Islam [7]
9. Judaism [7-8]
10. Christianity [8]
11. Zoroastrianism [15]

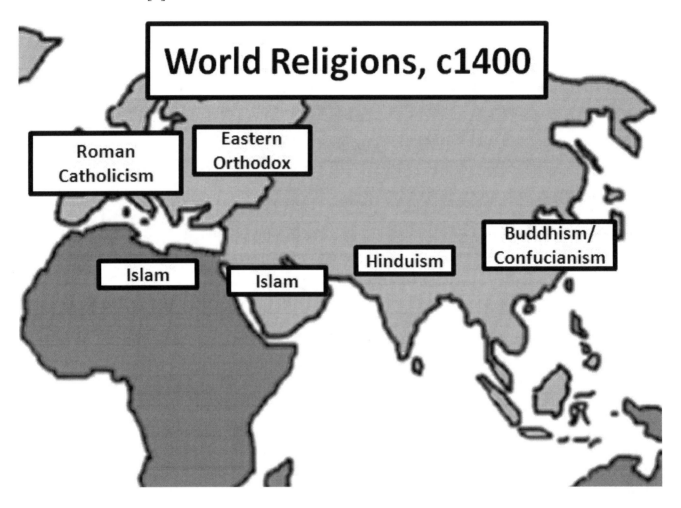

World Religions, c1400

Roman Catholicism

Eastern Orthodox

Islam

Islam

Hinduism

Buddhism/ Confucianism

Most Important Empires to Know (Pre-1820)

1. Han Dynasty [21-22]
2. Tang and Song Dynasties [22]
3. Ming Empire [23]
4. Mongol Empire [23]
5. Tokugawa Shogunate [24]
6. Khmer Empire [24]
7. Mauryan and Gupta Empires [25]
8. Mughal Empire [25-26]
9. Umayyad and Abbasid Caliphates [27]
10. Ottoman Empire [28]
11. Safavid Empire [28-29]
12. Empire of Alexander the Great and Hellenistic Culture [36]
13. Roman Empire [36-38]
14. Byzantine Empire [38]
15. Carolingian Empire and Charlemagne [42]
16. Ghana, Mali, and Songhai Empires of Africa [53-54]
17. Mayan Empire [55]
18. Aztec Empire [55]
19. Incan Empire [55-56]
20. Napoleonic Empire [75]

See Empires c1750 map on pg. 67

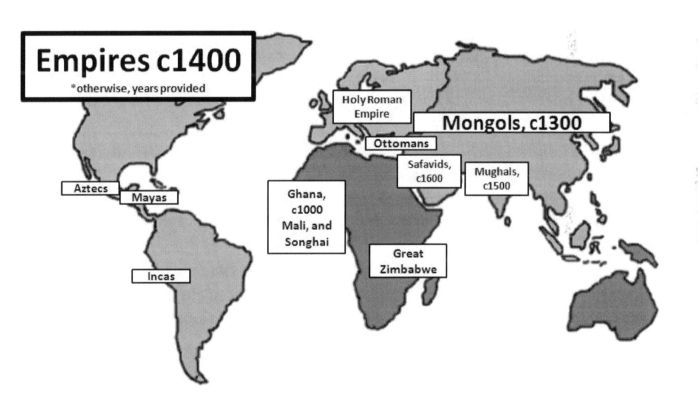

Wars and Conflict

1. Peloponnesian War [34]
2. Punic Wars [36]
3. The Crusades [44]
4. Hundred Years' War [45]
5. Thirty Years' War [64]
6. English Civil War [65]
7. Glorious Revolution [65]
8. French Revolution [72-74]
9. Napoleon's Invasion of Russia [75]
10. Unification of Italy [80]
11. Unification of Germany [80]
12. First Opium War [91]
13. Crimean War [81]
14. Boer Wars [90-91]
15. Sepoy Mutiny [91]
16. Boxer Rebellion [93]
17. Russo-Japanese War [93]
18. World War I [93-95]
19. Bolshevik Revolution [102]
20. Russian Civil War [102]
21. Mexican Revolution [96]
22. World War II [110-112]
23. Cold War [119-123]
24. Soviet-Afghanistan War [122]
25. Korean War [124]
26. Vietnam War [124-125]
27. Post Fall of Communism Conflicts [123]
28. Chinese Civil War [132]
29. Conflicts in Middle East [140-141]
30. Conflicts in Africa [142-144]

Twentieth and Twenty-First Century Human Rights Violations

1. Pogroms [101]
2. Russia's Bloody Sunday [101]
3. Armenian Massacres [96]
4. Ukrainian Famine [103]
5. Great Purge [103]
6. Nanjing Massacre [110]
7. Final Solution [114]
8. Ethnic Cleansing in Bosnia [123]
9. Khmer Rouge [125]
10. Cultural Revolution [133]
11. Tiananmen Square Massacre [133]
12. Amritsar Massacre [134]
13. Taliban [142]
14. ISIS [141-142]
15. Apartheid [142]
16. Rwandan Genocide [144]
17. War in Darfur [144]

Geography

1. Why did civilizations develop near water? [13]
2. Why was Mesopotamia called the Fertile Crescent? [13-14]
3. What was the significance of the Silk Roads and trade on the Indian Ocean? [29]
4. What impact did being a group of islands have on Japan? [23]
5. What are the important aspects of Indian geography? [24]
6. How did Greece's geography affect its development? [34]
7. How diverse is Africa's climate? [53]
8. What is a physical map? [56]
9. Why couldn't Napoleon defeat Britain? [75]
10. Why did the Industrial Revolution begin in England? [82]
11. What does the Suez Canal connect? [140]
12. What are some of the environmental issues threatening the Earth today? [146-147]

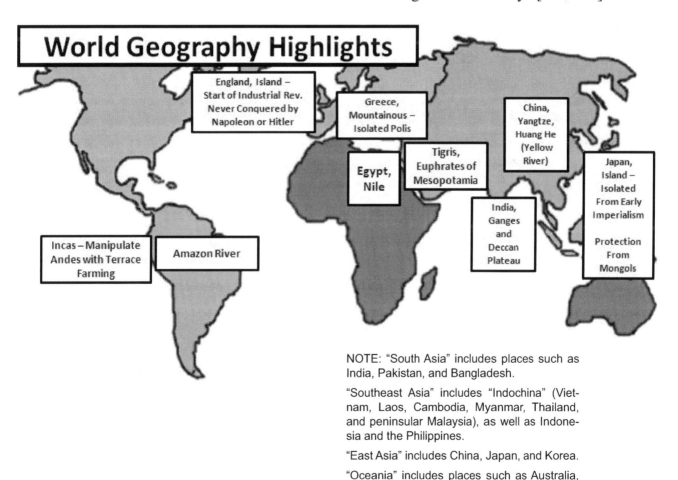

NOTE: "South Asia" includes places such as India, Pakistan, and Bangladesh.

"Southeast Asia" includes "Indochina" (Vietnam, Laos, Cambodia, Myanmar, Thailand, and peninsular Malaysia), as well as Indonesia and the Philippines.

"East Asia" includes China, Japan, and Korea.

"Oceania" includes places such as Australia, New Zealand, and other Pacific island nations.

Women's Rights

Increased:

1. Hatshepsut [16]
2. Wu Zhao [22]
3. Justinian's Code [38]
4. Peter the Great [64]
5. Mary Wollstonecraft [66]
6. Women's rights in 20th Century [83]
7. Mustafa Kemal Atatürk [95]
8. Soviet Union [102-103]
9. Mao in China [131-132]
10. Benazir Bhutto [135]
11. Aung San Suu Kyi [126]

Decreased:

1. Hammurabi's Code [14]
2. Ancient China [22]
3. Athenian Democracy [34]
4. Fate of Olympe de Gouges [74]
5. Napoleonic Code [75]
6. Taliban [142]

Examples of Cultural Diffusion

1. Definition of Cultural Diffusion [14]
2. Phoenician Alphabet [14-15]
3. Silk Roads and Indian Ocean Trade [29]
4. Muslim and Greco-Roman Architecture [28]
5. Hellenistic Culture [36]
6. Greco-Roman/Western Civilization [37]
7. Cyrillic Alphabet [38]
8. Hanseatic League [43]
9. Results of the Crusades [44]
10. Mansa Musa [54]
11. Columbian Exchange [58]
12. Mestizo Culture [58, 59]
13. Westernization of Russia [64]
14. Enlightenment in Latin America [76]
15. Industrial Revolution [81]
16. Meiji Era [93]
17. Global Interdependence [145]
18. Globalization [146]

Fabian Society: Favors democratic socialism in Britain.

ASEAN: Association of Southeast Asian Nations; social, economic, and political union

Cro-Magnon: Early form of modern humans

OAS (Organization of American States) Western Hemisphere organization

Rosetta Stone: Found by Napoleon's troops; can decipher hieroglyphics

Stirrups & Saddles: Both aided in riding a horse, or a camel in a desert caravan

Fluyt: Dutch cargo ship for merchants

Low percentage terms that could wind up on a test

Qanat: Underground irrigation technique used by Persian Empire

Tripartite Pact: Established the Axis Powers

Hague: Dutch Parliament and international court

Utopian Socialism - 19th Century movement that led to establishment of communities with social cooperation and a lack of property distinction.

Dowry: Marriage custom where woman's family provides money and goods

Champa Rice: quick growing allows for two harvests per season

Convention at Kanagawa: Opened Japan to US trade in 1854

Alliance for Progress – US economic support for Latin America during the Cold War

(EEC) European Economic Community: Was created before EU to bring economic integration to Europe

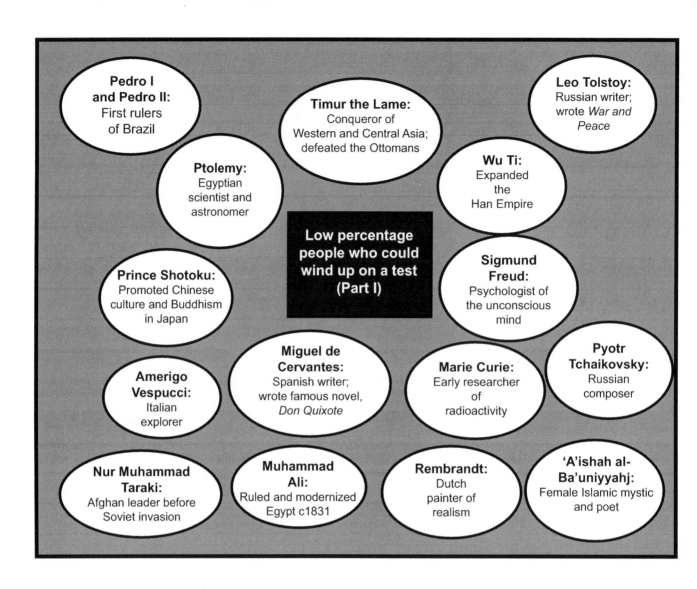

Pablo Picasso: Cubism artist, painted *Guernica* which protested fascist aggression

Sir Francis Drake: English Vice Admiral who helped defeat the Spanish Armada

Draco: Harsh legislator in the early years of Athenian government

Bernardo O'Higgins: Helped lead Chile to independence

Mamluks: Dynasties in Egypt and Syria c1400

Max Weber: German Sociologist

Low percentage people who could wind up on a test (Part II)

Fyodor Dostoyevsky and Alexander Pushkin: Russian writers

Queen Nzinga (modern Angola): Fought against the Portuguese and slave trade c1650

John Maynard Keynes: Economist, supported stimulating economy in Great Depression

Ngo Dinh Diem: Unpopular non-communist leader of South Vietnam

Xuanzang: Chinese traveler to India who translated Buddhist scriptures

Hugo Chávez: Venezuelan President, 1999-2013; supported socialist reforms

Mahmoud Ahmadinejad: 21st century leader of Iran

Celts: Early settlers in Europe; Influenced ancient Britain during Iron Age

Caligula and Nero: Harsh Roman Emperors

205

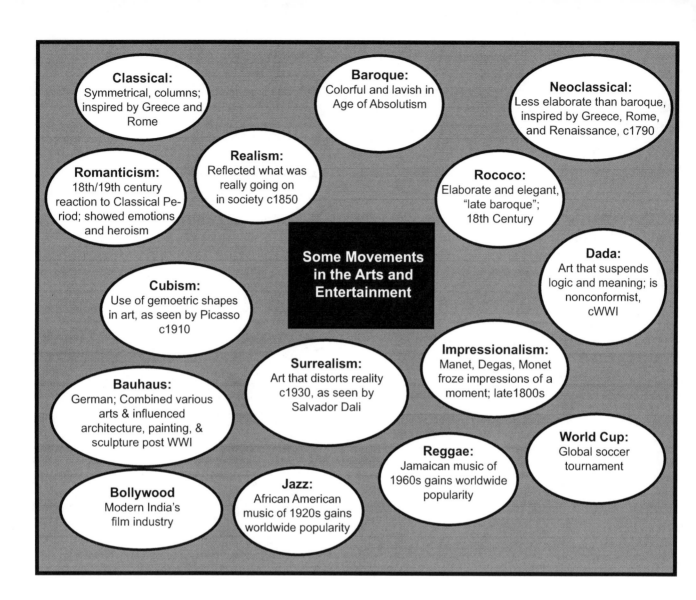

Classical:
Symmetrical, columns;
inspired by Greece and
Rome

Baroque:
Colorful and lavish in
Age of Absolutism

Neoclassical:
Less elaborate than baroque,
inspired by Greece, Rome,
and Renaissance, c1790

Realism:
Reflected what was
really going on
in society c1850

Romanticism:
18th/19th century
reaction to Classical Pe-
riod; showed emotions
and heroism

Rococo:
Elaborate and elegant,
"late baroque";
18th Century

Some Movements
in the Arts and
Entertainment

Dada:
Art that suspends
logic and meaning; is
nonconformist,
cWWI

Cubism:
Use of gemoetric shapes
in art, as seen by Picasso
c1910

Surrealism:
Art that distorts reality
c1930, as seen by
Salvador Dali

Impressionalism:
Manet, Degas, Monet
froze impressions of a
moment; late1800s

Bauhaus:
German; Combined various
arts & influenced
architecture, painting, &
sculpture post WWI

World Cup:
Global soccer
tournament

Bollywood
Modern India's
film industry

Jazz:
African American
music of 1920s gains
worldwide popularity

Reggae:
Jamaican music of
1960s gains worldwide
popularity

Comparative Timelines — c1700-BCE - c1000

Region	c1700 BCE	500 BCE - 200 CE	200 - 500	600	1000
East Asia	Shang - c1500-1050 BCE	Confucius - c500 BCE Reign of Shi Huangdi - c220 BCE Han - 202 BCE-220 CE			Wu Zhao - c700 Tang - 618-907 Heian Period in Japan - 794-1185
India	Mohenjo-daro and Harappa exist until about 1500 BCE Aryans settle c1500 BCE	Mauryan - 322-185 BCE Ashoka - c250 BCE	Peak of Gupta Rule - 320-550		
Mid-East	Hammurabi's Code c1750 BCE	Jesus Christ - c30		Muhammad - c622 Islam begins to spread - c622 Umayyads - 661-750	
Europe	Mycenaeans c1600 BCE	Athens under Pericles - c450 BCE Twelve Tables of Law - c450 BCE Socrates, Plato, Aristotle - c400 BCE - c332 BCE Alexander the Great - c330 BCE Punic Wars - 264-146 BCE Julius Caesar - c50 BCE	Christian Persecution ends in Rome - 313 Fall of Rome - 476 Justinian's Code in Byzantine Empire - c530	Charlemagne crowned - 800 East-West Schism - 1054 Battle of Hastings - 1066	
Africa	Ancient Bantu Migrations - c2000 BCE Egyptian New Kingdom - c1550-c1070 BCE Hatshepsut - c1460 BCE		Aksum conquers Kush - c350	Golden Age of Ghana c800-c1050	
Americas	Olmecs emerge c1200-c400 BCE			Anasazi - c200-c1300 Mayas peak - c250-900	

Comparative Timelines — c1200 - c1700

Region	1200	1400	1500	1600	1700
East Asia	Song - 960-1279; Genghis Kahn unites Mongols - c1200; Khmer peaks - c1200	Koryo in Korea falls -1392; Zheng He explores - c1400		Tokugawa Shogunate takes over Japan - 1603; Ming fall - 1644	China and Japan continue policy of isolation
India		Islam continues to spread through India	Mughals strong - 1526-1707; Akbar the Great rules - c1600		
Mid-East	Abbasids - 750-1258 (Golden Age of Islam); The Crusades - 1095-1291	Ottomans emerge - c1300	Constantinople falls to Ottomans - 1453; Safavids - 1501-1722; Suleiman rules - c1530	Shah Abbas - c1600	
Europe	Magna Carta - 1215; Marco Polo - c1270	Gutenberg Printing Press - c1440; Spanish Inquisition begins - 1478; Columbus finds New World - 1492; Hundred Years' War - 1337-1453; Renaissance - c1350-c1550	Luther's 95 Theses - 1517; Act of Supremacy - 1534; Scientific Revolution c1550-c1700	Philip II - c1580; Galileo - c1600; Thirty Years' War - 1618-1648; Glorious Revolution - 1688; John Locke - c1690	Louis XIV rules France, Peter the Great rules Russia - c1700
Africa	Mali - c1200-c1450; Kingdom of Zimbabwe - c1220-c1450	Mansa Musa - c1300; Ibn Battuta - c1350; Songhai - c1375-1591		Atlantic Slave Trade - c1500s-c1800s	
Americas		Aztecs control Mesoamerica, Incas control Andes of S. America c1492		Cortes conquers Aztecs - 1521; Pizarro conquers Incas - c1533; Middle Passage goes to New World, Columbian Exchange, Encomienda, Mercantilism emerges - c1550	

Made in the
USA
Middletown, DE